Conversations with Robert Stone

Literary Conversations Series
Monika Gehlawat
General Editor

I0642303

Books by Robert Stone

A Hall of Mirrors. Boston: Houghton Mifflin, 1967.
Dog Soldiers. Boston: Houghton Mifflin, 1974.
A Flag for Sunrise. New York: Knopf, 1981.
Children of Light. New York: Knopf, 1986.
Outerbridge Reach. New York: Tickner & Fields, 1992.
Bear and His Daughter. Boston: Houghton Mifflin, 1997.
Damascus Gate. Boston: Houghton Mifflin, 1998.
Bay of Souls. Boston: Houghton Mifflin, 2003.
Prime Green: Remembering the Sixties. New York: Ecco, 2007.
Fun With Problems. Boston: Houghton Mifflin, 2010.
Death of the Black-Haired Girl. Boston: Houghton Mifflin, 2013.

Conversations with Robert Stone

Edited by William Heath

University Press of Mississippi   *Jackson*

For my good friend Jim Vincent

www.upress.state.ms.us

The University Press of Mississippi is a member
of the Association of American University Presses.

First printing 2016

∞

Library of Congress Cataloging-in-Publication Data

Names: Stone, Robert, 1937–2015, interviewee. | Heath, William, 1942– editor,
  interviewer.
Title: Conversations with Robert Stone / edited by William Heath.
Description: Jackson : University Press of Mississippi, 2016. | Series:
  Literary conversations series | Includes index.
Identifiers: LCCN 2016020065| ISBN 9781496808912 (hardback) | ISBN
  9781496808929 (epub single) | ISBN 9781496808936 (epub institutional) |
  ISBN 9781496808943 (pdf single) | ISBN 9781496808950 (pdf institutional)
Subjects: LCSH: Stone, Robert, 1937–2015. | Authors, American—20th
  century—Biography. | Novelists, American—20th century—Interviews. |
  Stone, Robert, 1937–2015—Technique. | Civilization, Modern—21st century.
  | Civilization, Modern—20th century. | BISAC: BIOGRAPHY & AUTOBIOGRAPHY /
  Literary. | LITERARY COLLECTIONS / American / General. | LITERARY
  CRITICISM / American / General.
Classification: LCC PS3569.T6418 Z88 2016 | DDC 813/.54 [B] —dc23 LC record available at
  https://lccn.loc.gov/2016020065

British Library Cataloging-in-Publication Data available

Contents

Introduction

I like men who dive.
—Herman Melville

Robert Stone published eight highly praised novels, two collections of short stories, and a memoir. Since the following interviews cover all six decades of his career, the purpose of this introduction is to provide perspective on three topics of particular importance: the author's comments on the art of fiction, his remarkable life, and his major novels.

The Craft of Fiction

In 1974 I attended a NEH Seminar on Contemporary American Literature at Amherst, where Robert Stone was teaching. During a visit to his home we discussed several issues that appear in the interviews that comprise this book. I remember best what he said about the origins of literature. He pictured cavemen sitting around the campfire telling stories, which implied that they had, at least in part, a collective consciousness. Talking about the dark, mysterious things that threatened them must have provided a source of strength. Exchanging stories demonstrates that we are not alone. We share the human condition.

"I like talking about writing," Stone told one interviewer.[1] Throughout the interviews collected in this volume, Stone repeatedly discusses the importance of telling stories: "The purpose of fiction is to help us answer the question we must constantly be asking ourselves, who do we think we are and what do we think we're doing?"[2] Stories are essential to human survival. "Because life is painful, we want . . . [our] suffering to signify something."[3] But there is a permanent gulf between words and the world. "Language makes its flying leap at life, but it is not life. . . . Literature won't pull you through, although it's there to help you."[4] With or without literature, we have to live as best we can. The novelist refines reality—which "as a phenomenology, as a primary process, does not have any meaning"[5]—into art. Thus "on some level the world's consciousness gets that tiny bit higher."[6]

As a boy, Stone "really, really wanted to write. I loved language. I loved literature."[7] Joseph Conrad and F. Scott Fitzgerald were his acknowledged masters; less obvious influences included John Dos Passos, with his multiple plots involving various characters, and Nathanael West, with his dark vision of the American grotesque. Stone studied Ernest Hemingway's sharp dialogues and grace-under-pressure situations. Charles Dickens's vivid imagination and verbal virtuosity made a lasting impression, and he praised Samuel Beckett and Louis-Ferdinand Céline for their mordant artistry.

Stone's novels focus on a few characters whose lives unfold in juxtaposed sections until their story lines intertwine. He always opens his novels with incisive dialogue as well as evocative descriptions of people and places that draw us into his world. A love of the theater—Stone spent one summer playing Kent in *King Lear*—helps explain Stone's craft. "You have to try to imagine your way into all the characters. . . . It's like ventriloquism."[8] Stone refers to taking the "soundings" of his characters, to knowing who they truly are. He deliberately writes about complicated characters, creating unsympathetic, even psychotic people. Stone tells Charles Ruas, "There's an American way of being like that. . . ." Pablo Tabor in *A Flag for Sunrise*, for example, is an attempt "to recognize the importance of the rootless, affectless, emotionally crippled individual in American life."[9]

Stone both sympathizes with and judges his characters. Usually his male protagonists are referred to by last name to ensure distance—Rheinhardt, Converse, Holliwell, Walker, Browne, Strickland. Each character is to some degree Stone's alter ego, but that does not keep him from exposing the character's flaws. "The axiom 'Character is fate' is literally true in my fiction."[10] His central characters are their own worst enemies. Put in extreme situations, they face disturbing aspects of their personalities. The veneer of civilization is stripped away, reducing them to primal emotions such as fear and anger. They must cope with their own folly plus external forces that threaten them.

Judging characters requires moral standards. "I really believe people are responsible for what they do,"[11] Stone says. Often his characters are forced to realize how hard it is to behave decently in the modern world. "Most people are more like chimpanzees than they're like Socrates, including myself. Our collective perception of what we're like is considerably at variance with what we're really like."[12] To illustrate, Stone quotes what André Malraux heard about the human condition from a wise old priest: "people are much more unhappy than one might think. And . . . there is no such thing as a grown-up."[13]

Coming to terms with the realities as well as the mysteries of existence is central to Stone's artistry. Yet, there is a miracle at the core of things: "that the very mud of the earth could somehow come to consciousness. There is some kind of significance there."[14] While asking such ultimately unanswerable questions reveals Stone's religious dimension, he remains an agnostic who resists dogmatic belief: "I don't think faith is saying, 'Well there's one God, and there are three persons,' and the rest of the catechism. That's not faith. Faith is an attitude toward things themselves, or the universe that somehow, on some level, there's some kind of meaning."[15] Stone cites what King Lear says to Edgar, pretending to be Tom in the storm: "'Thou art the thing itself. Unaccommodated man is no more than such a poor, bare, forked creature as thou art.' The thing itself; that to me is the center of all English literature."[16]

As his admiration for Shakespeare implies, Stone understands that major writers have the ability to make words sing. "Language is the medium, the music."[17] Consequently, he devotes years to each novel to achieve a distinctive style, adhering to Conrad's maxim: "Fiction must justify itself in every line." At his best, Stone writes with lyrical precision. "I see myself as being a kind of poet," he says, "but I put it in the prose."[18]

Robert Stone's fiction is not for everyone; his novels are character-centered, and his vision of life is grim. His sensibility has been stamped by the sixties. A friend of Ken Kesey, Stone was present at the creation of that decade's counterculture. His signature is his ironic tone— an on-going sense that there is something going on here, but Mr. Jones don't know what it is. You and I do, however, because we're hip, authentic, in the know—not square, inauthentic, and out of it. In Kesey's phrase, we're "on the bus." As Stone explains to Woods, "Irony is my friend and brother. 'To know true things by what their mockeries be.' There's only one subject for fiction or poetry or even a joke: *how it is*."[19] Irony implies levels of meaning—what life appears to be as opposed to what, if truth be told, it really is.

Stone's craft demonstrates his deeply personal vision. A diver, he loved to explore coral reefs, and his vision, like that of Melville before him, is strongly influenced by his experiences. "How do fishes live in the sea? As men do on land. So the bottom of the sea, to me, means primary process of nature, nature being most itself. Although it is innocent, it is full of dangers and frightening."[20] The best way to confront the horrors of existence is through art. "The very act of writing is a positive act. The dynamic that's present in most of what I write is *perception*."[21] Robert Stone's reputation rests on his mastery of the craft of fiction. The questions still to be asked are where his deep and disturbing sense of life came from and how well his individual novels fulfill his artistic standards.

West Side Story

How Stone's early life shaped his art is a central theme of the interviews in this volume. Robert Anthony Stone was born in Brooklyn on 21 August 1937 to C. Homer Stone and Gladys Catherine Grant, who never married. His father, a roustabout railroad man, abandoned his son before he was two. A schoolteacher with a cultivated manner, Gladys lost her job due to schizophrenia and thereafter had to support herself and her child on a small pension. During a three-year period, Stone boarded at St. Ann's, a Manhattan school run by the Marist Brothers. His most autobiographic story, "Absence of Mercy," details the harsh treatment he received there. During that time he lived in fear and developed a life-long anger about how he had felt "completely out of control and pitted against forces at whose mercy [he was]."[22]

The boy and his mother lived in a variety of dingy single room occupancy hotels in New York between trips to New Mexico, Canada, and Chicago. The people he observed during these ramblings exemplified the underside of American life. If not sinister, they certainly were down-and-out. Since his mother was his "contact person for reality," Stone "got some confusing signals. . . . I always used my imagination as a kind of alternative life."[23] Sometimes his mother would slip into delusions that "I was not supposed to know about."[24] He became acutely aware of the way words could create their own reality. "I had to develop a model of reality in the face of being conditioned to a schizophrenic world." As a result, "I always had a vaguely dreamlike sense of things. There was not a strong distinction for me between objective and imaginative worlds."[25]

As a student at St. Ann's into his senior year, Stone read books constantly but rarely did his homework. He was in and out of several street gangs, one of which was called the Saxons. Another, his friend Marco "Freddy" Vassi recalled, had clashes with their "natural enemies,"[26] the Puerto Ricans, where several boys were killed. Stone did not participate in these battles, but like many a rebel in search of a cause in the fifties, he dropped out of school and enlisted in the Navy.

Stone frequently refers to his years in the Navy. When drill instructors yelled at the young recruit he would instinctively cringe, a humiliating vestige of his beatings at St. Ann's. He next went to radio school in Norfolk and served as a journalist third class for Operation Deep Freeze III in the Antarctic. "I was a romantic at heart," Stone says, "and I wanted to see the world."[27] He read numerous books while in the Navy, most notably *Moby-Dick*, *Ulysses*, and *On the Road.* During the Suez War of 1956, at Port Said, Egypt, Stone witnessed French bombers strafing civilians. He visited major Mediterranean cities, albeit more as a drunken sailor than a discerning Henry James. Like Melville, Stone saw the watery part of the world, meditated on mysteries of the deep, and used his seafaring years as his Harvard and his Yale.

While working as a copyboy for the *New York Daily News* in the late 1950s, Stone took a writing class at NYU with M. L. Rosenthal. He met his wife Janice Burr in the class, and the adventure-seeking couple moved to the French Quarter in New Orleans. Stone was initiated into the demeaning grind of the American assembly line at an instant coffee plant and a liquid-soap factory and sold encyclopedias in black neighborhoods. For a while, he and Janice worked on the New Orleans census: "We were really seeing the horrid side of white Louisiana, the sweet side of black Louisiana," he recalled during an interview with Robert Solotaroff.[28] Upon his return to New York in 1961, Stone began his New Orleans novel, *A Hall of Mirrors*, which earned him a Wallace Stegner fellowship to Stanford.

California in 1962 was Paradise. "It was a garden without a snake. It had snakes, but I didn't know about them at first."[29] He began "goofing" with Ken Kesey and the Merry Pranksters, first on Perry Lane and then at La Honda—a period memorialized in Tom Wolfe's *The Electric Kool-Aid Acid Test.* "I spent a lot of my time, when I should have been writing, experiencing death and transformation and rebirth on LSD at Palo Alto. . . . It's hard to stay away from religion when you mess with acid."[30] Taking drugs made him ponder the nature of reality. Not surprisingly, most of his protagonists are substance abusers.

Stone's interviews are rich in lively comments on the sixties: "Sometimes I feel like I went to a party one day in 1963 and the party spilled out and rolled down the street until it covered the whole country and changed the world."[31] In *Prime Green: Remembering the Sixties*, his eloquent, understated memoir, Stone's wry humor underlines his insights. From serving in the Navy to working as a stringer in Saigon—with memorable stays in New York, New Orleans, Palo Alto, Hollywood, Paris, and London—he captures much that is essential about the decade by keeping the focus on personal experiences. The centerpiece is a striking portrait of his friend Ken Kesey, whose relationship with Stone comes up frequently in the following interviews. Already the author of two acclaimed novels, Kesey seemed to embody unlimited promise: "If American literature had a favorite son, distilled from the native grain, it was Kesey."[32] His charisma drew followers, inspiring him to become a guru for a generation. If only he had put "his progressively revealed mythology in novels," Stone concludes, "he might have become a writer for the age."[33] Stone, on the other hand, stayed the course, often drawing on his memories to shape his distinguished career.

Robert Stone's Fiction

Although the New Critics warn of "the Intentional Fallacy," mistaking an author's apologetics for what a work has actually accomplished, I have always found what writers had to say about the creative process of great interest. Stone naturally puts the best face on his creations as he makes many astute comments on the art of fiction. What follows is a brief overview that provides critical perspective on Stone's novels and helps clarify references to them in the interviews.

The first two parts of *A Hall of Mirrors* (1967) represent one of the most auspicious debuts in American fiction, featuring vivid characters and evocative images—the sights, smells, and sounds of New Orleans. At its heart is Stone's authentic voice and his chilling vision of a devolving, predatory world. Rheinhardt, the book's protagonist, has abandoned a promising career as a clarinetist to become a disc jockey for a right-wing radio station. The novel plays variations on the parable of the talents. Out of "tremendous spite," Stone says to Charles Ruas, Rheinhardt "has rejected his own talent. . . . There's a constant process of choosing the darkness."[34] A street-savvy guy whose "dynamic is perception," Rheinhardt's life is "an exercise in sheer existential amorality."[35] He's like Bob Dylan with his put-ons, put downs, and hostility to genuine desire. When Rainey, a sincere Christian, asks why Rheinhardt works for a reactionary radio station, he remarks: "The pop heart and mind demand assurance. Unusual times demand unusual hustles. The explanation number is very big."[36]

Geraldine, whose hard-luck story is a country western song, is one of Stone's most memorable women. In her case a newspaper ad for "TALENT" means only one thing, and the moment a pimp presses his brass knuckles against her cheek is pure terror. She loves Rheinhardt for all the wrong reasons—he's cool and "far out"—but he's bad news, a demonic drunk who makes himself as unlovable as possible to drive her away. Arrested as a vagrant and faced with her own demons, Geraldine's suicide is utterly moving. Her suicide moved Stone as well, "it was like a death had really occurred."[37]

"*A Hall of Mirrors* was something I shattered my youth against,"[38] Stone says. Since he was immersed in the counterculture at this time, the novel's realistic opening and surrealistic closing are no surprise. "I definitely think taking acid affected the book. . . . I felt released from the restrictions of the realist mode."[39] He "was carrying things to their logical, absurd conclusion" by switching "into the hallucinogenic."[40] In his effort to satirize the lunacy of power-hungry reactionaries, however, Stone resorts to surreal effects that weaken the novel's moral force, redeemed only by the powerful depiction of Geraldine's suicide. In spite of its flawed ending, *A Hall of Mirrors* brilliantly displays its author's gifts as it distinctively captures what life on the wild side was like in the sixties.

Stone's next book, *Dog Soldiers* (1974), which won the National Book Award, is closely analyzed in several interviews. In May 1971, Stone traveled from London to Vietnam on assignment for *Ink*, a short-lived periodical. During what he called "the baroque period of Saigon,"[41] there was a lull in the fighting, but the drug trade flourished. Stone says that he was "up to my ears in smack."[42] He was a quick study and a few weeks in Vietnam were enough to inspire new characters. John Converse is another ineffectual, feckless Stone hero. An unfulfilled writer, he finds himself "outside his own moral tradition."[43] After a fragmentation bomb attack in Cambodia reduces him to "a soft, shell-less, quivering thing," he is lured by Charmian, who "had taken leave of life in a way that he found irresistible,"[44] into smuggling two kilos of heroin back to the States. To succeed, Converse needs his Marine buddy Hicks, a worthy successor to the dog soldiers, a Great Plains Indian warrior society. If fear is the core of Converse's being, Hicks doesn't "know the meaning of scared."[45] He has trained in martial arts, absorbed Nietzsche's notions of the superior man, and developed a code of conduct. In living out his "Samurai fantasy," he has "the strength of his own illusions."[46] When the drug deal proves to be a set-up, Hicks overpowers two hardened ex-cons in the pay of corrupt drug enforcement official Antheil and escapes with the dope as well as Converse's strung-out wife Marge. To keep Marge from total panic, Hicks gives her heroin, and they begin a relationship based on "need and revulsion."[47] In one chilling scene Hicks gives an overdose to an author curious about drugs. "I didn't really mean for him to kill Gerald,"[48] Stone explained to Eric James Schroeder in 1984, but the book suggests otherwise.

In a violent grand finale, Stone ramps up the rhetoric as Hicks engages in combat with drug agents, rescues Converse, protects Marge, and retains the dope. Hicks then forfeits the reader's sympathy, if not the author's, when he shoots his former guru Deiter, who urges him to surrender the heroin. At *Dog Soldiers'* conclusion, Stone revealingly provides Hicks with some memories drawn from his own youth. Converse and Marge survive, but whether they have learned anything of value from their harrowing experiences remains problematical. Although Stone overreaches at the end, his novel captures the souring of the sixties and brings the evils of the Vietnam War home.

A Flag for Sunrise (1981) originated in a scuba-diving trip to the Bay Islands off Honduras in 1976, followed by visits to other Central American countries. "I could see that really bad things were going to happen, and there's nothing to stimulate a novel like a sense of general fear and paranoia."[49] Holliwell, an anthropologist who feels alienated from the human family, is a complex protagonist, and Tecan, the novel's fictitious country, displays Stone's ability to conjure up a sense of place. The most memorable scene comes when Holliwell dives to a coral reef and has a sudden revelation: "a terror struck the sea, an invisible shadow, a silence within a silence."[50] Stone's characters sometimes get "little glints of what may or may not be God," but in this case Holliwell senses that "what's down there is evil itself."[51]

Another admirable character is Justin, an American nun seeking transcendence, who secretly supports the revolution. She has a "hunger for absolutes,"[52] but in her spiritual crisis is no longer sure how to find them. Holliwell falls in love with Justin, but he betrays her to the CIA on a promise that they will protect her from Lieutenant Campos, who ultimately rapes and kills her. Stone's presentation of this horrific scene from Justin's detached point of view is concise and moving. Her last words, "Behold the handmaid of the Lord,"[53] are stunning.

Sequences involving Pablo Tabor and Father Egan are less effective. Pablo's sensibility consists of resentments and paranoid fears that everyone is trying to turn him around. When Holliwell kills Pablo to avoid being killed, his death comes none too soon. Father Egan, a whiskey priest sloshed in Gnosticism, protects a serial child killer in the deluded belief that he can save his soul. This sub-plot detracts from the main action. The simmering rage of the people of Tecan on the eve of a revolution already packs the novel with sufficient menace.

Stone discusses his scriptwriting and movie business experiences in several interviews. He considers *WUSA*, the Paul Newman film of *A Hall of Mirrors*, an unmitigated disaster but feels better about *Who'll Stop the Rain?*, based on *Dog Soldiers* and starring Nick Nolte. Stone's caustic insights about Hollywood are poured into *Children of Light* (1986), set in Baja California during the filming of Kate Chopin's *The Awakening*. Stone writes that the parties involved want an art film that might turn a profit. "A vestigial social impulse was being discharged"[54] for cynical reasons. Stone's novel might have been subtitled "fear and loathing on location," since the dialogue is relentlessly nasty, with spite and hate being the dominant emotions.

The protagonist Gordon Walker travels to the Mexican coast, purportedly to oversee his script but actually in quest of Lee "Lu Anne" Verger, who plays Chopin's heroine Edna Pontellier. A dissolute substance-abuser, Walker "brought trouble with him," Stone explained to Michael Silverblatt.[55] Lu Anne is schizophrenic; she keeps her spectral familiars, "the Long Friends," in check by medications, which she stops taking to enhance her performance. Her director approves: "She has a way of being crazy . . . that photographs pretty well."[56] Stone draws upon his mother's madness to make Lu Anne's insanity convincing. In a Grand Guignol climax Lu Anne reprises Lear's mad scene on the stormy heath with her own blood-smeared rantings, as well as Edna Pontellier's death by drowning. Walker survives, probably to snort coke and quote more Shakespeare.

Outerbridge Reach (1992) was inspired by the story of Donald Crowhurst, who in 1969 faked sailing alone around the world before committing suicide. In the story's combination of "heroism and folly"[57] Stone designed a plot with an elemental diagram of sea, sky, boat, and one man's mind that raised ultimate questions. Owen Browne, a Vietnam vet turned yacht salesman, lives comfortably in Connecticut with his wife, Anne, and their daughter, Maggie. An All American boy, Browne yearns to satisfy his "heroic longings"[58] and enters a race to circumnavigate the globe. He wants to "test his true resources," since "the sea is the bottom line,"[59] an ultimate, existential situation. Browne will pit his Emersonian self-reliance against a merciless Melvillean ocean. Anne admires her husband and anticipates success. She also knows that if she discourages him "it will be with us the rest of our lives."[60]

Ron Strickland is hired to film the story. A confirmed cynic with an eye for human weakness, to him everyone is a phony, and he uses his cunning to skewer them. The "squeaky clean world of the Brownes, Mom, Dad and little Sis, self-absorbed, oblivious,"[61] is his meat. He pins their photos on his wall just as prehistoric hunters conjured up their prey with cave paintings. Like Satan in the biblical story of Job, he plots to destroy "the man of rectitude with a faithful wife."[62] He embodies the demonic aspect of Stone's artistry. Wised-up to a fault, Strickland's art is fueled by fear and rage that originated in a childhood similar to Stone's own. Fear, Strickland admits, was "truly the mother of sensibility."[63] The novel's second half juxtaposes Browne's ill-fated voyage—first his boat breaks down and then *he* does— with Strickland's seduction of Anne. Browne does resemble Job, since every day at sea is a trial of mind, body, and spirit. Meditation and water are wedded forever, Melville tells us, and, as Browne ponders, he deconstructs himself and becomes delusional. By lying about his true position, Browne does "something almost blasphemous," Stone says. "He's creating a universe . . . of singularities . . . an absolutely arbitrary, godless, meaningless, unfathomable world."[64] Finally, Browne immerses himself in the destructive element and drowns.

As Owen sinks, Anne succumbs. Touched by his hard childhood and obvious attentions, she misreads Strickland's malevolence: "Owen was at sea. Ashore she was beset, outmaneuvered, of questionable morale."[65] Still, it is one thing to have a drunken tumble with a talented seducer, another to wake up in love. Anne's transformation is too sudden. Not until sixty pages later does she express regret. "She's just astonished at what happens," Stone says.[66] Anne is very observant; if Stone had added more self-analysis to her musings, falling for Strickland might have made better sense. Yet despite Stone's questionable "soundings" of Anne's character, *Outerbridge Reach* is the author's finest work.

The origin of *Damascus Gate* (1998), Stone's longest novel, was a trip to Egypt followed by a stay in Jerusalem, "the very place that stood for everything I have been writing about," Stone told Robert Birnbaum in 2003.[67] Stone's hero Chris Lucas notes that Jerusalem is "the center of the world, where earth touches heaven."[68] Various characters are on the road to Damascus seeking salvation. A part-Jewish lapsed-Catholic, Lucas is researching "the Jerusalem Syndrome,"[69] people in the city on largely delusional divine missions. The novel has three main components: Lucas's fitful romance with Sonia Barnes, the cornucopia of cults he encounters, and a conspiracy to blow up the Temple Mount. A biracial nightclub singer and a Sufi, Sonia insists that Lucas share her beliefs before he share her bed. What follows is a kind of *Clarissa* theme: to convert or not convert. Will Lucas take a leap of faith? Sonia is more appealing as a talented chanteuse than a true believer, and the novel's unruly cast of international characters quickly becomes confusing. One sub-plot follows Raziel "Razz" Melker, who is grooming Adam De Kuff as a Christ for the new millennium. Unfortunately, arcane belief systems are Stone's catnip; he can't resist swatting them around. When Razz regurgitates esoteric lore, Stone recounts it all without irony or satire.

Damascus Gate fits the Hollywood adage: the first half of a film belongs to the director to develop the characters, while the producer owns the second. Gun running, dope smuggling, random murders, rioting Palestinians, Israeli agent provocateurs—capped by a convoluted plan to blow up the Temple Mount—these sensational events swamp the latter part of the book. The result is a plot that is too clever by half and a novel where less would have been more.

Bay of Souls (2003) is set in a college town in Minnesota, where Professor Michael Ahearn fears his life lacks meaning. Enter Lara Purcell, a Caribbean professor of third world issues. "She looks crazy," Michael says, and is told, "She is. And she makes other people crazy too."[70] We know where this plot is headed. Michael learns that she has lost her soul, her *ti bon ange*, now in the possession of either her dead brother under the waters of All Souls Bay in Guinee or of the wild goddess Marinette. Instead of running from the room, Michael abandons his family to join her. As the plot thickens, the book implodes. When a chastened Michael returns from his year of living dangerously, he has learned nothing. "I wanted more,"[71] he says. Despite a strong opening and other distinctive scenes, this is Stone's weakest novel.

Stone's final work, *Death of the Black-Haired Girl* (2013), exposes town-gown tensions between an elite college and a decaying city. Professor Steve Brookman has recently ended a year-long affair with a student, Maud Stack, who wants Brookman to leave his wife. Combative by nature, Maud mocks the self-righteous anti-abortionists in an incendiary article. As these two plot lines converge, she is raging outside Brookman's home when she is hit by a car. Although her death is an accident, this is New England; Puritan ghosts walk. Faced with nothingness, even a God of Wrath has appeal. If we are innately depraved and *deserve* to die, then sudden loss has a kind of meaning. Maud's father Eddie Stack blames his sins for Maud's death, thinks of killing Brookman, and battles the Church to have his daughter's ashes placed beside her mother's. The most sympathetic figure is Jo Carr, who brings common sense and compassion to the situation. A neo-noir novel with a metaphysical slant, this book delivers unsettling news about the human condition.

Stone also wrote provocative short stories, most notably "Helping" in *Bear and His Daughter* (1997) and "High Wire" in *Fun with Problems* (2010). His articles and reviews will be published as a book in the near future. The interviews presented here are complete. Mistakes have been silently corrected. See www.williamheathbooks.com for a list of additional interviews. The contributions of the interviewers are apparent; they provide acute insights while covering a wide range of important topics. Stone responds to their probing questions about each of his major works, adding insightful comments on the craft of fiction and his own life. Most impressive is the poised and thoughtful way he answers each question as truthfully as he can. John Cheever once said that reading quality fiction constitutes the most mature form of conversation among human beings.[72] An author candidly discussing his distinguished career is a comparable treasure.

I want to express my gratitude to the interviewers for their gracious cooperation as well as to Katie Keene, Monika Gehlawat, Shane Gong Stewart, Steve Yates, and the rest of the staff at the University Press of Mississippi for making this book possible. My beloved wife Roser and long-time friend Frank Bergon provided invaluable assistance. And a special thanks to Janice Stone for her support.

WH

Notes

1. Maureen Karagueuzian, "Interview with Robert Stone," *Triquarterly 53* (Winter 1982): 256.

2. William Crawford Woods, "Robert Stone Interview," *Writers at Work: Eighth Series*, George Plimpton, ed. (New York: Viking, 1988): 364.

3. L. P. Griffith, John Schultze, and Stephanie Anderson, "Robert Stone Interview" in Memphis, 29 September 2006.

4. "Me and the Universe," *The Writer in Our World*, Reginald Gibbons, ed., *Triquarterly 65* (Winter 1986): 229, 231.

5. Eric James Schroeder, "Keep the Levels of Consciousness Sharp," *Vietnam, We've All Been There: Interviews with American Writers* (Westport, CT: Praeger, 1992): 111.

6. Stone, "Me and the Universe," 233.

7. Christopher Bollen, "The Total Anti-Totalist," *Interview Magazine*. 2014. http://interview magazine.com/culture/robert-stone-death-of-the-black-hair-girl.

8. Griffin et. al., Stone interview.

9. Charles Ruas, *Conversations with American Authors* (New York: Alfred A. Knopf, 1985): 275.

10. Karagueuzian, "Interview," 249.

11. Ibid., 255.

12. Ruas, *Conversations*, 282.

13. Kay Bonetti, "Robert Stone Interview," *Conversations with American Novelists*, Kay Bonnetti, Greg Michaelson, Speer Morgan, Jo Sapp, and Sam Stowers, eds. (Columbia: University of Missouri Press, 1997): 12.

14. Ibid.

15. Griffith et. al., Stone interview.

16. Robert Solotaroff, "An Interview with Robert Stone," *South Carolina Review* (Fall 1993): 47–48.

17. Bonetti, *Conversations*, 17.

18. Griffith et. al., Stone interview.

19. Woods, *Writers at Work*, 350.

20. Ruas, *Conversations*, 292–93.

21. Bonetti, *Conversations*, 13.

22. Steven Benson and Robert Solotaroff, "Talking Sense," *KUOM*, Minneapolis radio interview, 1 May 1992.

23. Woods, *Writers at Work*, 353.

24. Solotaroff, "Interview," 28.

25. Woods, *Writers at Work*, 360.

26. Marco Vassi, *The Stoned Apocalypse* (New York: Trident Press, 1972): 37.

27. Bollen, "Anti-Totalist."

28. Solotaroff, "Interview," 38.

29. Bollen, "Anti-Totalist."

30. Woods, *Writers at Work*, 347.

31. Bonetti, *Conversations*, 22.

32. Robert Stone, *Prime Green* (New York: Ecco, 2007): 93–94.

33. Ibid., 161.

34. Ruas, *Conversations*, 276.

35. Robert Stone, *A Hall of Mirrors* (Boston: Houghton Mifflin, 1967): 251.

36. Ibid., 250.

37. Ruas, *Conversations*, 277.

38. Woods, *Writers at Work*, 347.

39. Solotaroff, "Interview," 39.

40. Bollen, "Anti-Totalist."

41. Schroeder, "Levels of Consciousness," 109.

42. William Heath and Michael Berryhill, "An Interview with Robert Stone at Vassar," 20 February 1975.

43. Ibid.

44. Robert Stone, *Dog Soldiers* (Boston: Houghton Mifflin, 1974): 24.

45. Ibid., 141.

46. Heath and Berryhill, Vassar interview.

47. Stone, *Dog Soldiers*, 114.

48. Schroeder, "Levels of Consciousness," 114.

49. Bollen, "Anti-Totalist."

50. Robert Stone, *A Flag for Sunrise* (New York: Knopf, 1981): 227.

51. Ruas, *Conversations*, 292.

52. Stone, *A Flag for Sunrise*, 343.

53. Ibid., 416.

54. Robert Stone, *Children of Light* (New York: Knopf, 1986): 12.

55. Michael Silverblatt, Interview with Robert Stone on Bookworm, 27 July 1992. http://www .salon.com/1997/04/14/stone_2/.

56. Stone, *Children of Light*, 110.

57. Benson and Solotaroff, "Talking Sense."

58. Silverblatt, Bookworm.

59. Robert Stone, *Outerbridge Reach* (New York: Ticknor & Fields, 1992): 139.

60. Ibid., 190.

61. Ibid., 134.

62. Benson and Solotaroff, "Talking Sense."

63. Stone, *Outerbridge Reach*, 193.

64. Benson and Solotaroff, "Talking Sense."

65. Stone, *Outerbride Reach*, 293.

66. Benson and Solotaroff, "Talking Sense."

67. Robert Birnbaum, "Interview with Robert Stone," 11 May 2003. http://www.identitytheory .com/robert-stone/.

68. Robert Stone, *Damascus Gate* (Boston: Houghton Mifflin, 1998): 484.

69. Ibid., 42.

70. Robert Stone, *Bay of Souls* (Boston: Houghton Mifflin, 2003): 47.

71. Ibid., 234.

72. John Cheever in a conversation with William Heath, Vassar College, 26 April 1979.

Chronology

1937	Robert Anthony Stone born 21 August at Good Samaritan Hospital in Brooklyn to C. Homer Stone and Gladys Catherine Grant. They never married.
1939–1955	Abandoned by his father. Stone lives in Manhattan with his mother, who has a small pension after losing her teaching job due to her schizophrenia.
1942–1955	Attends St. Ann's School in Manhattan; resides there from 1943 to 1946. In his senior year he drops out of school.
1955–1958	Enlists on 9 August 1955, in US Navy. During Suez War in 1956, on the USS *Chilton* in Port Said, Egypt, when French planes strafe civilians. Stone is senior enlisted journalist in 1957–1958 on the USS *Arneb* during Operation Deep Freeze III to the Antarctic.
1958–1959	Works as copyboy and caption writer for *New York Daily News*. Takes a writing class with M. L. Rosenthal at NYU.
1959	Marries Janice G. Burr on 11 December.
1960	Lives in the French Quarter of New Orleans from February to October. Works in an instant coffee plant and a liquid-soap factory and as a census taker and a seller of *Collier's Encyclopedias*. Daughter Deidre born on 15 June.
1961	Returns to New York. Lives at St. Mark's Place. Begins *A Hall of Mirrors*.
1962–1964	Stegner Fellow at Stanford University. Meets Ken Kesey. Takes psychedelic drugs and parties with the Merry Pranksters on Perry Lane.
1963	Son Ian born on 24 May. Kesey moves to La Honda.
1964	Awarded Houghton Mifflin Literary Fellowship. In mid-July Kesey's bus of Merry Pranksters arrives at Stone's apartment on West 97th Street in New York.
1965–1967	Writes for tabloids *National Mirror* and *Inside News*. Travels to Europe.

1966   Travels to Manzanillo, Mexico, to report for *Esquire* on Ken
            Kesey in exile.

1967   *A Hall of Mirrors* published. It is a Book-of-the-Month Club
            selection.

1968   Receives the William Faulkner Foundation Prize for the best
            first novel of 1967.

1968–1971   Lives in London but in Hollywood to write a screenplay for *A
            Hall of Mirrors*. In May–June 1971, Stone is a stringer for *Ink*
            magazine in Saigon, where drug use is rampant.

1970   *WUSA*, the film version of *A Hall of Mirrors*, starring Paul
            Newman, released.

1971–1972   Guggenheim Fellow and writer-in-residence at Princeton
            University.

1972–1975   Teaches at Amherst College.

1974   *Dog Soldiers* published. It wins the National Book Award the
            following year.

1976–1977   Scuba-diving trip to Honduras. Visits several Central Ameri-
            can countries.

1977–1978   Returns to Amherst College.

1978   Writes screenplay (with Judith Roscoe) for *Who'll Stop the
            Rain?*, a film based on *Dog Soldiers,* that featured Nick Nolte as
            Hicks.

1979   *Who'll Stop the Rain?* nominated by the Writers' Guild of
            America for best script adapted from another medium.

1979–1980   Teaches at Stanford University and at the University of
            Hawaii–Manoa.

1981–1983   Teaches at Harvard University, the University of California–
            Irvine, and NYU.

1981   *A Flag for Sunrise* published. It receives the John Dos Passos
            Prize for Literature and the Los Angeles Book Prize. Finalist
            for the Pulitzer Prize, Pen/Faulkner Award, and National Book
            Award. Stone stays in Westport, Connecticut, until 1998.

1982   Receives the American Academy and Institute of Arts and
            Letters Award. Plays a prominent leadership role in the PEN/
            Faulkner Foundation for the rest of his life.

1983   Receives NEA fellowship.

1986   *Children of Light* published.

1987   Receives Mildred and Harold Strauss Living Award.

1992   *Outerbridge Reach* published. Receives Ambassador Book Award. Finalist for the National Book Award. Edits *Best American Short Stories* 1992.

1993–1994 Teaches at Johns Hopkins University.

1995–2002 Writer-in-Residence at Yale University. Lives in Westport and Key West.

1997   *Bear and His Daughter* published. Finalist for the Pulitzer Prize.

1998   *Damascus Gate* published. Finalist for the National Book Award.

1999   Moves to Manhattan.

2003   *Bay of Souls* published.

2005–2015 Honorary Director of the Key West Literary Seminar.

2007   *Prime Green: Remembering the Sixties* published. Receives the Ambassador Book Award.

2010   *Fun with Problems* (stories) published. Endowed Chair in the English department at Texas State University–San Marcos.

2013   *Death of the Black-Hair Girl* published.

2015   Dies 10 January of heart failure in Key West. Stone, a chain-smoker for many years, suffered from emphysema.

Conversations with Robert Stone

An Interview with Robert Stone

William Heath and Michael Berryhill / 1975

Printed by permission.

At my request and for an absurdly low fee, Robert Stone came to Vassar College and met with students from classes in American literature and creative writing taught by Michael Berryhill and myself. Stone was remarkably poised and gracious as he fielded a wide variety of questions about both *A Hall of Mirrors* and *Dog Soldiers*, as well as his early life, the craft of fiction, and his experiences in the sixties.

Heath: Would you give us the background on how you became a writer?

Stone: I went into the service. I started out in the Navy as a radio operator, and then I became a journalist third class, which is what I was officially called. Then I became a petty officer, and I went to Antarctica on Operation Deep Freeze. I wrote a series of official reports about that operation. I got out of the service in my early twenties, and I went to work as a reporter for the *Daily News*. I started going to NYU, but I dropped out, left the *News*, and then went South and worked at a lot of different jobs in and around New Orleans. I continued that and wandered around for a while until it seemed to me that I had a sense of what the beginnings of a novel should be like and, on the basis of this beginning, got a fellowship to Stanford. When I got to Stanford there were an awful lot of curious things going on that made it much more fun to do almost anything else than write. So the novel was a long-delayed process. It was finally published in '67. So as far as my relationship to writing goes, that's it. It took me about five years on and off to write because I quit writing it a lot and then would begin again. I've published a couple of stories and the most recent novel [*Dog Soldiers*]. In the meantime I've done certain journalistic gigs on and off, and I'm now writing a third [novel].

Heath: How did you go about researching *Dog Soldiers*?

Stone: I didn't really research it. I didn't know what I was doing when I began it. I knew I had experienced certain people's lives around me, some of whom were fairly close to me, some people not. But what the moral of the damn thing was I didn't know. At a certain point I got the opportunity to go to Vietnam, and I had been sort of messing around with these people, with their story, and what their lives were like. It occurred to me when I got there that I was seeing the other side of American reality in the sixties, but this suddenly forced me into a recognition of what things were actually about. Now that may be a literary conceit, and how much it could be experienced in terms of reality, I'm not sure, but that was the sense I had. When I came back from there I had worked out whatever the moral was, whatever the direction was, and in the course of working it out, I think it changed my politics a lot. It changed a lot of my attitudes. I wasn't really sure what it was up to until I came to the end of that book. I was finally satisfied at the end that what was there was a true thing, that those people were true, and that what attached to them was true. So it wasn't exactly a matter of research beyond trying to figure out exactly what I'd seen, once I got back, in terms of the nomenclature of weaponry and so forth. It wasn't the kind of book that you have to research.

Heath: What about the sequence at the end, where Hicks gets up on the mountain with Dieter and so forth? What are the origins of some of those people?

Stone: I don't think there is any personal origin in any one person I know for Dieter. It certainly is not Ken Kesey, which has been suggested. Dieter isn't anything like Kesey at all. True enough Kesey had a house out in the woods with a lot of curious things that was wired, so possibly there were some physical origins for what the plan of that place was like, but certainly Dieter was not Kesey or anything like him. There were a lot of people in various places in the late sixties who were trying to organize what everyone else was trying to find out. Dieter is meant to be one of those people. There was a sense at a certain time that traditions were crumbling and that people would have to develop centers to stay in and work within, like the ninth-century monks. That somehow things would have to be renewed through the spiritual efforts of a number of dedicated bands of people. That sounds rather fatuous now, but didn't at the time for a lot of people. Dieter has seen that it's a failure. It's a failed experiment, and Dieter is a failed experimenter. I mean for him to be, I suppose, rather pathetic, but I also mean for him to have a certain kind of nobility, a certain kind of basic humanity.

Berryhill: You mentioned that you started with the characters and then you found a moral center for the novel. I was wondering is the moral center *in* any of the characters? We start with Converse, and then our attention is switched to Hicks, something as basic as that. How do you conceive of those two men in terms of moral attitude?

Stone: To have a common situation that involves three people, through a sequence of events, three people say, and by changing the center of the palimpsest you change the consideration on the balances totally. If you don't get then the total experience, you get a kind of dead reckoning sense of what the moral center of the situation is. I think that it is literally true in the novel that character is fate. The people are what happens. It is a very different thing in life to figure out what is going on. And sometimes it is even a difficult thing in life to figure out who anyone is, even who you are yourself. In working out a novel you are kind of recapitulating the problems that go on in real life, or life that is as real as it gets. This sense of action carrying a certain moral weight. *Moral* gets to be a curious word, and you say, "What do you mean by that?" I mean people acting on each other in situations that are in extremis, or even situations that are not in extremis. This strange charge is being raised. People are putting promises to each other in certain possibly inchoate ways. People are representing themselves to other people in some kind of performance. This process that we don't exactly understand goes on, and we can see this in life. That is what the novel's about. It is an inquiry into that process so that all of these people take on a certain responsibility for their own actions. And the general effect of that is what the novel is about. It's not so much to say, "What is the moral center of these events and to these people, and is there such a thing as a moral center?" It gets down to questions that are very difficult to answer, so it's a thrust in the direction of an answer or answers.

Berryhill: There's a series of confrontations, Converse and Marge, a series of moral actions. Right from the beginning, when Converse propositions the missionary and going on down the line. So that finally what comes about is that they are going out into the desert on what they know is a kind of hopeless mission.

Stone: They suspect, although they are never sure, any of them, that what they are doing is not merely a gesture. In a way Converse and Hicks are opposites. If you can postulate three directions, rather than four, Hicks and Converse, at least, are opposites. Because Converse is like a great many people now. He is thoroughly conversant with the moral language of the time. One of the strange things about the last ten years is that there has never been so much consciousness of what is right to do, so much outrage against injustice, so much sense of the moral priorities, and so much total disregard of them. There has been a tremendous seeming increase in moral awareness, and at the same time there's been this abandonment of moral principles, that I think you can actually experience in reality. So Converse is a guy like a lot of people who really speaks the language of moral awareness and knows how the game is played and is thoroughly outside of it. Hicks has a much simpler basis in it. He buys a whole lot of myths in toto. In a way he's sounder. But he's accepted the acting out of this mythological structure that was given to him, which is a fairly primitive one, as a moral base. And for him it works. Converse is outside his own moral tradition. He practically has none at all. He ends up in a way being led. These people are doing things, and they're not even convinced of the reality or meaningfulness of what they are doing. They're making gestures, or for all they know they're making gestures. So that both Converse and Marge in their respective ways are cooled out. They can only make gestures. And Hicks knows only gestures to start with.

Berryhill: A lot of the gestures, the heroic gestures, come out of things that you quite pointedly refer to. What I mean is literary and cinematic motifs. For instance, it's no accident that the one film quotation is from Hawks. *Only Angels Have Wings* is on TV while the two agents are torturing Converse, and the other one is John Wayne in *The Searchers*—the lonely hero, isolated from the community, and things of that type. And the Hawks thing is "Are you any good?" Support your buddy, or you never cry over your buddy's death because he wasn't good enough. There are these kinds of literary motifs built into it, and I was wondering how conscious you were when you started the novel. I mean, "Are my obligations to Joseph Conrad?" What kind of impulse is there? Could you talk a little bit about these motifs?
Stone: I think the motifs come right out of the writing. Hawks has done more than describe the situation of men acting in terms of a code. To some extent the code may not have existed before Hawks. As naïve or strange as it sounds, or as naïve an attitude of mind as this may seem to reflect, Hawks

has really told a lot of people how they are supposed to behave. And they do. People do act on the basis of what they see in movies. Certainly people of a certain age, they actually do. It's true. And a lot of what Hicks is acting out is trivial, but in a way it's also rather moving. A lot of things that compel a guy like Hicks is the romanticism of a certain kind of film, which is just as sound a cultural tradition from his point of view as any other. But still the tradition has to be in touch with something real. It's not just to say that the guy is acting in a way he's seen people act in movies. But he's kept in touch with a certain tradition of behavior that he's seen referred to in film. It gets referred to because it is a part of his cultural equipment. It's part of what's operating in the underworld of the book. I don't think there are any similarities between the kind of writing I do and Conrad's. But I certainly do feel that something about the writing of the novel I learned from Conrad. I have a feeling that I know more about writing novels from having read Conrad, who is a favorite writer of mine, than from almost any other novelist I can think of. I learned something about how novels are supposed to go, or at least what I like about novels, what I like about the novel, from reading Conrad.

Berryhill: You've got the same situations, like rapacity in the jungle. Conrad's Marlowe had a constant fever like Converse, little things that are just part and parcel of writing about the same world. But also Marlow's old aunt who sends him off, and the old woman knitting in front of the door. I think of Charmian and the missionary woman—foils of each other, kind of guardians of the portal as Converse goes for his trip into hell. They're a kind of signpost.
Stone: Yeah, I think that's true. Their respective attitudes toward women are significant because Converse's sexuality is indulgent and generally directed. His attitude toward women is totally different from Hicks's. Hicks is looking at women as a kind of prize, as a possession, in a very old fashioned primitive way. Well that's what he thinks, or so he thinks. Because in fact his relation toward Marge or his attitude toward women are somewhat different to that. There are a whole lot of things that it seems to me that I know about Hicks and how he thinks about women that are not exactly in the book, that have to do with Hicks's mother. It's not out there, but I believe it. It's not in the book, but I believe it. I profess to know about it.

Berryhill: Could you say something about how you create a character?
Stone: I could say something about it, but I may be just making it up on the

spot. Obviously, I think you have to know a lot more about a character than you put in the book. I think you have to believe in a character completely. I certainly believe in these characters. I believe in the characters in *A Hall of Mirrors* to the point where I got very upset when one of them committed suicide, and I'm not kidding. I really did. I believed in them. I have to get a certain investment in them in order to work with them at all, because they really dominate my world while I'm doing it. And I have to believe in them and know a lot about them. I have to know them as intimately as I can know them and persuade myself that they're not fiction, but almost at a certain point that they are some kind of spirits, as though they have some kind of reality in the universe. I know they haven't, but I have to persuade myself that they have. And sometimes I can. I think you have to be able to answer a lot of questions necessarily to yourself about how these people are, and what their origins are. You must know them as thoroughly as they can be known, being the ephemeral creatures that they are, finally.

Berryhill: How do you know what to leave out when you know a lot about a character?

Stone: It's hard to know what to leave out. I think it's a matter of balancing. It's a matter of balancing passages, because I like to do the sections or the chapters or whatever in a certain kind of relationship to each other. You get to a point where you feel that you've gone on too long, that somehow less is better. If one has a heavier weight than the one following it, or the one before, I think there's an impulse toward symmetry, to just sort of cut that out, to say, "All right, you don't need it," that it's going to work better against the other section or that other chapter if you leave just that much out. I think it's always a necessity to be as precise as you possibly can be. Because past a certain point you are just parading attributes in front of your reader. You're decking out a character with a whole lot of history and equipment, and it becomes obtrusive. Or it becomes obtrusive to me at any rate when I am at the point of establishing the credentials of such and such a person as a real person. I feel that I'm going beyond the necessities of story-telling at a certain point, so I'll just strike it out. I think it's a very important thing to know what you should have out there and when you should stop. But I don't know how the process really works. I think it's fairly intuitive.

Heath: Wallace Stegner said about your first novel [*A Hall of Mirrors*] that you don't appear in it and that you never will appear in one of your fictions. Do you find that helpful? I find your fiction distinguished by its ability to at once love and judge your characters. No one gets off the hook, and yet obviously you care about them all. Is keeping yourself out a part of that? Although I also feel that you get judged in there too in various guises of yourself.

Stone: I think that's an inevitable part of the process. In a way I've always thought about these people that I wouldn't have done what they did. I wouldn't have to be them if I could make them up. I think there have always been certain possibilities in any character I'm close to in my novels that has to do with me, but I've never had the feeling that any of them in any sense could ever be said to be representations of me. While in no sense are they me, they do certain things for me that I might do in their circumstances, or might have done, and yet as long as I can keep them doing it for me, I don't have to do it. I mean that I am in and out of them is necessary, because if I can't get behind that person's eyes, then I don't know what they are like. They have to be at least enough like me—any of them, all of them—for me to experience what their reality is like. And that I do love them is generally true. Judgments are passed. I think especially in *Dog Soldiers* there are references to the business of writing, to the business of feeding on grief, on war. The question of what is the morality of taking a situation like a war and people's sufferings and turning it into a book, that is addressed, and that should be addressed in the book. Because I was aware of that. When I was in Vietnam I felt I knew a lot of people who I thought very highly of, and I thought that I was sort of turning my back on them when I left, which I was in a position to do, and that I was going off finally to take this and make a book out of it. All those things bothered me on some level, and they are referred to in the book.

Heath: A lot of the characters in both of your novels talk about how the old moral values just don't apply anymore. They really are at a loss on how to cope with a sense of a chaotic world coming down on them. From what standpoint, then, do you manage to judge? Because the judgment is felt, and yet is there moral confusion in you, too?

Stone: Yes, it's mine. Yet I presume to try and work out a standard by juxtaposing one of them to the other and by putting them loose in a world where action is important. Where actions are definitive and are finally definitive. But their moral confusion is certainly mine. I really don't know properly what standards to apply, and partly the books are an attempt, in the palimpsest effect, to try to apply different points of view and different standards to things that are being done. The moral relativism in these books, and also some of the stories, is very important. That echoes a kind of moral confusion, because I don't properly know what to bring to bear. I think that's a common condition unless you go ahead and accept a moral frame of reference. If you say, "All right I am a Marxist and the advancement of social engineering, or putting forward the historical process, is my morality." Or unless you embrace a religion and you take the moral structure of that religion. People are actually, actively doing these things now. They are turning to the moral structures of religions and the moral structures of political systems. And to attempt to stand outside these things, I think, is very difficult, and it demands a constant redefinition. An awful lot of people who I know, or I have been close to, have become either actively political or they have become religiously oriented. I've watched them do this. I've watched this process closely. And it's partly I guess what I'm talking about and what I'm referring to in the book.

Berryhill: This brings us to the problem of where a writer belongs. If you become, say, a Marxist or a religionist, what happens to the objectivity of your art?

Stone: I don't think that it's necessarily true that you lose it. In a way there is no objectivity, finally. Because you do get into a place that you're speaking from. It's possible for an artist to be a Marxist and an objective and a sensitive artist. It's possible for an artist to be a religionist and still have the necessary objectivity. There are examples. It's always a matter of that curious rule in the world that nothing is free. And that whatever confidence you may gain in the world from taking on a certain point of view, you will somehow give up something for it. But it works the other way around, because you have to give up a certain kind of certitude in order to keep your place on the shifting moral grounds and comment on what's going on around you. I don't know that the condition of the writer now . . . I mean, I'm not even sure that the condition of the world, that the condition of western society, is so qualitatively different now. It seems to me that it is, but I don't know. I can't know that. I suppose the people that I've known in the last twenty years have been self-dramatizing people, and that I've been one, too. We've all been going around telling each other the sky is falling, western civilization is coming to an end, the revolution is at hand, and the millennium is upon us. It's been a lot of fun. But how true that is I'm not altogether certain. I suspect that it's probably true, that we are at some furious impasse, but I'm not altogether sure of that.

Berryhill: Doesn't Marge say it's going to go on for a million years?

Stone: Yeah, I felt that when she said that, that she was right.

Heath: I notice that both your novels are laden with a great number of references to Christianity and especially the more prophetic books of Christianity. Is that just because it's in the culture, or does it have a special appeal for you to bring all those in?

Stone: No, probably that's reflective of me. It's certainly in the culture. It's a part of the culture that I refer to a great deal because when I was an adolescent I was very involved with religion. I was personally very religious, and on some level or other, continue to be so. I think my attitude toward things in general is a religious one. Maybe it's just a superstitious one. The religious culture of the West has always been fairly important to me, personally as a writer, so it is something I refer to a great deal. A lot of the moral language that comes most easily to me is religious, so I do employ it.

Heath: What will become of Rheinhardt?

Stone: I've often wondered what it would be, and I'm not really sure. I know he's come to this particular pass where he's going to the Mile High City. I think it is not out of the question that Rheinhardt can somehow move into something else with greater strength, but I'm not really sure of that. I don't know if he's thoroughly undone. He keeps saying, "Defend me, friends. I am but hurt." And on a certain level he believes it. You know, that's the eternal optimism of Claudius in *Hamlet*. He really wants to believe, even though he's just been run through, that he's all right. Rheinhardt is quoting Claudius there, who is a character in a tragedy who has been skewered, but who clings to a kind of almost perverse joie de vivre. He would like to believe that on some level he can go on. And yet what he has experienced has been a thorough-going despair. I'm not sure. I don't know what happens to him. I think it's open-ended.

Heath: If he continues to survive, would it be a victory?

Stone: It would depend on what happens next. In a way it could be a humiliation. It really is open-ended.

Heath: What did you think of the movie *WUSA*?

Stone: I'll tell you about that. I'll tell you two things: my name is on the screenplay, and the lines spoken by the actors have very little to do with anything written by me. In a way I suppose I've been informally alibiing that movie for years and years. I'm sorry about it; I really am. It's a lousy movie. There's no question about that. All I can tell you is, it's not my fault. It really isn't. I did write a script for it. That script was cut up and thrown around, and I didn't have the sense to take my name off. So I feel very badly that it has my name on it. And because it has my name on it I probably owe everybody who has ever seen it an apology, so I do apologize. It is a god-awful movie.

Heath: How were they allowed to change the rally scene?
Stone: They just did. I'd say, "You can't do that," and they said, "Yes we can." It's as simple as that. You just don't get control. I was off miles and miles away when those decisions were made. There was a time when I was around when I would see the rushes after a scene, and I would complain. People would say, "Oh, you don't like that scene? Well, we'll shoot it all over again. What do you think of that?" And of course the set would have been taken down by then the day before. So you just don't get that kind of control. It's very tempting to try and translate something from book into film, if you like film, and I like film. And I think the experience is very satisfying in a lot of ways, but it's also deadly. Or it can be. I had a shot at it. The circumstances were really wrong. There wasn't much I could do about it.

Berryhill: What about *Dog Soldiers*?
Stone: Well, to the extent that the book is a different thing, I don't care. I have no feelings about them buying the book and making a film out of it. As long as my name's not on it. Now if you saw *WUSA*, it has my name on it. People might think this is what Stone thinks is a good movie. And that bothers me. But that the book is bought, that it is made into a film, doesn't bother me at all. It's a totally accepted thing. If I were to try to do a scenario for it, that would be another matter. Then I would worry a lot about whether it's any good or not. As a film that is simply an adaptation of my book, I don't care.

Berryhill: Do you think it would be hard to make *Dog Soldiers* into a good movie?
Stone: It would be very difficult with *A Hall of Mirrors*. With *Dog Soldiers*? Very difficult. If there is one good movie in it, there are ninety-nine bad ones. And they'll make the ninety-nine bad ones first before they get to the good one. To the people in the industry I think it looks deceptively easy.

It is much less a realistic novel than it may seem to be. There are a lot of pitfalls in it. It's more difficult than it may appear. I think it's a very tough thing to get a good movie out of it. There's always the danger that you get into this vulgarization, this trivialization, the characters flatten out. Because you can't have that undergrowth in it, you can't have that level which is symbolic. You've got to rely totally on the director to do the visual, associative, symbolic equivalent of what you're doing in the little throw-a-ways, in the associations of your prose. Unless you've got somebody who can do that with a camera, in terms of your own intentions, everything's going to flatten out. And you're gonna get this trivialization. And it's very difficult to avoid.

Berryhill: It's a highly visual book. I think of something like the sticker stuck to the bottom of the shoe that Converse sees or your use of alternation, especially toward the end, cutting back and forth between Hicks and Marge, and Converse. Simultaneous action.
Stone: That's true, but it doesn't necessarily recapitulate the process of the camera. I mean, something with the mind's eye is not exactly the same as something with a camera. All the writers I am most fond of, some of whom go back to long before movies were ever thought of, do that kind of thing with the mind's eye. Whether you can do quite the same thing with a camera, I'm not certain. Maybe you can. It would be good. I'd like to see it made into a good film. I don't know whether that's possible. There is a director who's interested in it named Karel Reisz [*Who Will Stop the Rain?* (1978)].

Heath: Are there any scenes in *Dog Soldiers* that would be especially difficult to shoot?
Stone: Some of them are impossible. You can tell which scenes simply by reading the book. Any kind of internalized concept would be difficult to film. There are characters whose heads are filled with associations. There's no way you can film that.

Berryhill: Could you tell us about the title, *Dog Soldiers*?
Stone: There was a society of the plains Indians, specifically of the Blackfeet, called the "Dog Lodge." These were people whose function was ambiguous; they opted out of the tribal society on one level and on another level they were particular protectors. They took away all their responsibilities as tribal citizens, but they were regarded to behave as people who were already dead. So it was a case of a society allowing for an opting out, a kind of desperate opting out, yet at the same time making those who had opted out

become its own particular protectors in war. They were expected to fight as though they were already dead. They were permitted all manner of license within the tribe, but at the same time their function was partly sacred in the same way as the shamans of some other tribes were permitted their license because their function was priestly and sacred. That's what I was thinking, and it seemed kind of heavy-handed to write an introduction about that so I just didn't say anything about it.

Berryhill: They also do things on the hunt. Aren't they a communal order for hunting?
Stone: It's been a long time since I read about them. I think they had a lot of spiritual priestly functions within the plains Indians tribes that are interesting and ambiguous.

Heath: Conrad is one of your favorite writers. Who are some of the others?
Stone: I've always loved Dickens very much. Dickens is an underrated writer in a way. I like Conrad very much. Although there are a lot of writers that I like and admire, I don't think they are very similar to me as writers. Among contemporaries, I think William Gass is a very fine writer. I think Bob Coover is also. Mark Costello, whose work I admire very much, has written a book called *Murphy Stories*. I think there was tremendous power of imagination in Dickens, an ability to realize the absurd, to make visual, to make palpable, these figures of his imagination. That's a process that I've always admired. Obviously there wasn't a great deal of depth and spiritual insight in Dickens, but he did have a sense of things like evil in the world. He had a romantic attitude toward it, but it did make it very real and very palpable and very frightening to his readers. That's something I admire very much.

Heath: What about writers like Flannery O'Connor or Nathaniel West?
Stone: I haven't read very much of Flannery O'Connor, but certainly West was a writer that I admired very much and who I think had a very brilliant sense of American reality.

Student: From reading *A Hall of Mirrors* and *Dog Soldiers* I notice that you have a lot of interest in altered states of consciousness. How do you write about drugs?
Stone: I think you'd have to make it as experientially true as you can, in terms of your own experience. It is given to everybody, I suppose, to have

certain insights whether they want to or not into extreme states of consciousness, through intoxicants or through drugs or through happy or unhappy circumstances. I guess it's simply a matter of bringing those to bear on one's awareness and consciousness. If you can really remember, if you can bring to bear, what it's like to be drunk or be stoned or be injured or be afraid, that's your priority in terms of balance. I think it's just making it true to other people's lives as you've seen them or true to your own as you've seen it. I mean, it must be true, as true as you can make it.

Student: Could you say something about your own experience in the sixties, the drug scene then? Where you got your material for *Dog Soldiers*?
Stone: I took a lot of dope [said jokingly]. I was a friend of Ken Kesey, I still am, and in the early sixties a bunch of us in California used to associate together and take rides and go on trips and generally enjoy ourselves in a rather enthusiastic and possibly fatuous fashion. We learned a lot, and we had a very good time.

Student: Could you talk more about the sixties and the function of Dieter in the novel?
Stone: I think there was a time of great optimism, at least that I experienced personally. I don't know if I was as optimistic as other people were. Certainly there was a great surge of optimism. There was a time when a number of people thought, I thought, that the general level of consciousness could indeed be raised, that some kind of breakthrough in terms of people's relationships with others and the individual's relation with society could be altered, that a kind of spontaneity and a kind of warmth and a kind of in-touch-ness with one's self and with other people could be brought about. I know that one of the ways that we thought we could do this was through drugs. Another way was by taking the lessons of drugs and of spirituality and applying them, and there are a number of us around my age who are a little bit embittered that it didn't turn out better. Because it did seem possible at the time, and yet in so many ways there came a period when every lousy due bill came up for presentation, that so many things turned into their ironic opposites, that so many numbers were played out to their logically extreme absurdity. It began to seem as if the whole game was not really worth the candle, and certainly socially I think what hangs on now, in terms of the social condition of the United States, is the burnt end of a lot of these things—the empty commercialization, the vain indulgence of a lot of these cultural things. They're in a spirit of played-out dead ends. It is the failed

end of a lot of those optimistic thrusts of the sixties that are surrounding the world of the people of *Dog Soldiers*. It seemed to me at the time that all of this was going on while the war was going on, and it couldn't have ended up any other way. Nevertheless it did help bring an end to the war, if it did nothing else, so maybe it's quits, maybe it ends up sort of evening itself out.

I talked to a guy . . . not very many of the people I knew who used to take acid a lot take acid anymore for the obvious reasons because I'm sure you know as many people as I do who are burned out and really in bad shape from taking too much acid, but I talked to a guy a couple of years ago who was just coming down from a trip. He was down and together, and he said, "It just occurred to me that I've taken acid about thirty times, and I needed everything I ever learned from acid to get through that last trip." So it's kind of canceling out. If he doesn't take acid again he'll have the feeling that he just quit even. Maybe that's what happened in the sixties, maybe we needed all that spiritual thrust just to get through the times because they were so awful. I don't know. That's a collection of responses and feelings that I have about that time and about how I felt about my participation in the counterculture.

Student: Does what went on in the sixties have any positive influence on us now?

Stone: I don't know what's happening now. And I don't know what's going to happen tomorrow. Some things will not be lost, and I think that exists even in the book on one level and, one time anyway, where Converse tries to save Marge at the very end. In spite of everything there is something. There's us, and that's what he tries to articulate, that kind of grain of a sort of humanism, of a sort of sense of the value of what is human in the face of that which is not human. One of the positive directions of all of these people is their humanity. Even if they are perverse and even if they are acting out something that is evil, they are all human on a certain level. There is some-thing, some value in their humanity—all of them. That's what Converse is trying to articulate in that small moment of the book. Marge immediately puts him down, and I didn't really feel entitled to somehow raise that banner again. I thought I would be getting too didactic if I suddenly had somebody come on and say, "Just a moment, in spite of everything I still say there is something." I had him say it, and I had it dismissed. But it does reflect an attitude that I do experience and that I do feel, and it is an undercurrent in the book. It's a minor chord. I don't see it as thoroughly despairing, even though it is very ugly, and it did cost me a lot of unpleasant moments in a way. There were a lot of bad things that really worried me and that upset me to write about, but they were pretty much reflections of actual things, of things that were true about somebody sometime.

Heath: Would you say something about the moral responsibilities of the writer? Should he be a kind of dog soldier of his society?
Stone: I think there is a certain kind of ministry that writers should be willing to accept. They have, or should have, a certain role like that. I think at their best they do. In extreme situations in a lot of places in the world I think they accept that. Of course the other extreme of this is simple pretentiousness, but the answer is yes. I do think they should have a sort of special role, a moral role. It's only as good as they can make it. It's only as good as their own ethos, but I think they should ideally.

Student: Hicks is a fascinatingly contradictory person. Would you comment about him?
Stone: He wasn't a pure concoction. He was based on a whole lot of people in varying forms who I have known since I was fourteen or so years old. It seemed to me there was a certain kind of man that I had known since I was fairly young, you know, from my time in the service, from my time in high school. There was in this a certain image or attitude represented by all sorts of people, in a way, certain individuals. There was an attitude that was worth somehow articulating. I thought it desperately difficult to find Hicks's voice, and I only got it from putting myself in Hicks's place. It's obvious that in no sense is he anything like me, but there are certain aspects of Hicks's life that are true about my life and certain other aspects of his life that are true about the lives of other people who I knew well. He's trapped in a kind of condition that always fascinated me that I was never trapped in, but it seemed to me I understood enough about that condition to try to make him a vehicle, a moral vehicle of perception, who not only locked within a certain apprehension of the world but took strength from that apprehension. I mean a man who in a way has the strength of his own illusions.

Student: Have you changed your moral position from *A Hall of Mirrors* to *Dog Soldiers*?
Stone: I think that must be true, but I never seem to be able to hold on to it. That has to be true, that I come to vacillate between one passage and another. Yet I think that in a way it's an extension; I don't feel there's a great deal of difference, you know any kind of contradiction, between what's said

in *A Hall of Mirrors* and what's said in *Dog Soldiers*. I think they really are extensions, but how that relates exactly with the passages that I've come through I'm not sure. Only I continue to do the same thing. I think we should just raise the question and suggest a multiplicity of answers, and because I have a fondness for irony these answers tend to contain the seeds of their own confounding in them. My apprehension of things in general is like that; that's true. There's really nothing that I can bring to bear in writing except what I've come to and how I think at this point. That's really all there is to it finally.

Student: Will you continue to rely upon your own experiences in your novels?

Stone: I reserve the right to spend the next ten years on top of a mountain and write of all sorts of unearthly things. I mean, experience takes its different forms. On a very narrow fact level it's easier to write about a lot of situations if you've experienced them or are close to them, but I don't think it's necessary . . .

Student: Who were some of the sixties people you knew?

Stone: I don't know if you could call Neal Cassady a nonliterary figure or not, since he's occurred in so many works of literature. He was a certain person I knew who I thought a lot about. There are a great many people, who are nonliterary people, who I knew in different parts of the country and on the west coast who had to do with the sixties. It's really impossible not to fall into these media categories. There's so much of a constant feedback and a constant process of reporting going on that it's so hard to tell the reality from its instant summing up. I find it a little difficult in a way to talk about that time. It wasn't necessarily happening to me at the same time that it was happening to everybody else. I recall the early sixties as a particularly good and rich time, but it may be just because I was younger then. My life was somewhat different then than it is now. It was much more open-ended. I got around more. I guess I had the energy to. I did know Cassady. I'm still a friend of Ken Kesey. A lot of his friends are my friends. They were an awful lot of really incredible people. To talk about those people would be a project in itself. There were a lot of extraordinary people around.

Heath: There are a couple of references to Charles Manson in *Dog Soldiers*, I'm sure with great deliberateness, because I take it he represents one of those people who carried to its logical absurdity certain things that began good, began hopefully, in the counterculture.

Stone: There's no way around it; he was an absurd reduction of a lot of the extreme directions in sixties spirituality. In a way it's a little bit too neat to say, "All right, Manson suddenly sums up everything. This is the direction we were all going to." I get into that in a kind of facetious way, in the story I'm going to read later tonight ["Aquarius Obscured"]. It's a little pat to say "All right, it all comes down to Charlie Manson." Nevertheless he does stand even in time as the nightmare parody of all these directions—the benign leadership principle, the refracting of reality so as to make the mythological instantly present. There was an awful lot of the things that happened in the sixties that had a lot to do with psychedelic drugs. He had everything to do with psychedelic drugs, so the connection there is obvious. This kind of un-structuring of the mind, this evoking of the irrational as a principle, is not totally without its dangers. Everything is relative, and this can get very strange. If moral responses are obviated, the possibilities are not only liberating they are also sinister. It's common sense, really. So he is inescapable. It's too much to say that the murders he committed ended everything and disillusioned everybody. Yet, you know, they are so closely related to other things that were going on that I don't think it's impossible really to think about the sixties, unfortunately, without thinking of him. I think you have to.

Heath: Is *Dog Soldiers* meant to be set right after the Manson killings?
Stone: It's set in '71.

Berryhill: Would you say something about Danskin. The name itself conjures up leotards. I've always thought it was one of the big jokes in the book.
Stone: It does conjure up leotard, that's true. But also when the Vikings used to come and raid the coasts of the British Isles, they used to flay people. In old British churches in the ninth century they had on display what was known as a danskin, that is to say a Dane's skin. That was a token of the flaying of the Vikings when they came to loot and pillage the population.

Berryhill: He makes the statement that in prison there wasn't anything happening outside that wasn't happening inside. That strikes me as probably true, but it might strike some readers as a bit far-fetched.
Stone: I'm acquainted with people who spent part of that period in Agnew

in California and McLean. People like that, many of them, felt very close to the core of the culture development of the time. It's a bit of a joke, but it's also, I think, literally true.

Student: Is there any particular reason for the name "Converse"?
Stone: There's no particular reason but the in and out, backward and forward suggestions . . . reversing ground, convolutions, reversal, upside down, that sort of thing.

Heath: What about Rheinhardt?
Stone: I named him for Django Reinhardt, the guitar player. And I gave his name as many letters as I possibly could.

Berryhill: How about the cop, Antheil?
Stone: You can say "An Til" as in George Antheil, or "Ant Heil." I liked that because he's the composer of the *ballade mecanique,* and his name looks like "ant heil" which conjures up the idea of ants saluting each other, so it was for those combinations of circumstances.

Berryhill: At the end of the novel, we see the couple going off in their stage-coach, a Land-Rover. Then we see the two corrupt cops, some kind of a parody of the end of *Casablanca* or any number of adventure stories, going off kind of wary of one another—that seemed to me to be a fine resolution, a way of avoiding the problem of that romantic leave-taking.
Stone: It's an alternate romance. It's another couple—yet another coupling, a variation on the coupling that goes on. I thought it was the coupling to end on.

Berryhill: I was thinking too when the character says, "People have left office under more compromising circumstances." I wonder how far was Nixon from your mind at that point.
Stone: That had to be in there somehow [laughs]. There's always the temptation to go off on a great Nixon trip. I tried to avoid that.

Heath: There's a delightful moment in *A Hall of Mirrors* after Rainey has just confronted Minnow, and he says, "I've got you on tape."
Stone: Yeah, I've thought about that. I had a very strange feeling through the past several years that that's the character, Minnow, that I thought I should sue somebody for plagiarism, or they should sue me for liable. It just

gave me the feeling that I must have been right about some things in that book.

Heath: Today you were talking to several of us about details of the heroin smuggling ring from Vietnam. I take it that the situation that Hicks falls into was actually going on.

Stone: When I arrived in Saigon I had one name to look up. A friend of mine told me you've got to look up this guy, so I spent a couple of weeks looking for him. When I found him I found that he was a junkie, that he lived in a pad on Tu Do Street with a lot of famed journalists, some with Vietnamese girlfriends, and they were dealing in heroin. When I located other people that I knew there, nobody wanted to know him or wanted him anywhere around. I discovered that in the hotel where I was staying people were doing a lot of opium smoking. I just generally found myself, as far as I could see, up to my ears in smack—in all ways, in all directions. It changed the feeling of what I was going to write about, because I ended up knowing much more about the heroin business in Saigon than I wanted to. I mean, at one time it defied fiction. It is a fact that heroin was smuggled into the United States in corpses, in the coffins of dead soldiers. It seemed to me that this was just too much. That's the truth. The American dead were being sent to Aberdeen, Maryland, with heroin concealed in their coffins. So it's something that fiction can't possibly do justice to. You wouldn't make that up in a novel. It would look like something beyond necessity, that it was just too blasphemous, yet that was the fact of the matter. Philip Roth wrote an essay that says that American reality is very hard to match in fiction, because no matter how freakish the event you can think up is, something even more freakish eventually happens.

Heath: Was it also a fact that the narcs in California were drug dealers themselves?

Stone: In the days before the Federal Drug Administration took over, there were various state bureaus modeled on the Federal Bureau of Narcotics, which was in the Treasury Department, that agency compared with the FBI, favorably and unfavorably in certain ways, depending on your point of view. There were many more incidents of corruption in the old Federal Bureau of Narcotics and in the state agencies modeled on it than there were among the FBI. To remedy this, this organization had been put with the department of Health, Education, and Welfare. It has been restructured to some extent, but it was certainly a fact that in the old Federal Bureau of

Narcotics under Harry Anslinger there were numerous cases—cases that are in the press, documented cases of the collaboration of these officers with the smuggling of drugs.

Heath: The Great Elephant Zap sounds like another one of those things that had to be true because no one would believe it if you made it up.
Stone: Yes, that is true.

Berryhill: What about the Battle of Bob Hope?
Stone: That's also true, about somebody I know very well, and the fragmentation bombs, the South Vietnamese planes dropping those Elephant Feet on Cambodia. I mean, a lot of that, a lot of those things are true. The bomb at the tax office is also true.

Heath: How long were you in Vietnam?
Stone: Just a couple of months, something under three months, which is, I admit, not very long, but all I can tell you is every day was different.

Berryhill: You talked earlier about kicking around New Orleans and finally realizing you had enough to write a novel. What would you say to a young writer? You obviously didn't get a college degree, yet you're sitting here in a room with people who are getting college degrees.
Stone: I had the sense, before I began that novel that writing a novel was one of the greatest things that anybody could do. That was the way I felt at the time. I thought it was a really great thing to do. I had the sense that because I liked to write that perhaps I could do it. I think I may have read *The Great Gatsby* and thought to myself this is an incredible thing to have done, and I would really like to be able to do something like this. I think I made something like a false start. I was intoxicated with the structure a few times, and then it occurred to me that I just hadn't seen enough life cast in time. I was not precocious. I really had no way of knowing that I would ever succeed in getting anything published. I didn't start very early. I was always writing, but I never succeeded in getting a story together to my own satisfaction until fairly late in my twenties. By then I realized that I had seen enough life lived in time to get the sense of that process—of life lived over time, in depth, in time—in a novel. Then I began writing, but it was a long, ongoing process, the writing of *A Hall of Mirrors*. So I think it was at first an intoxication with the form; I knew it was something I wanted to do before I was really able to do it. Then I was able to do it.

Berryhill: Was your time at Stanford worth it, or did you consider a lot of it distraction?

Stone: It was a lot of fun being there and also different from anything I had experienced. California was very different. It was a very pleasurable time in my life. It was helpful to have that fellowship, because it enabled me to just write. It was the first time in my life that I had been able to just write and not have to hold down a job. When that was over I had to go back to work, and that delayed the process even more. So it was very valuable to me in terms of the friendships I made there and the fact that I had time to write. I got some kind of feedback and some kind of support, which I had never gotten before, so I feel very good about that year.

Student: Now that you've had two novels published will you change as a writer?

Stone: I think it scares me, because it's true all right that you can never go back to that business of being just yourself and the kitchen table, to that total sense of privacy when you don't really believe anybody is going to read it. You write it, and you say, "all right, I'm writing a novel," but you don't really believe that it's ever going to be read by anybody except your friends. That's something else. I don't think I really believed it. I hoped for it, but when I was writing, it was more or less fantasy—the idea that anybody beyond myself and my friends would read it. It's very hard to recapture that kind of situation. When you are writing something else, and you have read reviews of your own writing, and you know that it's going to end up in the public, you suffer a loss of innocence from the time when you never seriously believed that it would ever get published. I mean, that's true. The idea is not to let that come down on you, because it can really crush people. It can be a very intimidating thing.

Berryhill: Speaking of reviewers, do you think they made any sense on either of the novels?

Stone: I liked some of the reviews more than others [laughs]. I was pleased when the reviews were good, and I was disappointed when they weren't. Some of them I really responded to. Others, even though I was pleased with the fact that they were favorable, I really wasn't able to understand. There are a couple of reviews that I pick up every once in a while, and I try to figure out what the guy is awed about and goes on about, and I don't really know. But others I take as somewhat personal and very special responses to what I was trying to do.

Heath: Are you finding that other contemporary novelists are now getting in touch with you, and are you finding yourself playing a kind of encourager role to people who are beginning to write and send you their work? Is that level of fame arriving?

Stone: Not really. I don't get many letters from writers, from people who are trying to write. I have gotten a few letters from people that pleased me very much. But no, not really, I'm not at that level of fame, fortunately, because I would find that hard to deal with.

Berryhill: Would you say something about your teaching at Amherst?

Stone: I have done that, and I enjoy it. It has its moments, and many of them are very satisfying. I'm not doing it after the end of June. For the most part I enjoy it. I didn't find it boring. I don't know. In a way I was a little bit disappointed in some of what I got because I thought it was so intellectualized, more from other fictions than from life. So overall, although I wasn't that bored, I wasn't that stimulated either. But I guess when I'm through with it I'll know more about it.

Interview with Robert Stone

Maureen Karagueuzian / 1980

From *TriQuarterly 53* (Winter 1982): 248–58. Reprinted by permission.

Robert Stone guards his privacy carefully and has seldom been interviewed. This conversation took place late in the summer of 1980, in the small New England town where he has made his home for the past seven years. At the time, he was nearing the end of his third novel, *A Flag for Sunrise*, which takes its title from an Emily Dickinson poem.

The interviewer and Stone had talked briefly earlier in the summer, after Stone read from his forthcoming novel at the Berkeley Writers' Conference. He reads well—hesitating, changing his accent, even shouting, as his text requires. His scuffed cowboy boots, which seem a poor fit, and his spotless but carelessly selected shirt and pants belie the care he gives to other areas of life. At the week-long conference, where the pace is intense, Stone had a reputation for scrupulous attention to each student's work. That seriousness about writing, about responsibility, is also revealed in the interview.

Interviewer: I notice that the setting of your fiction has moved south. You were born in Manhattan: but *A Hall of Mirrors* takes place in New Orleans, *Dog Soldiers* at least partly in the Southwest and Mexico, and *A Flag for Sunrise* in a fictional country in Central America. Do you feel that that movement south enhances your themes?

Stone: I think that the move to New Orleans did. I wasn't really ready to write a novel when I went down there. But I got a certain vision of American reality from that particular city and my life in it that made me ready to deal with this country and people's lives lived out in time and in a special kind of place. It gave me the arena that I wanted, and I was able to draw from my experience of a lot of different people and put them together in the three main characters in my first novel. I put a great number of people together—not precisely, for they're finally imagined characters. But they're based on my experience of people. So it was very valuable for me to go there.

As for the move to Central America, it's a way of examining America—America overseas. The people in *A Flag for Sunrise* are all Americans, or at least North Americans. There are no main characters who are local people. It's about America and America's role abroad and about people who represent aspects of the American condition.

Interviewer: I remember you said at Berkeley that you were patriotic.
Stone: I'm concerned about America and its responsibilities.

Interviewer: I think it was Faulkner who said that there's a certain pattern in an author's work that emerges both in the individual book and in the work as a whole. I would see *Dog Soldiers* as being a much more positive book than *A Hall of Mirrors*. Do you agree?
Stone: Yes, generally, I agree. I think there's a great deal of similarity between my first two novels—not so much in milieu, but in plot. If you take the three major characters in each book as aspects of the American condition, they're different; but their relationships are not terribly dissimilar. *Dog Soldiers* is a much more spare, less freewheeling book. There are a hundred little stories coming on in *A Hall of Mirrors*. It's a much more panoramic book because I'm trying, really, to address the whole country. Also, I was younger when I wrote *A Hall of Mirrors*, ready to meander more, to wander about. That book has an almost picaresque structure, while *Dog Soldiers* is very tightly structured. It's very precisely plotted, less expressionist, more realistic—although I don't consider it an altogether realistic novel.

Interviewer: It's so metaphoric. Do you think primarily in images? How do you begin?
Stone: I begin with character. If I can understand characters, who they are and what they want, then events will proceed from the characters. You know, the axiom "Character is fate" is literally true in my fiction.

Interviewer: Did you pretty much know that Hicks and Geraldine would die when you began the novels?
Stone: The first thing, really, that I knew about Geraldine was that she was going to end up that way because it was taken from life.

Interviewer: The events that led up to her death seemed to me inevitable.
Stone: Right. That sense of inevitability accounts for the characters. I'm either building toward something inevitable, or I'm building back, in a way, from the result, in order to discover its inevitability. I was very fond of Geraldine, and I was very thrown when she did die—even though I knew she was going to, all along. It was very taxing emotionally, and it was the same with Hicks.

Interviewer: You said that *A Hall of Mirrors* started with the fact of Geraldine's death. Was there something similar that *Dog Soldiers* started with?
Stone: Something that turned out to be *Dog Soldiers* was in my mind before I went to Vietnam. I was in England at the time. Of course, being in Vietnam brought it all together, and I got a clearer picture of what I wanted to do. Before I went to Vietnam, I had the idea of somebody in possession of something that represented ultimate need. The Vietnam War was an event of such widespread consequence that it was very much on my mind, along with the idea of possessing something, of a person putting himself in the position of possessing this thing in a kind of feckless moment and having to bear the consequences. When I went to Vietnam and, as it were, saw the war, things became clear to me as a result of what I saw.

Interviewer: Would you say that *A Flag for Sunrise* is moving in an even more positive direction than *Dog Soldiers*?
Stone: I don't think so. It's about something different. I think that Marge and Converse, even in their extreme condition, have an insight. They have learned something. They do come out at the other end of all that having—at least it's imminent—a kind of realization. They have made a series of discoveries, they are seeing more clearly, and the chance for them to bring that insight to bear is definitely there. The insight presents itself in a kind of odd and reversed way when Converse says, "In spite of everything, there's something." It's deliberately made inarticulate and kind of nonsensical, but that's what the positive dimension is.

Interviewer: Marge doesn't know what he means?
Stone: He says, "There's us," by which he means not just the two of them. But she dismisses that. Nevertheless, he has it; and he may or may not do something with it. *A Flag for Sunrise* is more about the problem of living in a kind of meaningful, moral way in a world which is apparently godless.

Interviewer: The "War Stories" section and the section on Father Egan have been published. Who's the central character?

Stone: Holliwell is a main character. Egan is fairly important, but he's not quite one of the principals.

Interviewer: Sections from your previous novels also came out prior to publication. Does that give you a sense of how your current work is going? Is that your working pattern—to complete a section of a novel and send it out?

Stone: I work section by section, and I usually have the sections fairly complete without the necessity of a lot of rewriting. But I don't usually send them out unless somebody asks me. I want to see a section complete for myself, although I may work on it a bit for purposes of publication. If I round it out a little to make it an excerptible piece, then it will have its own existence. But I don't necessarily put it into the book the way it appears in the magazine. I feel quite free to change it.

Interviewer: What about "Porque No Tiene, Porque Le Falta," that wonderful short story in the 1970 Martha Foley collection—was it originally conceived as part of *Dog Soldiers*?

Stone: Or "Aquarius Obscured." But it's an independent short story that's been published.

Interviewer: How do you feel about the short story form versus the novel?

Stone: I think a short story is very, very difficult to write. In a way, it's harder than a novel. A novel takes years and a story takes weeks or months, at the most. But I think writing a successful short story is very difficult. Stories built out of anecdotes—and usually they are—don't occur to me very often. I like larger pictures and the convolutions and ironies of event—not what the short story is built on. The short story is something like a joke; at least it has the structure of a joke—or any sort of anecdote. The curve of its dynamic breaks, just like a pitch. And when it finishes, it has illustrated something. All short stories are the same. It's always: this is how it is. That's the unspoken. And to do that successfully, to make a statement in a relatively short space about how things are is very difficult; and the people who do it well have a great gift.

Interviewer: Is the writing process pleasurable for you?

Stone: It is sometimes, but a lot of times it's simply hard work. The writing process itself is slightly less pleasurable than the process that goes into dreaming it up. That's the nice part.

Interviewer: Do you keep a notebook?
Stone: I do. I don't keep it very religiously, but I write things down. And then the notebook gets mislaid, and so forth.

Interviewer: Do you write in longhand or at a typewriter?
Stone: I write at a typewriter. Sometimes I'll stop, though, and write something out in longhand if I really want to get it straight, if I think that it calls for very careful analysis so that I don't get it wrong. If I want to think it out very clearly, then I'll slow myself down to write it out in longhand—description sometimes and sometimes an attitude or a thought, a revelation of some kind that introduces itself into a character's consciousness. I'll do that in longhand because I want to get it right.

Interviewer: You said you don't do much rewriting?
Stone: Generally I write every chapter twice, and then I leave it until I go over the whole thing. I take two chapters a day when I start rewriting. I read the whole thing first and make notes, and then I'll take it chapter by chapter, two a day for a couple of weeks, until I've gone through the whole book.

Interviewer: Do you write the chapters in order?
Stone: I try to go sequentially, but sometimes—if I have a breakthrough in one direction—I'll follow through. I know what goes behind it. I have a kind of map written down.

Interviewer: An outline?
Stone: Yes, chapter by chapter. I eventually make an outline about a quarter to halfway in. Then I'll see what I've got in front of me because I want to balance it. I usually have simultaneous stories going, people over here and people over here, so I want to balance those episodes. And for that I have to make some kind of outline. I don't really make charts, brochures, or portfolios on characters, the way some writers do. But I do make a little written outline.

Interviewer: What is the most difficult part of writing for you?
Stone: Getting myself to do it. If I can't write, then I'll pick up something and start reading. But I have to get myself into the space—whether I feel like

it or not. I think the hard thing is just getting yourself going when you don't feel like it, when you'd rather be doing something outside. But it just doesn't finish itself. Plenty of people can think very moving and inspiring thoughts, but that's not the same as writing. No one can do it for you.

Interviewer: Do you work regular hours? Do you have a certain pattern to get going?
Stone: It's always hard for me to get going. I always start early in the morning, and I go on as long as I can. Since the Berkeley Writers' Conference, I've been working almost every day. I've taken a few days off, but I haven't done anything like taking a week at the beach. I'm reaching the conclusion and I've been anxious to finish, so I've taken very little time off.

Interviewer: You don't have to be in a certain emotional state in order to write?
Stone: I just don't feel I can afford to wait for the right emotional state. I think I feel guilty about how little I've produced. I don't know why I've produced so relatively little. I feel like I work all the time.

Interviewer: It must have taken a great deal of time to keep *Dog Soldiers* so precise.
Stone: I think so. And with my first novel, I didn't know a lot about control.

Interviewer: You've traveled in Central America, where your novel takes place?
Stone: By chance. I had done a reading at the University of Alabama, and I had $1,000 to play with. Since I was already in Tuscaloosa, I went to the Bay Islands, off Honduras. I started wandering around, riding on buses, traveling; and I ran into some people I knew who lived in Managua. So I caught a ride with them and stayed with them in Managua for a while. Then I went down the coast to Costa Rica. I went back to Central America later, researching, as it were.

Interviewer: You think that kind of thing is necessary in order to write?
Stone: It's necessary in certain circumstances. I don't write documentary novels, but I certainly want to have a sense of place. I have to know what I'm writing about, what the land looks like, what the mountains look like, what the towns look like.

Interviewer: There's no tendency to get back to Manhattan in your writing?
Stone: I never write about New York. I never write about my childhood or my adolescence—I just don't, for whatever reasons.

Interviewer: It's interesting that so many writers have to get that out first. Are you more concerned about social issues than emotional development?
Stone: No. I'm primarily interested in the individual's dealing with the world, and the people that I write about do so against a background of social issues. I don't make a choice between social issues and the concerns of the individual. I am interested in people against the background of social forces, but mostly in people. I personally am very interested in what's going on politically; so are some of my characters—at least they're affected by political events, whether they're interested in them or not.

Interviewer: What do you think about the current American scene?
Stone: I think it's very bad. I really think that the country is lacking in conviction and—not to belabor poor old Yeats's anti-Christ yet again . . .

Interviewer: The worst are full of passionate intensity?
Stone: And all that. I feel very pessimistic this particular summer. I know I can vote against Ronald Reagan's becoming president because I think it makes the country look bad, and I hate to see that happen. I don't think the man is qualified, or even a serious person. Anyone who says that Karl Marx invented the graduated income tax is so profoundly ignorant of Marxism and economics that it's just terrifying.

Interviewer: Why do you think we've come to this pass?
Stone: Well, partly it's the problem of democracy, which is an imperfect vehicle for government—although a preferable one. But I also think Americans are spoiled, probably more so than most people. But that may be the direction that the whole western world is going in. We take a lot for granted, and we don't want to put anything out for what we get. We have a number of social contradictions in our society that we've tried to resolve, but I think that they're rather too much for us. I don't know about our future. I think we're being outdone by forces in the world that are hostile to us, and I'm rather worried this particular summer. I can't tell if there's going to be a war or not.

Interviewer: If you were to advise a beginning writer, what kind of training and experience would you advocate?

Stone: Mainly reading. I read a lot aboard ship. I read when I was a kid instead of doing my homework. I'm still addicted to reading. I think the reading of good fiction is where you learn most about how fiction works. There's no kind of life that is of more advantage to a writer than another. Allen Ginsberg might go off to Peru or India, or San Francisco when he was younger, but Wallace Stevens went to Hartford Accident and Indemnity. I don't think there is one kind of life, but you obviously have got to have the sort of make-up that makes you listen. In addition to reading, you have to listen. The more kinds of people you know, the more kinds of voices you hear, the better off you are because you have these voices echoing in your head.

Interviewer: At Berkeley, you said you were well-acquainted with institutions, that you were brought up in institutions. In what sense?
Stone: I was in a school, more an orphanage, from the time I was six to the time I was about nine, and I was in and out, depending on my mother's circumstances at the time. I was in the Navy, which itself is a kind of institution. That's what I meant.

Interviewer: You went to parochial schools?
Stone: Yes. The place I was at was Catholic, run by the Marist Brothers.

Interviewer: Were they strict?
Stone: They were strict in the sense that they hit you. As those orders were in the forties and fifties, they were strict, and they were a bit physical.

Interviewer: Can you credit them with giving you an eye for imagery, for allegory?
Stone: I credit them with teaching me to spell and for teaching me grammar, which they did quite efficiently. They certainly gave me a grounding in language that was sufficient to carry me farther. It was practical, down-to-earth, and basic—and in its way, good.

Interviewer: What about the religion?
Stone: The religion I certainly absorbed. I don't know if I absorbed it so much from them as I took what I chose. I don't know if going to that school enhanced my religious convictions, but my religious convictions were pretty strong.

Interviewer: Did you get them from your mother?

Stone: No, my mother wasn't Christian. It may have had something to do with religious instruction. I certainly took it for granted. First I resisted, then I was kind of won over by it, then I became enthusiastic, and then I turned around.

Interviewer: You liked the ritual?

Stone: I liked all that. I also believed in it. There's a lot in my make-up, in my conditioning, that's the result of being brought up Catholic. Quite a lot, I think.

Interviewer: One reviewer has said that you're like one of the great nineteenth-century moralists.

Stone: I wonder what nineteenth-century moralist the reviewer had in mind. Dickens, Twain . . . I do write about what people do and what they ought to do or what I think they ought to do. I really believe people are responsible for what they do. That's why my principal characters sometimes do unsympathetic things and maybe why my books don't sell terribly well. I have people do things that they accept responsibility for.

Interviewer: How do you envision your audience?

Stone: I envision my audience as people who in sensibility are somehow like me. I think the imaginary reader, every writer's imaginary reader, is someone who is either similar in sensibility or who has the openness to accept the expression of another's sensibility. That's who my readers are. I'm fond of my readers. My readers feel strongly about my work, and I feel strongly about them. They're who I'm writing for. Because I'm not an immensely popular writer with a real mass audience, I feel that my readers are a relatively small band. That makes me feel all the more chummy toward them.

Interviewer: I think it also means your work will last longer.

Stone: I'd like it to. My first book is out of print, which I'm unhappy about—especially with the current scene, the political, evangelical groups. Although the political events, in a way, are dated, they were rather prophetic, if I may say so.

Interviewer: Do you reread your own work?

Stone: From time to time. I always think: How did I do this? I'll never be able to do it again. I reread *A Hall of Mirrors* when I was writing *Dog Soldiers*. I always get into a kind of despair about the book I'm writing. Sometimes I think it's the best thing I've ever done, and sometimes I think it's not.

Interviewer: For Norman Mailer, Hemingway is still the champ. What do you think about Hemingway?

Stone: I think Hemingway was a very, very good technician. He learned a lot about how dialogue works and, simply, how to write. He was a very gifted and wonderful technician, the kind of master you can learn from. He made what have come to be technical discoveries about how to utilize the difference between the way people actually speak and dialogue that reads like people speaking, which isn't the same thing. I have learned from Hemingway, from that kind of almost Latinate spareness of his. But, on the level of ideas, I think he was very trivial. I see Hemingway as really not a very wise or insightful man. His work is a bit adolescent, a bit impoverished spiritually. He never came close to writing something like *The Great Gatsby*. That's a damn near perfect novel. There's a great deal of wisdom in that book about the American condition. It's short. It's very rich. It has a character who is elusive and mysterious and, at the same time, perfectly understood. It's a great book. I first read it when I was a boy and didn't really understand it, and then I read it later just before I began *A Hall of Mirrors*. That's what made me want to write a novel, reading *Gatsby*.

Interviewer: Hemingway said he couldn't combine writing and teaching but that he admired those who could. You have no problem with that life?

Stone: I think it's easier to do that, although I don't teach regularly. I usually do it when I'm asked, but I've never looked for a teaching job. In some ways, I think teaching's good. It gives a certain structure to your week if you have to teach a couple of times, and it also discharges a lot of social energy. Writing is a very solemn and lonely business, and to be able to talk about writing isn't necessarily a bad thing. Especially if you're teaching writing, responding to student writing, you don't have a great deal of preparation. You have to read the pieces and think about them, but it isn't really very hard work. Something like a writer's conference is really very wearing because of its intensity, but teaching a course is different. And I like talking about writing.

Interviewer: You don't find the academic world an impediment to writing?

Stone: Since I didn't go to college, since—in fact—I didn't really finish high school, I haven't had time to get very irritated at the academic world. I went into the Navy at seventeen, and I got an equivalency diploma.

Interviewer: You said you like talking about writing. Do you like to associate with other writers?

Stone: It's interesting to talk to other writers, and I do know quite a number of writers. But American writers are very prone not to talk about writing. American writers like to talk about bear hunting and scuba diving and trout fishing and things like that rather than literature.

Interviewer: Do you read a lot when you're writing?

Stone: I read almost anything that comes in front of me. I read all the time. That's what I'm doing if I'm not out-of-doors. I was reading about Scott Fitzgerald in Hollywood fairly recently and some of his Pat Hobby stories. I read a lot of history. I have always read a lot about the Renaissance and the Reformation periods. I read a biography of Giordano Bruno by Francis Yates fairly recently, also a book about Renaissance mysticism and symbolism. I tend to read the same poets. I read Wallace Stevens and I read Yeats, and I have those books around. I also read the Bible. I usually have a Bible on my desk, Shakespeare handy.

Interviewer: When did you realize that you were going to become a writer?

Stone: I started, I think, with some kind of narrative compulsion when I was a child. I wanted to make a story out of what I was doing and what other people were doing. I think the first form that really arrested me was the radio play, the radio mystery, Sam Spade and that sort of thing. I started writing, just like everybody else did, science fiction things. But I don't know that I ever thought that I could properly become a writer. That didn't seem to be a good thing to do. Writers, painters, sculptors and such people were disapproved of where I was brought up. It wasn't the kind of thing that one aspired to be, so I don't think I ever went around openly wanting to become a writer. It was economic. It was also a suggestion that people like that were weird and a little bit nutty, undesirable.

Interviewer: It's not clear to me how you made the transition to writing.

Stone: In a sense, I had burned all my bridges behind me. I started at New York University and then went to New Orleans. I was back at NYU and in a writing class when I saw an announcement about the Stanford Program. In those days, it was very hard to get any of those things if you didn't have any academic credentials. But this was one that didn't demand any. You could get it on the basis of what you'd written, and I had written something that became part of *A Hall of Mirrors*. I was at Stanford in Wallace Stegner's program for two years. It was there that I started writing seriously. The fellowship helped me a great deal. But that time also set me back a little because I started hanging out with Ken Kesey and his friends and going on a perpetual party.

Interviewer: You were involved in the counterculture? The antiwar movement?

Stone: Yes, I still see Kesey fairly often. I wasn't any kind of leader. I was, as they used to say, just another body. I didn't pay my taxes for a number of years until they came and confiscated my teaching salary, which was all right with me. That's what I expected them to do.

Interviewer: Didn't you hate to give up large sections of *Dog Soldiers* in the movie *Who'll Stop the Rain*?

Stone: I had no illusions about it. *A Hall of Mirrors* was made into a film too, but the film made from *Dog Soldiers* was a lot better. It's not deathless, but I think it's rather good. It had some wonderful performances. Of course, I hated to leave things out, but those decisions weren't entirely mine. Writers don't have very much control over a film. I sort of quit and Judy Rascoe, who's a friend of mine, took over and really gave it the structure that it has. I did some additional dialogue after that. I went down to Mexico, where a lot of it was filmed, and worked with the actors a little and worked on the dialogue. The script owes more to Judy Rascoe than it does to me, although a lot of the new dialogue that isn't in the book was shared between us.

Interviewer: Which parts did you hate giving up?

Stone: The character of Marge. I don't think Marge makes any sense in the film. It didn't give Tuesday Weld the character that she could have delivered on. I think Marge in the book is much more interesting than in the film, but what they were trying to do was make her more sympathetic, an innocent victim of circumstances rather than a person who is responsible. The book, of course, demands that people be responsible for their actions. So the change in Marge's character is a violation to me. Oh, I have no great quarrel with the film. But, in a book, there's no limit to the dimension which you can bring to bear. Words reverberate. They have chains of association. The experience of reading is a much more elaborate and complicated one than watching a film. When you limit it with a camera, you're making it much smaller, whereas in a book things go on and on reverberating.

Interviewer: That's what the images in *Dog Soldiers* did.

Stone: That's what I try to do. In a film you can't do that. It becomes extremely limited. It goes so far and no farther. It flattens out. This is true of the filming of anything. If you take the scene in *War and Peace*, where—who is it?—where Andrey Bolkónsky first sees the French colors and the line of French infantry on the distant high ground and then he gallops back—and it's all on the crisp autumn day—the experience of that is going to be much richer and immediate when you read it than when you just have a bunch of people dressed up as the Russian hussars or the French infantry. Then you automatically limit it to what you can see. If you've got the Battle of Borodino in your mind, it has all the dimension, the complexity, the richness of real life. When you have the Battle of Borodino filmed, then all you get is what you see.

Interviewer: What plans do you have for the future—after *A Flag for Sunrise* is finished?

Stone: There are a number of things I wanted to do— a couple of books. a play. There's also a film I would like to do pretty much for fun. I may find myself in California next year. I'm ready for a little urban living again. I've been here seven years, with a little time out for teaching. I may go back out and work at Zoetrope, the film complex Francis Coppola owns.

Interviewer: Would you work on adapting your own novel?

Stone: No. I'll adapt somebody else's novel—preferably a Zane Grey western. Adapting your own novel is thankless, and you end up worried about traducing the book. I don't want to go through the characters twice. I wanted to have done with them. I don't want to be a party to the process of flattening them out, vulgarizing them. The work in itself is fun as long as you don't take it seriously and cannot be broken by it. But you can't make any emotional investment in it. You have to realize that it's an industrial process, often supervised by people who don't have a very clear hold on what they're about. If you're prepared to not take it too seriously and simply enjoy it, it's O.K. I'd like to do that. There's a trick to writing a screenplay, but you're working with other people and it's not nearly as hard. I like film, although I take it more seriously as a moviegoer than I do as a screenwriter.

A Conversation with Robert Stone

Charles Ruas / 1981

From *Conversations with American Writers* (New York: Alfred A. Knopf, 1985): 265–94.
© Charles Ruas. Reprinted by permission.

For the past ten years Robert Stone and his wife have lived in Amherst, Massachusetts, where he teaches creative writing. The interview was set at my loft in Soho during one of his periodic visits to the city. The conversation occurred over two days, so that each of us would have a chance to return to what had been discussed.

Robert Stone is of medium height and build, with the ruddy complexion of the country life. His thinning red-brown hair and free-growing beard give the impression of an academician, or of an outdoorsman in town for the day. This is reinforced by his reserve and shyness. He is soft-spoken and precise in his choice of words and has a wonderful speaking voice.

During this extensive interviewing, Robert Stone was disarmingly straightforward in answering the questions, which he often used to explore his own ideas.

CR: Your novels are set in New Orleans, on the West Coast, in the Southwest, and in Latin America. But you are that rare exception, a native New Yorker.
RS: Yes, I was born in Brooklyn and then moved to Manhattan when I was quite young and grew up mostly on the West Side. My mother's family had been in the tugboat business in New York; not so much in the business but working on the tugs. I still have a lot of relatives in Brooklyn, in Broad Channel.

CR: I know you had a Catholic schooling. Was your family religious?
RS: My mother was a nominal Catholic with a real dislike for the clergy and for the church. Her family was Irish and Scotch.

CR: Was that combination of Scotch and Irish also Protestant versus Catholic?

RS: My mother's father was a Presbyterian; he was an alcoholic Scotsman who worked on the tugboats. My grandmother was an Irish farm girl whose family had been in upstate New York for quite a long time.

CR: It was she who wanted you to go to a Catholic school.

RS: I went to a parochial grammar school and to a Catholic high school. I really didn't get on with the Marist Brothers, and they didn't get on with me—we didn't relate to the fifties. It was the kind of Catholicism which doesn't exist anymore, I hope. I just couldn't get it together in school, so I left high school without finishing it. Then I joined the Navy when I was seventeen. I was a so-called minor enlisted man. I got out when I was twenty-one.

CR: Was this during the Korean conflict?

RS: No, it was in 1955 that I enlisted, and 1958 when I got out, so it was just after.

CR: Were you a journalist in the Navy?

RS: First I was a radioman, but there is an official rank of journalism in the Navy. You can be a hospital corpsman or a journalist. Because I passed the test, I was officially certified Third Class Journalist. I had the insignia on my arm to prove it. Essentially I was a correspondent for the Armed Forces Press Service; that was my last year and half in the Navy.

CR: Was it right after that you worked in the Merchant Marines in New Orleans?

RS: I did a couple of trips out of New Orleans. Most of the work I did in the Merchant Marines was in fact pierhead work, unloading, because I had low seniority in the union.

CR: When did you turn to writing? Or were you writing all this while?

RS: I had always, on some level, wanted to write, and I had always been writing a little bit. I didn't do much when I was in the Navy. I wrote one short story the whole time I was in. But I had won a contest when I was in high school. Because my upbringing was in what you'd call a working-class context, I had the impression that being a writer was unsubstantial and not altogether respectable. But it was basically what I wanted to do, even though I didn't realize it when I was younger. I always wrote. I always had a kind of narrative impulse to try to make sense of things by telling stories about them, and I guess I also always had a certain facility with language and was always kind of in love with language. One thing that the Catholic school system did for me was to really teach me how to read and write thoroughly and grammatically. All this time I was mainly writing poetry. So in New Orleans I did things like read poetry to jazz, which was the thing of the time. The jazz, I suspect, was better than the poetry. My wife and I ended up taking the 1960 census in New Orleans. It really saved our bacon, because we were terribly broke. We got hired at a buck eighty a household to go all over town and just talk to the population of New Orleans—which is some population! What you would find behind a particular door would be completely unpredictable. It was an interesting job, sort of fun, even though all it consisted of was taking down names, ages, and so forth. It was fascinating to see the city on that level and be able to go into everybody's house and figure out their story; marvelous.

CR: New Orleans is the setting of your first novel, *Hall of Mirrors*. Had you started writing at that point?

RS: I wasn't ready to write a novel at that point in my life. I started the novel when I must have been about twenty-six, and prior to that I had not enough sense of life lived in time, the shape of people's lives; there was no pattern that I saw in things until I got to be that age. When I was twenty-one, twenty-two, I was not Carson McCullers—I did not have any vision, I just didn't know enough.

CR: How did you start the actual writing of *A Hall of Mirrors*? Was it when you were involved with Neal Cassady and his friends?

RS: Marginally, because Janice, my wife, was a waitress in the Seven Arts Café on Ninth Avenue, and that was a hangout for everybody. She had a day job in the RCA Building as a guide. So she would get out of her uniform and put on her black stockings. We both worked nights. I would get out of work about one a.m., and that's when I would run into the poets and musicians of the late fifties. LeRoi Jones, as he was known then, and Gregory Corso would read there, for example. Our living in the Quarter in New Orleans is the genesis of *A Hall of Mirrors*. When we moved to California, which struck us as a marvelous sybaritic place where you could live cheaply, that's when we met Ken Kesey and his friends. I was in the process of writing *A Hall of Mirrors*, and that process was sort of interrupted by this encounter with all these people, and I spent a lot of time doing funny things in my head and hanging out.

CR: Were you also dropping acid at the time?

RS: Yes, with the result that the book, which began as a traditional, realistic novel in the manner of Dos Passos or Steinbeck, began to change as my perception of reality was altered. I don't know how much importance to ascribe to that. It would be wrong to say that I started it as a realistic novel, took a lot of drugs, and then it went funny—that's not really true. It probably would have taken a lot of the turns it took anyway. It changed in my hands as I worked on it over a long period of time. I was never sure that it would be a finished book. I expected it would be one of those ongoing novels that you're always writing, writing for the rest of your life, and it would never be finished. I made a contribution in that direction by not working on it for a long time. I finally left California, where I had a fellowship at Stanford, because I was having a terrific time, but I wasn't getting any work done. I came back east, and the writing of the novel was interrupted by periods when I would have to go to work. I would work for twenty weeks, and I would go on unemployment. Sometimes I would take turns with my wife—she would work, and I would work on the book. That's the slow way to do a book. Rather to my surprise, it did get finished in '66, and it came out in August of '67.

CR: *A Hall of Mirrors* deals with alcoholism. Is that something you felt was a literary subject? That was a popular romantic concept.

RS: In a way, it's something that I'm trying to get away from. I was in the drug culture—not so much the criminal end of it, although you always run into some pretty bad people sooner or later. The drugs that run through all my stories and in my novels are a reflection of people I knew who did take a lot of drugs, so that I am really reflecting what I've seen around me. People are constantly drinking, they're constantly doing stuff throughout the book, but that's what these particular people would do. In the case of my protagonist, Rheinhardt, there's a lot about him that represents the shadow part of my life, in the sense that it wasn't my life but, in a way, it could have been. I inflicted on Rheinhardt all the things that I was afraid would descend on me so that he was literally my scapegoat; he was a kind of alter ego. I didn't make the choices that he made. I did everything else that he did. I more or less stopped drinking a lot, which I used to do. I was a kid who went to school drunk in high school, and I quit doing that.

CR: The culture of the fifties had a romance with drinking.

RS: Drinking was it and, as you say, it was romantic. And it was my first novel. I don't think I was ever an alcoholic, but if I hadn't made the choice not to be, I would have drifted that way, as had a lot of people that I knew, such as Kerouac and a lot of lesser-known people around the scene, whether in New Orleans or in New York.

CR: Someone was telling me about the drive you took in the desert. Tell me the story.

RS: Tom Wolfe describes a ride I took with a guy named Ken Babbs and his wife and children who were aboard. We drove from Manzanillo to Nogales, Arizona, all the way up Route 5. We were doing lots of speed, smoking lots of grass, and wildly hallucinating on the Mexican desert. We kept seeing these machines which looked like road monsters. Once we encountered this thing standing in the road—it became necessary, if we were to continue, to drive right into it, and we had this moment of sheer terror when we thought that we were either about to drive into another dimension or into this beast—we were going to do a Jonah and disappear into the belly of the creature. Somehow we got through the ride. Neal Cassady, in those days, was pretty shot—I never knew him at his best. He was gone on stuff like Methedrine, so he never shut up—he just went on and on, out of his head.

CR: Could you still distinguish the charisma that made so many writers captivated by him?

RS: I have used Cassady-like people in my books, but I was not captured by the romance of Cassady. He looked and seemed to be like a guy who'd done a lot of time. I read *On the Road,* and I see how Neal was like a hero, but he was somewhat older than me. I always had the feeling of a guy who's on his way to being—I hate to say this—but on his way to being an old-time street guy, short of breath, who was really hustling to keep up with these younger people. I've seen some of the movies that Ken took, and it really showed in that footage—how old and pained Neal looked in those days, and how everybody around him was so much younger and just full of this infinite energy. He was taking all that speed, in my opinion, basically to stay up—to get in there with these crazy kids. I remember an encounter between the people in the bus and Jack Kerouac, somewhere on Madison Avenue. Cassady was driving the bus, and Kerouac, Ginsberg, the Orlovskys, and a couple of other people, including a guy who claimed to be Terry Southern and wasn't, were in this party. Kerouac had reached the stage of being very alcoholic and embittered—boy, he hated us. He was jealous that Ken Kesey had grabbed Neal as a bus driver. These people were just a bunch of California hippies. He did not see us as angels, seraphs, and all the terrific things that he saw his own generation as. It's true that in a way we were the opposite—we were a lot healthier and California-like. We were just not a New York number. There was a lot of the hayseed, cowboy element in Kesey that clashed with the Eighth Street commando—an East/West Coast culture clash of ages. Kerouac was eloquent on what jerkabouts we were.

CR: But Neal Cassady affected all of the Beats, and, as a young writer, could you identify with their experience of encountering someone much more raw with all his poetic vitality?
RS: Their encounter took place in the forties. *On the Road* is set in 1949, to a large extent. They were young people at Columbia who were encountering, in Cassady, the American West, the outlaw and the life of the road. I can see how the young Cassady could appeal to them. He just knocked them out by being such an American original. I don't think their attitude towards him was patronizing, but there was something of the discovery of the genuine, unschooled American. Their perception of him was aesthetic—they were seeing all those traditions reenacted in one individual. In a way, he was always performing for intellectuals. He had this role of American original thrust on him, and enjoyed it, and always, on some level, had to work at it. Which doesn't mean that their friendships were false or that their feelings for each other weren't valid; there was a lot of mutual respect.

CR: Were you writing prior to *A Hall of Mirrors*?
RS: I started writing *A Hall of Mirrors* in New York in '62. On the basis of the beginning of it I got a fellowship at Stanford. When I went to California, it was like everything turned Technicolor. California in 1962 was a different world, of course. Somebody described being in San Francisco as like being stuck on an escalator in Lincoln Center. There were people there who had gone there to get away from crime—it sounds absurd now. But it was a much more easygoing place than New York. The sixties hadn't really happened yet. The worst and strangest thing around was us. We were, when you come right down to it, pretty harmless.

CR: Did that affect your writing?
RS: Yes, it did. It's hard to say, but I think it did affect my writing because it changed my life and circumstances and it gave me a view of what is

practically a different kind of culture. It changed my perspective; it enlarged my experience. It made me think, as acid did, made me consider questions of reality—the difference, as somebody said, between words and silence. It also brought back what I think were a lot of latent religious feelings in me that I had really turned my back on. What got me into trouble at school was my rather naïve, militant atheism. But, in fact, I was basically religious. Even though drug mysticism is a vulgarism of the real thing, I think it did make me come to terms with my own religious impulses. There is some element of the religious in almost everything that I've written.

CR: In *A Hall of Mirrors* your style is all there, and it won the Faulkner Prize for a first novel. I was wondering if you had a sense of coming into your own when you were writing?

RS: I was creating myself as a writer in that book. I put everything that I knew—or claimed to know—into that novel, as one will with a first novel. That book was like a process—rather than being something that I sat down over a period of time and wrote, it existed in my life and parallel with my life for a number of important years. I was learning to be a novelist in the course of writing it, I was developing a style, and I was also pursuing a vision of things. I wasn't sure what I was after when I began it, but as the characters came into existence I began to play them off against each other. I realized that I had attitudes about the relationships between people. I had something to say about how people are with each other—how they seem to promise things to each other and, most of the time, don't come through or come through and don't quite manage it or come through in the face of expectation and sense. The attitude towards the world and towards fear and towards violence were things that I had something to say about. By the time I was halfway through it, I really had myself and my novel. It sounds funny to say, but it has to be true about any novel: it's something that you make up as you go along. With *A Hall of Mirrors*, I knew pretty much how it would end, but a lot of what was in the middle I didn't know. If you'd asked me then what I was writing about, I would have said, in a kind of Kerouac-like romantic vein, America. If you'd asked me if I had a writer I was emulating, I would have said Gogol. It would have been presumptuous to say all those things, but I was trying to make a statement about America.

CR: With Rheinhardt, you first introduce the potentially psychotic character that he reveals himself to be, which is something that fascinates you. Where does that aspect of your fiction come from?

RS: The affectless person is a person that fascinates me. That's the result, in a way, of when I was young. I spent three years in an orphanage, basically because my mother was schizoid—she wasn't a sociopath or a psychopath in any sense of those terms, but she was schizoid. I grew up, in those years, with people who were going that way—these affectless, institutionalized sociopaths were the people right around me. When I was in the Navy at seventeen, there again I ran into military people like that. Those things frightened and fascinated me. There are people like that always with us. There's an American way of being like that, which I presume differs from the French or German or English way of being like that. Is it too much to say that there's a little bit of that person in everybody? I think it is too much say that, but maybe there's a little in me.

CR: Do you see it out there in the culture?
RS: Exactly. Because of the lack of tradition and the general rootlessness and transience of American life, that character plays a larger role, is more in evidence, and is, to some degree, celebrated. That character is a contributor to the American experience. Not only have we the Frontiersman and the Puritan and the Outlaw, but we have the Sociopath as a major cultural type, and there is a certain reference to him in American society. I think what I was trying to do was to recognize the importance of the rootless, affectless, emotionally crippled individual in American life.

CR: Rheinhardt is both a brilliant musician and a confidence man in his ability to infiltrate any society, and yet he chooses the derelict's life of a drifter.
RS: He's able to live in it, like a fish lives in water, because he's chosen it. Rheinhardt is a man of tremendous spite who has rejected his own talent because, as he says, he feels he lacks the energy and manhood. By that I mean that he just doesn't have a moral substance to be what he should be—a great musician. In an act of spite, he leaves his family, leaves art, and, ultimately, leaves good. He chooses the bad. Spite is what drives him to destroy himself, to move towards all the forces of darkness because he's turned his back on everything positive—all the things of light. I was once going to call that book *Children of Light*, and I wish I had.

CR: I focused on the fact that his intelligence is always used provisionally. He knows, without thinking about it, that he can do a newscast, and still he prefers the oblivion that drink promises.

RS: His dynamic is perception, and that's one thing he can't turn off. He's doomed to witness and to be intensely aware of what is going on around him. His condemnation, this doom that he's going towards, is all the more painful because of his self-awareness. Every time he deliberately makes an immoral choice, he is aware of the difference. There's a constant process of his choosing the darkness. He has to experience doing that.

CR: From the narrator's point of view, neither Morgan the social worker nor Geraldine is innocent. Is that part of your vision?

RS: They have their price. They're both hungry, they're both victims of spiritual hunger, and they both come into contact with Rheinhardt, who is on his way as far down as he can possibly go. Geraldine has the bad sense to fall in love with him, which is, of course, going to sweep her away. Her price, in a way, is him.

CR: Your characters are helpless but the society explodes. Was that a political statement?

RS: No, it's a surrealistic ending. At the time I wrote about the riot, before '64, as best I recall, there hadn't been any. I was carrying things to their logical, absurd conclusion. Unfortunately, the logical, absurd conclusion turned out to be what happened.

CR: Was that ending also a resolution for you as a writer?

RS: I take satisfaction at having done it. I haven't read it now in a couple of years. But I remember it very clearly, because it was harrowing to write. When Geraldine died it was like a death had really occurred. It really upset me, and I stopped writing for over a month while at that scene. There is humor in the book that I can't help bringing to bear, because it's one of the ways that all of us get through life. Emotionally, it really knocked me out—the years of writing it—it was like a rock. By the time I'd finished it, I was in a different place, and in a different head. I was living in the real world and I was living in a fictional world. Reflections of my real experiences, my feelings, my politics, my attitudes toward people and towards life and towards America were all going in there.

CR: Was that when you went to England?

RS: After that I went to England. I was trying to begin another novel, and I didn't know what the novel was. I had a wonderful time in England; I was drinking too much, partying too much. Then, of course, Vietnam was in progress. It began to occur to me that if my subject was America, and if I was going to be faithful to the subject that I had chosen, I had better get over there. I knew I was going to have to write about people who had been there. I got accreditation from a now defunct English imitation of the *Village Voice* called *Ink* to go to Vietnam as a correspondent.

Nineteen seventy-one was an odd period in the Vietnam War. It was not a time of intense combat, although there was some near Saigon and up north. I think my going out to the line, which I did on the back of somebody's motorcycle, was really a gesture. I just thought, I can't really stay in Saigon. If this was going to have any validity, I really should get out there and see the line. So I did. Somebody like Michael Herr saw twenty times as much combat as I ever did. Michael really paid his dues over there in a way that I didn't, but I thought I had to pay some dues, so I went out.

CR: In Saigon, while reporting, did you consciously look for the subject of a novel?

RS: Well, I really didn't know quite what I was after. I was writing for *Ink*, and I had a good, close, scary look at the drug scene and the black market in Saigon, partly because, more or less by chance, I ran into some people who were connected with the shady side of Saigon. The shady side of Saigon was quite as frightening to me as the stuff that was going on on the line in 1971. It was the time of Vietnamization, and American troops were being taken out of Vietnam. The ARVNs were still fighting and dying, to speak of the allied side, and certainly the other side was. But the love of combat was not intense for most people. Then I began to see what this book was going to be and who these people were going to be.

CR: Were the people there trafficking more desperately?

RS: A surprising number of respectable people, or apparently respectable people, were involved, to some degree or other, in both drugs and gold. A lot of people carried things back and forth to Laos, for example, or carried gold from Laos—and that includes diplomats and civil servants, members of the press corps, and the military, too. There was a lot of profiteering, more than one might think. There was a large press corps, and some of it marginal. I am by no means speaking of everybody, but there were plenty of people in the press corps who were into drugs—who were using them and, to some extent, dealing. By 1971, there was a heavy drug scene.

CR: While you were there, did you have the images of war that we did here, watching it on TV every evening?

RS: We were all part of the antiwar movement, but I was getting my perceptions of the war through the medium of the English press and television. That is why I think, when I came to America, I saw the impact of the war on the whole country more clearly, because I had been away. I hadn't experienced it as a gradually increasing thing. It was still going on when I came back in '71, the same year that I had been over there, and came back to what was the beginning of post-Vietnam America. To me it seems that, with the war and the drug explosion and everything that happened in the sixties, the world seems so different than it was before the Vietnam War, before the drugs, the music, before all that wild thing went through. It's almost like living in the aftermath of a revolution—as one might talk about "before the revolution" and "after the revolution." This is a different country. It's easy to confuse one's personal circumstances with circumstances in general, but that's the way it seems to me.

CR: Since so much of your information came from outside this country, did you find double motives as you focused in on the book?

RS: It was this corrupting force that even those honestly involved in it—who, from traditional motives, participated in the war—were involuntarily contributing to the corrupting of American society all the way through. What was worst in America was acted out. What is best about America doesn't export. Yet I have to say that a funny thing happened to my antiwar position as a result of being over there. It wasn't that I stopped being against the war, but I began to feel about it in a different way. Suddenly it was not something abstract. I knew what it looked like and I knew what it smelled like and I knew more about Vietnam than I had known; and it occurred to me that the other side, who had always been my good guys, were, in fact, not such good guys after all. I began to encounter and to hear about some of the atrocities that they perpetrated. One feels one is taking leave of one's senses to talk about whose atrocities were worse. But the image of the North Vietnamese or the Vietcong soldier as representative of humanism and progress, which a lot of us allowed ourselves to entertain, was not a correct one. I began to feel an ambivalence that was reflected in the book. Suddenly there was no more a question of right or wrong, there was just this awful event. In V. S. Naipaul's *A Bend in the River*, two characters are talking and one of them says, in effect, "Sometimes it seems as though there is no right or wrong here." The other character says, "It isn't that there isn't any right and wrong, it's that there isn't any right." That's the way I felt. It is extremely difficult to discover where right is. It keeps disappearing—you think you see it, you've got it in your hands, and then you don't—that old ambivalence comes down and you're compromised. It's just that the ambiguities of life are infinite. Everybody's talking morality, but there aren't a whole lot of people trying to practice it.

CR: Were you also disillusioned by a lot of the leaders of the antiwar movement?

RS: Yes, I was. I think that one of the lessons of the sixties, the war and that period, was that so many of the leaders of the alternative societies and the alternative methods—those systems and ideas which were offered—were quite as ready to lie and as corrupt in their way as the leaders of the so-called establishment. All the leaders, all the gurus that I'm aware of, turned out to be questionable. So where was the true way? It wasn't there. There was damn little that one could do, and life was, finally, as it always is, a lonely and dangerous business in the last analysis.

CR: The character of Hicks becomes the protagonist even though Converse is convinced that he's a psychotic. This paradox you created in *Dog Soldiers* is a recurring theme in your work.

RS: Hicks is absolutely determined to be true to himself and to what he perceives to be his code. His code may be assembled—it's homemade—and some of his sources may be vulgar, but he's going to act morally in his own terms. That makes him look crazy to somebody as relativistic as Converse. Sometimes he does violent and impulsive things, which he then regrets, but he's trying to follow his own code.

CR: By the time you introduce Hicks and he encounters the criminals of the heroin traffic, he becomes a warrior, and the war is brought back to America in the book.

RS: There's more than a grain of truth in it. The social fabric—to coin a phrase—was struck a blow, either as a result of the war or as an indirect result of the war, that it hasn't recovered from. There was an undermining of the society. It was partly economic, and it was partly spiritual. I think everybody must be aware that this society is a whole lot shakier now than it was before the war. I was trying to examine the process of that blow's falling on America in *Dog Soldiers*. *Dog Soldiers* is about a whole lot of dreams that went bad. It's about people pursuing sensation and experience for their own sake; people doing things that they did both in Vietnam and in America, as they still do—doing things that they never thought to see themselves do in the name of experience.

CR: What is heroin?
RS: It's not only a manifestation of moral sleaze. If you want to take and abstract all human desires and make a paradigm out of them, that would be the pattern. It activates the pleasure centers of the brain. It is pure abstract desire. It takes the place of money, sex, and company. It's a magic and powerful substance that is charged with its own mystique. If you've ever read junkie poetry, people have this love for heroin, and they fear it. People speak of it as though they were speaking about God. It is the Big H—a mixture of love and adoration, and it's really awful.

CR: In Hicks's total distrust, did you see the war as catching up with and destroying the counterculture that grew out of the protests?
RS: Yes, it finally did. Another thing that *Dog Soldiers* is about is that nothing is free. There was America having this party at the same time as the war was on. We were going to do three things at once—we were going to fight a successful war in Asia, we were going to reform society, and we were going to have a terrific party at the same time. That just wasn't so.

CR: Were the authorities, the hijackers, and the narcotics dealers reflecting your own feelings about the government?
RS: The characters are not themselves officers of the war, but they are the kind of people who are always around them—stoolies and gofers. They are the place where the cop meets the criminal subculture. They represent that side of the law. I was using a situation that was true about certain law enforcement officers, agencies, and individuals as a reflection of the general corruption and uselessness that I was seeing in the government. I am not a radical, and I think the American Constitution is one of the great documents of the eighteenth century. In theory this system is terrific. In practice it has a lot of good things about it, but I am not an admirer of the American government.

CR: From the Vietnam era we have a distrust and fear of power.
RS: I have been observing power in its application through all my novels. I am suspicious and fearful of organized or institutionalized power, whether it is "alternative" or "establishment." I have learned, and I hope that others

have learned, the truth of the old dictum—"Trust is good, not to trust is better." It's a brilliant proverb.

CR: You portrayed the corruption of society in all your novels, so that your view is of the underside of events.

RS: I have an attitude towards institutions and power, and I really suspect that, deep down, nobody knows what the hell they're doing. A lot of correspondents in Vietnam, when they were writing about the war, would say, "We're writing this up, and it gets put in neat columns of print. We are attempting to make sense, and we are making sense, of something that cannot be made sense of." In a way, all life is like that, in that most people are more like chimpanzees than they're like Socrates, including myself. Our collective perception of what we're like is considerably at variance with what we're really like. We are cleaning up our own act in our collective perception of ourselves. That has its amusing aspects and its terrifying aspects, but I believe that is the case. It is very hard for us to put one foot in front of the other, so to speak. It is very hard for us to behave rationally, let alone well.

CR: In the way you portrayed how Hicks died in the desert, did you see him as a martyr of his own code?

RS: Yes, in that he insists on coming through. In remaining true to himself, he does terrible things that he would never have thought he would do. The violence of his nature emerges in the pursuit of his own code, and it becomes an end in itself. It becomes something beyond morality, something more important than life. He's just determined to live up to this construction of himself, and that is in a way noble but also pathological.

CR: There are elements of rage against America in characters such as Hicks. Does it represent an essential trait of the culture?

RS: They are, in their way, particularly American characters, and they represent a number of forces in the society, in the myth and the reality of America. There is a lot of rage against America, and it is there for the obvious reasons. I love America, so it enrages me—if I didn't, I wouldn't be so angry, nor would I make America my subject.

CR: Who are the writers you read and learn from?

RS: The first person who gave me what I would call a literary experience, who taught me something about how language works and what writing is about, oddly enough, was Carlyle. I must have been in the eighth grade when I read Carlyle's *French Revolution*. My first reaction to it was "I can't understand a word of this. It doesn't make sense to me. What a strange way of writing this is." But as I read it, I began to really enjoy it, and I began to understand it more. It really struck me as most unfamiliar, provocative, and strange. That was the first time that I was really struck with language. I learned about the variety of textures that prose could have, about the liberties that could be taken with language, that one could depart from the conventional rhetoric of English and in so doing produce a strong effect.

And, of course, Dickens. The characters in his books are in a kind of alternative world that you can get into, and when you're into it you're really seeing it. Someone described Dickens as a visionary. His imagination is so visual and so verbally skilled that you cannot refuse his reality, and you know, by reading him, that his experience of his fictive world was very rich and immediate and present. He was obviously immersed in his books. That's his greatness. He was afraid of so many things as a Victorian, but writers as different as Dostoevsky and Kafka saw themselves as attempting to emulate Dickens. He really has a sense of evil—he just never forgot that blacking factory. It must have terrified him—the prospect of tumbling into the proletariat in the Victorian age of primitive accumulation. You can imagine that it must have been scary for him, but it did him a lot of good as a writer.

When I was a teenager I read Dos Passos's *U.S.A.* trilogy, and I still have a habit of beginning to write about many different characters. When I was in my early twenties I found the reading of Kafka's *The Trial* a revelation. Finally, I think the writer who influenced me the most, even though I don't share anything of his vision, was Conrad—as a storyteller. I learned the art of the novel from Conrad and Scott Fitzgerald: the novel as being full of strategic as opposed to tactical considerations. There's nobody writing, under a certain age, who wasn't influenced by Hemingway. My favorites are, I think, every writer's favorites—that is, Beckett and Borges. They are the greatest writers in the world to me.

CR: What are your work habits?

RS: My work habits are fairly rigorous. I start early in the morning. I'm usually out in the woods with the dog as soon as it gets light. Then I drink a whole lot of tea and start as early as I can, and I go as long as I can. Right after I wake up, I feel I'm at my best. I feel like all the systems are going. I exercise regularly. I don't drink a lot. That's perhaps one of the reasons why my characters are always drinking and taking drugs, because I am not.

CR: Is Mrs. Stone also a writer?
RS: No, she's a social worker.

CR: And do you read your material to her?
RS: Yes, she's always the first person to read it. I use her if I'm uncertain, if I have trouble with something I'm writing. Writing is a constant process of decisions, and as a writer I feel I have to make the decisions. Once in a while, something will be too close to call, and I will take it to her. Among civilians, it's only my wife who will read it.

CR: Nabokov once said that he wrote for a small group of people, most of whom were friends. Who are your books written for?
RS: Somebody who is like me but obviously cannot be me. I have to trust the hypothetical reader. I am trying—in a good cause—to crowd people out of their own minds and occupy their space. This is an incantatory process. I want them to stop being themselves for a moment. I want them to stop thinking, and I want to occupy their heads. I want to use language, and I want the language to reverberate. I want to use the white spaces between the lines. I want it to be the total experience that language can be. That's my ambition. I may not always do it, but that's what I'm trying for. If I didn't write for people, my proper business would be meditation. But my business is writing for people. To me, it's an act of affirmation.

CR: Critics have commented on the originality of your style. Can you define your particular style?
RS: One doesn't consider style, because style is. I can see myself not being able to write because I'd be thinking about style. Style is form. My style of writing is part of my way of being, and it's a reflection of what my mind is like and what my relationship to language is.

CR: Faulkner once said that he owed his style to a fifth of bourbon.
RS: I cannot write intoxicated in any way. Somebody once asked Ken Kesey, "Well, you're a young man, and you've written two major novels in a short period of time. How have you been able to do that?" He said, "Speed."

CR: Do you work things out by rewriting?
RS: I'll write a very rough first draft of every chapter; then I will rewrite every chapter. I try to get it down in the first rewrite, but some chapters I

can't quite get right the third time. There are some I go over and over and over again. For example, the Naftali chapter in my last novel—I must have done it five times. There was always too much of something. It was too long, or it was too short. It was either too sentimental or too lacking in sentiment. I couldn't get it right.

CR: What mistakes do you rewrite out?

RS: If you've been writing for a while, you begin to indulge yourself. You begin to think that minor things of concern to you are going to be of concern to everybody.

CR: When you work, does your imagination begin with language or with images?

RS: In imaginings, when I'm walking down the street, I begin to make language of it at a fairly early stage. I make it verbal. Language is a code system, and for writers it's their medium, so I begin to impose language on phenomenology very quickly because it is how I make sense of things. I like to write dialogue, so I'm always listening to people talking. But there are some people that you should listen to, and there are some people that you should watch because you're going to learn more about them that way than from what they say.

CR: Does the material of the novel create its own form, or do you begin with a sense of structure?

RS: I think I have a sense of structure at the beginning. I am not certain what will happen in terms of specific incidents, but I have a sense of the rhythm of it. When you begin, it's a little open—what the ultimate beat is going to be. As soon as I know who the people are and as soon as I begin to write, I can sort of catch the beat. One is improvising when one writes, and you pick up in the same way a musician starts to improvise and detect the inner structure of what he's playing—that's the way I think it works in the writing of a novel. You pick up the beat.

CR: Are the strange and frightening things you write about the things that you fear?

RS: It's a commonplace idea, isn't it, to be drawn to the things you fear? The reader and I will consider how strange and frightening things are, and we will laugh about it, having no other alternative, and thus transcend it and assert the positive part of our humanity and perhaps make it less fearsome.

If you read Beckett or see one of his plays, it seems as though he is pushing despair, but the strength of his insight leaves you feeling kind of elated and comforted by the fact that there is a sensibility that is aware and can go down to that depth and bring up pure art. I want to share that sense of the terrifying nature of things with my hypothetical reader and, as a result of our sharing it, produce a positive experience that gives rise to hope and transcendence. That's what I'm trying to do.

CR: That's art as sublimation?
RS: Well, sure it is, it's what Malraux described, as in all art. It's a response to the silence; it's a response to loneliness, and it's also reassembling our lost God. It's part of the process.

CR: How did you go about creating a whole country for *A Flag for Sunrise*?
RS: It's not so hard to create a country. All you've got to do is think of a name for it. [Laughs.] I don't want to be facetious in my answer. I wanted a combination of countries to go with what I had seen and what I wanted to do. Tecan is representative of all those places in the world, particularly in Latin America, that are beset with the American presence and that are ill-governed. People die and they are unhappy with the world. So it is what it is—an unfortunate Latin American country—and also it is the world and things as they are.

CR: I was wondering which specific countries you had in mind for Tecan?
RS: It's not a portrait from life in prerevolutionary Nicaragua nor is it Honduras nor is it Guatemala, but in certain ways it resembles all those places.

CR: Was this a subject you had in mind for a long time?
RS: Well, I once gave a reading at a university and ended up with a thousand dollars in my pocket. I thought, I've got to go somewhere, where shall I go? I found out there was this flight down to San Pedro Sula, Honduras, so I thought what a gas it would be if I got on a plane to San Pedro Sula. I expected a town out of *The Wages of Fear*, and that's exactly what I got. There it was! I started traveling from there by bus, met some people, and ended up, after some weeks, in Costa Rica. In the course of that trip, just listening to people, keeping my eyes and ears open, I became aware that there was a lot going on down there that was extraordinarily interesting. So I went back.

CR: What were you sensing there?

RS: The situation began to remind me of Vietnam. I was sensing the American presence in the underdeveloped world, and I was again seeing this vaguely irrational sense of mission which Americans are consumed with when they are about their business in the underdeveloped world: anthropologists, missionaries, contractors, deserters, crazies, druggies—various people.

CR: Was it all out in the open, and were they all visible?

RS: They were all visible to me in the course of my several trips. In 1976, when I set out, the Nicaraguan revolution had not begun, nor was it expected. No missionaries had been murdered; these things occur in revolutions. So I've been overtaken by events in the worst way again. It was not due to any great prescience on my part, because anybody who was down there at that time could feel those things in the making.

CR: It's not surprising that you mentioned Conrad before. *Nostromo* deals with a revolution in a Latin American country. Were you thinking of that novel?

RS: No, I wasn't. I haven't read *Nostromo* in a long time, and I tried to put *Nostromo* out of my mind. It was not in any way a model or even an influence, nor is it one of my favorite Conrad novels. I admire *The Secret Agent* and *Victory* and *Lord Jim* and the beginning of *Under Western Eyes*, which I think are marvelous.

CR: Is Graham Greene a favorite of yours?

RS: He is not a favorite of mine. When I went to a Catholic school, I was always abjured to read him, together with Evelyn Waugh and various Catholic writers, for the salvation of my soul. While it's true that we both have guys in white cassocks staggering around under palm trees, the similarities really do end there.

CR: I was thinking of the preoccupation with the moral concerns of your cast of characters in *A Flag for Sunrise*. The book opens with Father Egan, in his despair, encountering such extreme violence, and that's the drama that unfolds.

RS: One of the things that I want to establish, for my purposes, is the *homine lupus*. I want to deal with extremes of brutality, yes, that the innocent suffer at the hands of people or forces driven by ignorance and greed. It's against that background of innocent suffering that the action takes places. It's representative of life in Tecan with a vengeance. It is the place that Father Egan has to start from, where he stops being a declining, cowardly, aging alcoholic and begins to reach out towards God for the first time in years. It practically costs him his sanity. The constant memory of this not only shakes his soul and fills him with terror, but it also moves him out of despair towards the numinous. This element of the numinous is always there for all of the characters in their various ways, just on the edge of their vision. They're always getting little glints of what may or may not be God. All of them are pursuing something beyond themselves. Holliwell thinks, Well, in the end, is there justice? Pablo, in his primitive way, is after it. Sister Justin is after it in politics, and she finds it not in politics but in martyrdom. And all these people are striving for and occasionally glimpsing a transcendent realm which they desire passionately. Everybody's after a new morning: What do we have to run up and salute tomorrow?

CR: That's the meaning of your title.
RS: Right.

CR: Holliwell discovers that all these people have been through Vietnam and are doing the same things in Latin America.
RS: Such a brotherhood exists, and he is part of it and so are those others. It's like a recurring dream, not quite being able to remember the past and being condemned to repeat it. It's a condemnation, on the wheel of existence, to relive, in a much more frightening and a more dramatic way, Vietnam. It's as though he's paying dues that he didn't necessarily pay the last time.

CR: When you have him make those statements about American culture—is that parallel to your ideas that the worst is exportable but the best is not?
RS: It's a lament for an America that may be lost, a lament for the integrity, for the grandeur of the inner spirit of America—it's a lament for that, which takes the form of a diatribe.

CR: When Sister Justin sleeps with Holliwell, is it a gesture of despair more than of love?
RS: Love is such a strange thing—it has so many crazy forms that some loves are reflections of despair. Holliwell says they are both looking for a warm, soft place, in every sense. They're looking for shelter. They don't know if there is such a thing as love—how much of a word it is, and how much of a

real thing. But she doesn't consider herself to be a nun any more, and he is going to probably assume that she can act out a rejection of her vows.

CR: In the same way as Father Egan despairs of God.
RS: She despairs of God and turns to man and finds God. One of the things she has to do is go the whole distance in rejection.

CR: Catholic priests and nuns know that despair is a sin, and their training arms them against entering that state as your characters are driven to do.
RS: The underlying loss for everybody is Gnostic rather than Catholic. In Gnostic theory we are all lost, all separated from our true selves—we are components of a divine entity. The myth of Gnosticism predicates this great battle between good and evil, where some divine being was destroyed in a cosmic destruction which created the world and created us. We are the ruins of a vanished God and our necessity is to reassemble that God.

CR: The escaped killer, Pablo, journeys down to Tecan. Is that just another aspect of the American presence?
RS: In some ways, I'm thinking of what Porfirio Díaz said about Mexico: "Poor Mexico, so far from God, so close to the United States." But every time this colossus of the North turns on the edge of its bed, poor little Tecan is practically overthrown. This American presence—its turns cause all this upheaval—it's almost unaware of itself, unaware of its effects. It doesn't specifically mean to cause harm. It's serving its own interests as it sees them, but it is inflicting great hardship and great harm on Tecan. It's a due bill coming up for payment. We've been getting our bananas, we've been getting our potassium to stave off our sense of existential dread, we've been sending in Marines, pushing people around in Central America, and we're going to eventually have to pay the price of it. It's already happening.

CR: The whole structure of the American presence in Vietnam is moved to Latin America.
RS: Right. They're doing their job in the same way that the Soviet police state proceeds. It acts. It spies on its people; it tells them lies; and it does that while, at the same time, rationalizing and justifying its doing so. All its officers, all its functionaries do what they always do. The sum total of that is by way of being a misfortune of the country. There's no exact parallel here, but it is rather the same with the Americans who deal with Tecan. They're doing things that they've always done.

CR: Both Lieutenant Campos, who preys on young women, and his American counterpart, the child murderer, confront Father Egan. You have these blind, deadly forces turning to a spiritually bankrupt priest for help.

RS: They're both part of Egan's parish now because of what he witnessed and collaborated in—this is his ministry. He is now a party to the most fearful side of humanity, and that is where his mission lies as a priest now. Father Egan has found his way to the kind of Gnostic mysticism which presumes that all material existence is flawed and basically evil. These men are both, in their separate ways, human pathology, and at the same time rather innocent, like forces of nature. They're wounded humanity who do evil without particularly wanting to. Again, it's that disconnection between impulses, between motivation and its result. So he's confronting another failure of humanity, the flaw in things as they are.

CR: In the scheme of nature within the novel, the landscape is reflected by the offshore reef where each character who dives down experiences terror.

RS: But this is nature, and there is a predator down there. It's more than a shark. It's more like a killer whale. It's an elemental force—perhaps the opening to hell. The implication on a realistic level is that there's a shark or killer whale there. But this is where Father Egan dropped the body of the girl. What's down there is evil itself. I was thinking of the speech in *Richard III* where Clarence, just before they drown him in the butt of malmsey, says, "I have passed a miserable night, / So full of ugly sights, of ghastly dreams, / That, as I am a Christian faithful man, / I would not spend another such a night, / though 'twere to buy a world of happy days." And he describes his dream, which is of a thousand men that fishes gnawed upon, and skulls with jewels, and so forth.

CR: You suggested the coral reef inside man—is that something you've perceived?

RS: Yes. It's in imagination because brain coral looks like brain tissue when you see it. It's enormous and round. This idea that the mind is an undersea thing, going deeper and deeper, is something that came to me one day when I'd been up for about thirty-six hours.

CR: The sea is the image of the subconscious.

RS: This is the undersea reflection of the world. How do the fish live in the sea? As men do on land. So the bottom of the sea, to me, means primary process of nature, nature being most itself. Although it is innocent, it is full of dangers and also frightening. It's a paranoid nightmare of looking over your shoulder. No matter how beautiful it is, you're always on the watch for some dreadful monster.

CR: Contrasted to these blind and innocent forces of nature, there's human history, which your characters try to grasp. What is your concept of history?
RS: It's a bitter and ironic reflection that Holliwell has from his experiences. He understands it now, if he didn't before. Anyone who has been witness to history and its aspects should be proof against surprises, will not be affrighted by anything that happens. He's talking about Vietnam, and he's talking about what happened in Tecan. He's talking about history in general. Everybody's giving their interpretation. Sister Justin, who is coming into a kind of Marxist frame of mind, is after the same thing. Whether one is religious or whether one is Marxist, one is committed to the idea of history as positive. It's Christian dogma that the world is not evil, that the world is good. It's God's creation. The combination of Darwinism and the Christian world view is the essence of Marxism. So these characters are fighting to maintain their view of history as a positive force, and I am carrying through my skepticism, not only about religion and humanism but about history as a positive force.

CR: The irony is that in the end Holliwell and Pablo, adrift in a boat, become the absolute mirror images of each other. Is this duality about the underlying anarchy of human nature?
RS: What one would have thought as the most unlikely thing is what happened. Holliwell, who certainly doesn't want to kill anybody and certainly doesn't see himself as a violent person or murderer, kills Pablo. Pablo thinks that his spiritual education is still in progress, and he's going to be saved. For reasons which Holliwell can justify, but which obviously are unknown to Pablo, Pablo thus becomes the innocent victim. There is a kind of mirror. As unlikely as it seems, they have much in common—the murderer is murdered. All the killings that take place are a reflection of the violence of that part of the world. There, realities are stripped, and, without any veneer over things, it is a primary process. In places like that there is much seeking after God and yet the feeling of His tremendous distance.

CR: I was wondering, what are the implications for you?
RS: It reflects, I guess, my own attitude toward the state of God and man—the possibility of, the absence of, the unknowableness of, or presence of

God. Whether He is there or not there, He certainly is physically extant and physically absent.

CR: How far away are you from any kind of faith, really?
RS: I'm not much crazier than anybody else, but I'm not much saner. So, I thought, I'm really feeling crazy today. I think I'll go see a shrink. I called my GP and asked, "Who's a good shrink?" He gave me this guy's name. He was everything that a psychiatrist should be: a Jewish psychiatrist who was very together, very humane. I went to him, and I talked to him. He said, "What you need is religion. What you should do is go to Uttar Pradish in India because in Uttar Pradish the ground is holy and if you walk on it—the ground is so holy that the vibes coming up from the ground will clear up your head."

An Interview with Robert Stone

Kay Bonetti / 1982

From *Missouri Review* (Fall 1982): 91–114. Included in *Conversations with American Novelists* (Columbia: University of Missouri Press, 1997): 7–25. Used by permission of the American Audio Prose Library, Inc. All rights reserved.

Robert Stone . . . is in many ways an old-fashioned, big-theme novelist in the tradition of Joseph Conrad or Herman Melville. He writes novels of high drama, adventure literature that works on a theological level, often involving large historical developments and the crucible of individual morality. Proceeding from a biblical framework—he describes the Bible as "America's book"—his work has an eerie, apocalyptic flavor in its pursuit of the numinous, "seeking some kind of transcendental ground." His subjects are drawn from the corruptions of war and politics—the residue of Vietnam, political maneuvering in the Cold War, civil war in Central America, the culture of drugs and the drug trade. Almost always, the moral center of his novels is a woman, and it has been said that he writes better as a man about women than any other American writer. . . . This interview was conducted in Laguna Beach, California, in 1982, just after publication of *A Flag for Sunrise*, perhaps his most critically acclaimed book.

Interviewer: You're the kind of writer who is associated with the long haul, the big form. You have such a large vision that I was a little startled at the presence of short stories in your canon. How much do you work in the short story form?
Stone: Well, I started out writing quite a few. I find that I'm difficult to satisfy in terms of my own stories. I think I have destroyed many more than I have ever submitted. My stories are rather different from my novels. They're a bit more surreal. Perhaps there's more humor in the short stories. The concerns, though, are the same. Perhaps I find I don't have the opportunity to really address those concerns in what I consider to be a serious way, in

the story, in quite the same way that I can get to them in the novel because in the novel I can go off in different directions. I can find resonances by setting up things like parallel structures where two different sets of people are doing totally different versions of the same thing, whereas in the short story everything must be particularly impacted. So I'm always waiting for some story to occur to me that I consider to be inevitable. Because I don't actively pursue the form but rather wait to be struck by some story that will come together in my mind; I don't do many.

Interviewer: You said that the concerns were the same and by that did you mean the thematic concerns of your short stories?

Stone: I think there's a common element in everything I've ever written. I started out in my first book, and I think I was working my way toward the main subjects that I deal with. All of them touch on these subjects, and they are subjects that a great many educated people today don't take very seriously. I'm concerned with basic ontology, with questions that are perhaps more religious than political. I write about the presence or absence of God and the significance that the question of God's absence or presence has on people's lives. People's pursuit of the numinous, their desire for some kind of transcendent ground, seems to me to be a very large part of the human experience. It isn't something that is very often addressed in academic or literary or educated circles generally, but I think it's something that occurs in the lives of most people, even though they don't often talk about it.

Interviewer: Is this just your personal material, or do you see those issues as the fundamental business of the novelist?

Stone: I suppose every novelist finds his fundamental business, decides what his fundamental business is. That, I think, is mine.

Interviewer: What does this say to you about the fact that most contemporary novelists are somewhat embarrassed by this kind of subject matter, or consciously avoid it?

Stone: I understand why novelists do. It's very dangerous territory. It's very easy to be fatuous about transcendence and spiritual values. There's an awful lot of fatuous and sentimental stuff written about people's hunger for areas beyond their own ken. This is an area that you really can't fake. You come to it with either active belief or active disbelief or a position which takes its dynamics from somewhere in between. It has to concern you. If it doesn't, then you can't write about it. You can't, I think, effectively write about people's hunger for transcendence unless it's something that you yourself experience. It can't be done secondhand. It can't be rendered warmed-over.

Interviewer: You said that you think this is a central issue in most people's lives. I was wondering if you see yourself as writing to try to understand your culture within this frame of reference, or are you just trying to get down what you see? The phrase that comes to mind is Whitman's injunction to vivify the contemporary fact.

Stone: Of course I'm trying to do that. I'm writing about the American experience. It's very hard for me to keep politics out of what I write. I'm not an ideologue. I don't have an ideology, and yet I find it difficult to leave politics alone. I suppose because politics in America—politics of course anywhere—is the vehicle through which people attempt to act out their moral vision. I'm trying to render the American experience, which is particular, as there are specifically national ways of perceiving the world. The United States is a country which has always liked to see itself as representing a certain moral position. It's one of the countries in the world, like India and the Soviet Union and various others, that claim to represent a high moral purpose. At the same time, the United States and the people in it are very aware of the ways in which this claim to high moral purpose is compromised. This tension between the ways in which our pretensions, our protestations, of high moral purposes are compromised by the contradictions within the society is, in fact, the very stuff of American politics and a very large part of the American experience. We are all brought up with the idea that history, human events, is a kind of moral story. In this culture the basic book is the Bible. That's *the* book. And if you're brought up on the Bible, and even if we don't come from religious backgrounds, most of us have absorbed some of its basic assumptions from this society. One of the basic assumptions is that history moves to a purpose. There is such a thing as progress. The will of God, the will of history, is represented in human events. There is a moral charge to a historical event. That's something we have always assumed. Everyone who's ever written about our history seems to have accepted that politicians have, of course, vulgarized it and utter moral prophecy all the time. But there's this constant assumption of high moral purpose by the practitioners of American politics. I think probably a bit more here than in other countries. Of course all politicians claim to represent historical progress. The way in which it's done in America, though, is rather special. I think we do it more shamelessly. Our politicians engage in moralizing more shamelessly. Our newspapers, our media, talk a lot about morality. In fact, it seems that just lately there's more talk of moral purpose and morality in general than perhaps we've ever had before. There's not a hell of a lot of it being practiced, as far as I can see, but there certainly is a lot of talk about it. I mean, this is one of the things I'm trying to render. The contradiction between this high moral purpose and American reality.

Interviewer: The last line of one of your stories reads, "Momma's deluded." Do you think that there are any of your characters which are *not* deluded in some way or another?

Stone: Yes. There's always a character who is seeing as clearly as he or she can. Very often that character—I think, for example, Justin, in *A Flag for Sunrise*—really has a great deal of common sense. And she makes a rational decision to commit herself. She is a person given to commitment. She is, I think, an American who represents some of the best things about America, but she is undermined by the situation in which she finds herself. She's undermined by the other characters. Very often, I think, there are characters in my novels who are *not* deluded, who are as close to clarity as one gets. Frequently they find themselves, as in life, just undermined by these inescapable ambiguities that are involved in their relations with other people, or with the social situation in which they find themselves. It is very, very difficult to act morally and rationally at the same time. Usually one gives in the face of the other. One has to be a bit of an athlete of perception and a person of great strength and integrity to succeed in doing both.

Interviewer: It just seems that the undermining is so complex in your novels that one might at the end come away wondering if, as one critic said in reference to *A Hall of Mirrors*, the message is "despair and die." And yet other readers have said that despite all the horrible things that are done by people to one another in the name of some of the finest ideals in Western culture, one cannot come away from your novels with a sense of a black vision about the universe. That it's just simply not there. How do you explain these two radically opposing views of your vision on the part of many close and careful readers?

Stone: *Always* in these novels people are trying to get out of the box they're in. As in life, they don't often succeed very well. But they are always catching glimmers of something outside themselves that may be able to save them. They are always looking for the areas in each other that are positive. They are looking for love. They don't often get it, or if they get it, they run into its multiple faces and are confused. But my message is not despair; my message is, find out how bad it gets and begin from there. These people are looking for a place to start from. They pay the price of that. But what I'm not saying is that every time you try to do something worthwhile, disaster descends upon you. What I'm trying to underline is the great price one pays for action in the face of things as they are. I'm trying to define the tremendous difficulty of setting out to act decently. Most people, even the worst of them, have some level in which they want to see themselves as decent people. They have aspirations. There is always, I think, an imminence of a breakthrough. And what I'm writing about—basically what's in the white space, perhaps—is that breakthrough. What form it takes, I don't know. The characters don't know. But they're vaguely aware of it. They're getting some sense that there's a level in which one can break out of this box. They don't succeed in doing it; I can't have them succeed because I don't know how they'll be able to do it. I just don't know any more than they do. But every time I get in with those people, sit down and write them and get in with them, and they take on a certain reality for me, I am with them in their struggle to break through to something beyond the frustration of our social situation and our individual selves.

Interviewer: So then you do see Rheinhardt at the end of *A Hall of Mirrors*, Marge and Converse at the end of *Dog Soldiers*, and Holliwell at the end of *A Flag for Sunrise* as being on that moment? It seems to be most clearly articulated in *A Flag for Sunrise*. Holliwell looks into the sun and sees the eye of the universe and has that universal perception that what the eye is seeing is in fact what your eye is seeing in that eye. It's a very compassionate vision of a young child standing there holding a Coke can. You see them, in fact, as children at birth at that point?

Stone: I've always been taken with something that Malraux wrote in *Anti-Memoirs*. He talks about speaking with this old priest, and he asks what the priest's sense of human life is since he spent sixty years or so listening to confessions. And the priest says, "Well, in the first place, people are much more unhappy than one might think. And in the second, there is no such thing as a grown-up." In a way, I think that's true. We're not going to get anywhere by overlooking the difficulties that life presents us. We have got to start from an acceptance of the fact that we find ourselves beset, by our own natures which are imperfect, and by a world which is imperfect. We cannot simply decide to overlook and transcend these things in a casual way. If we try to do that we end up compounding our situation. That's why revolutions, for the most part, turn on themselves and fail. It's why complacent moralism ends up being vapid and useless. It's why prophets almost always undo themselves and are finally revealed as agents of dualism. We have to accept the human condition for what it is. And my understanding of the human condition is something like this: there was this mud, this substance. It somehow came into existence. Over a period of millennia, it became conscious of itself. It stood up on legs and started walking around, and talking and thinking and having aspirations of one kind or another. Now this is a miracle, that the very mud of the earth could somehow come to consciousness. There is some kind of positive significance there. In what I write, I try to be aware of that. That's why I think I'm not pushing a message of despair because I try to have everything happen in these books against the background of that miracle. That's an unspoken positive dimension. We are just mud, finally, that has become conscious of itself. That's a tough condition.

Interviewer: But "the jewel is in the lotus."
Stone: "The jewel is in the lotus." What the nature of the jewel is, I don't know, but I believe with Egan that it is.

Interviewer: But I wonder if the "despair and die" readers of Robert Stone are seeing another side of the coin. You were saying earlier that we believe in a progressive sense in Western culture. That's it in a nutshell, isn't it? Our conflict with an Eastern sensibility, as in *A Passage to India*, the muddle of India, the inattention to vaccinations, to taking care of disease, to the things that we all grew up in this culture with. I wonder if the "despair and die" readers of Robert Stone are having difficulties with perceiving those two worldviews as being present in your work?
Stone: I think so because people who interpret the underlying message in my writing as "despair and die" are mistaken. That is not what I'm telling people. That's not what I'm writing about. I'm not writing about how the world is just too awful for words. The very act of writing is a positive act. The dynamic that's present in most of what I write is *perception,* and I believe in the value of perception. I believe in a perception that faces things as they are, that looks it all in the eye. I believe very much in common sense. I think certainly it is better to have vaccinations and plumbing and leisure and affluence for working people and farming people, and the more that you can accomplish in that direction the better things will be. But embracing the philosophy that somehow, automatically, God is on our side, and things are just going to get better because that's the structure of history, I think that's

a big mistake. That's what I want to bring into question. I mean, what I am pushing for is that what keeps us going is our perception, our ability to reason down to basics, to somehow not delude ourselves into thinking we are more than what we are.

Interviewer: The terms "allegory" and "morality play" get called up over and over again in reference to your novels. What affinities do you feel with those forms, or, if not the forms, the way of looking at the world which those forms represent?
Stone: Allegory is something that you do almost unconsciously. The best allegories are not deliberate, but are stumbled on. In a way, I think it's less a matter of allegory than metaphor. Individual lives can often be taken for metaphors for the universal situation. I don't know how much I employ allegory. But I certainly do use certain situations as metaphors for the "basic situation" as I see it.

Interviewer: Is there a suggestiveness in your names, for instance, "Holliwell"?
Stone: Yeah, sure, Holliwell is twofold. He's Frank Merriwell gone to seed. But his name also literally means "a holy well."

Interviewer: Not a hollow well.
Stone: No. Well, there's a kind of hollowness too. You can't always control what's coming into your mind. I was thinking of Frank Merriwell, and I was thinking of holy wells, in the sense of somebody making a pilgrimage to a holy well. There are all kinds of holy wells. There's the kind that he is, in fact, named after, the ones in the British Isles, and then there are the holy sacrificial wells of the Mayans, which are less attractive in their origins. But there's a certain kind of hollowness in that name, too.

Interviewer: Who's Frank Merriwell?
Stone: Oh, he was the guy who played for Yale in those old books—*Frank Merriwell at Yale.* He was an all-purpose, all-American sportsman at Yale in books that I think were written in the 1890s. An all-American hero of popular fiction in the nineties.

Interviewer: What about Pablo Tabor? The word "tabor" means "drum."
Stone: It also is the name of an extreme Hussite leader in the wars of religion, about the time of the Reformation. The Taborites were a kind of

peasant army who fought the local nobility and also fought the church. They were one of the extreme factions in the religious wars of central Europe.

Interviewer: What about Morgan Rainey and Rheinhardt?

Stone: With Rheinhardt I was thinking of Django Reinhardt, the gypsy guitarist. I was writing about a musician. And Rainey was a name that I just associated with the Gulf Coast and the Gulf Coast sounds.

Interviewer: Morgan Rainey is one of these characters of clarity, is he not? I would question whether or not he was deluded by drugs or booze as opposed to ideals.

Stone: It's his own nature, his own rather masochistic vision of virtue that undoes him. I think the clearest-thinking person in that book is Geraldine. She sees things clearly enough. Rheinhardt seems to promise something to her that she very much wants, but she is the clearest-eyed of the characters in the book. She's most completely a victim of circumstances.

Interviewer: Let's go back to *A Flag for Sunrise.* There's that Pablo/Negus episode versus the Pablo/Holliwell episode. I want to know if you see a moral difference between those two episodes. In the first we have Pablo and Negus as the last survivors of the whole Callahan crew. Then you have Holliwell, the last survivor of the revolutionaries and the missionary-camp characters—the two survivors. In the first of the two, Pablo throws Negus overboard, and in the second Holliwell throws Pablo overboard.

Stone: It's that they're in situations where it's impossible; trust is impossible. They're impelled by fear and ignorance to destroy each other, which is a situation that a lot of the world is in, or close to being in, right now, so there in their individual relationship they just echo. Not to be too portentous about it, their situation is a bit like the situation in which the nations of the world find themselves right now. They're operating on ignorance and fear. Even Holliwell finally gives in to his own fear.

Interviewer: I'm maybe most fascinated by the character of Pablo in *A Flag for Sunrise.* To me, he's the most problematic character in terms of the way people read you. To me, Pablo is one of the scariest people I've ever run across in the world of fiction. My feeling when Holliwell threw him overboard was that Holliwell knew exactly what to do if he was going to survive. And indeed he didn't dare go to sleep, or Pablo would probably kill him at that point. On the other hand, in some ways we might see Pablo as one of the positive characters in this book, and see Holliwell as a "hollow man," that his act is selfish, stupid, and self-indulgent at that point.

Stone: I think both of those things are true. There's meant to be room there for—I mean, it's all true. Pablo is really crazy and dangerous. On the other hand, Pablo really means well. He always sees himself as a victim. When he is going to steal something, he's stealing because he thinks he's entitled. He sees the other people in the world as enormously powerful and himself as a constant victim. If he steals something, it's only him trying to get his own back.

Interviewer: But he's a speed freak.

Stone: He's a speed freak. He's a sociopath. He sees himself as meaning well. He sees himself as constantly having to defend himself by violence. At that point in the book, he really thinks that he has found a friend, just before Holliwell kills him. His belief is that he's completing his spiritual education, which he really believes in. He thinks he's found a friend who has addressed the central problems of his, Pablo's, life. Of course, he hasn't found a friend. He's found his ultimate enemy. And although it is wise of Holliwell to kill him, it is much safer for Holliwell to kill this dangerous speed freak, it is also Holliwell finding himself in the last position he ever would think to find himself, as assassin, as murderer. So he is guilty of Pablo's murder, even though his doing it was not an altogether wise act of self-preservation. And although Pablo, an hour later, might decide that killing Holliwell was absolutely necessary, he at that moment thinks he's found a friend. Okay, I'm making a comment on how it is with people.

Interviewer: You've mentioned common sense several times, and yet it seems to me that one of the central things about your novels that is absolutely pertinent to the condition of experience that most people of our generation find themselves in is that common sense doesn't seem to mean a darn thing.

Stone: That's the trouble, because people go for the answers that have capital letters. It's like common decency. Common decency and common sense are very hard to bring to bear on the large scale.

Interviewer: It's just that all the time, as people commit acts of decency in the world of your novels, anything good or bad could come out of it at any time. The good things that happen are random.

Stone: Right. As with so many things in history in general, and your history and my history.

Interviewer: But I think thus the confusion that readers come against in trying to figure out the nature of your vision. They know it's there, it's present everywhere, and you know it's not bogus. But it's very difficult to understand.

Stone: I can see where people might mistake what I am doing for the rather trivial exercise of saying that life is tough and no good. But it's just as trivial to say life is shit as it is to say life is roses. I mean, I pursue those questions because I'm interested in possible answers. But I really have to deal with the world and render the world as I experience it. I see a great deal of human life limited, poisoned, frustrated, by fear and ignorance and the violence that comes from it. I feel, consequently, that I have to address it. I think some of the people I write about are constantly trying to get above that and get around it somehow. They're always seeing these glimmers of transcendence which may be something, in fact, that is beyond ordinary life or it may be the better part of their natures or it may be the promise of care, love, concern from other people.

Interviewer: You're praised for being a writer in whom craft and vision meet, and yet it seems that lines in the contemporary fiction scene are drawn nowadays between the two. I think particularly of the running debate between William Gass and John Gardner over the question of "moral fiction." To what extent, in your view, is language per se the business of the novelist?

Stone: I don't know what the business of the novelist is if it isn't language. The way I learned it, you're supposed to have both. You're supposed to be able to write, and you're supposed to be able to think. Language is the medium, the music. Language makes the spell. It makes the situation. It makes the characters. You can't somehow get around the level of language in literature. It *is* language. It's a way of using language to invoke issues, individuals. Music can constitute a vision and painting can constitute a vision and literature constitutes a vision. You can't have music without a sense of sound, and you can't have literature without being able to wrangle the language.

Interviewer: What do you think about the debate, though, of the writers who insist that politics, morality, transmitting social values and things, that

that's a thing of the past as far as fiction is concerned, and that the only serious writers are those who are purely pushing language to its ultimate?

Stone: I don't feel that I have any part in that argument because I think that you're supposed to do both. A well-intentioned writer with a broad moral vision who can't write very well isn't very interesting. A writer who can write well but who has no subjects and isn't interested in reflecting life and people's lives isn't very interesting either.

Interviewer: One general criticism of your work, although critics seem hard-pressed to find things to criticize in your work, is that it's heavily plotted. Number one, how do you plot your novels, and from whom, if anyone, do you think you most learned plotting; and number two, do you think that's ever a legitimate criticism of a writer?

Stone: My favorite novels are in the grand tradition, in the old tradition. I think you have to tell a story. That's one of the reasons that people read books: they want to have a story. I would argue with a sensibility so refined that it can take its satisfactions beyond the level of storytelling. I yield to no one in my admiration for Beckett. But Beckett is a teller of stories, too. That it's heavily plotted, well, I do believe in plot. And I suppose I learned to some degree from all the nineteenth-century masters. I think I have some roots there that moved me very much when I was younger, when I was reading.

Interviewer: Care to name some names?

Stone: If I name the names, I feel like I'm trying to put myself in the same league with these people, which I'm not. I learned a lot from Conrad. I loved Stendhal, Flaubert. Certainly in the novels of the early twentieth century there's a great deal of story, of plotting. The plot in *The Great Gatsby* is a tremendously important part of the novel, and that's the American novel that at this moment I most admire. Its plot, which is so heavy with metaphor, is a very important part of its effect. So situation and plot, for me, are metaphor. I have to entertain myself while I am writing a novel, and in order to entertain myself, I have to tell a story, to keep the illusion of human events going. I don't *like* plot all that much. I sometimes find having to go back and say to myself, he does this because she did that because he did that, is a little tiresome, but you do try to recapitulate human causality.

Interviewer: A lot of people have brought up Graham Greene in reference to your work, and yet you've not mentioned him today in this list of writers.

Stone: I rather like *The Power and the Glory*, but Greene—the trouble with Graham Greene—is he was one of the writers who, when I went to school, I was adjured to read. I went to a Catholic school and he was a Catholic writer. But I never read a lot of Greene in the years that I was reading the writers who influenced me a great deal. I think our concerns are really very different. There's some superficial resemblances. Especially in *A Flag for Sunrise*, you have the idea of a priest staggering around drunk under a palm tree. The whiskey priest. But I think that's all very superficial. I don't think there are any stylistic influences. Admirers of Greene would say that's because Greene is so much better a writer than I am. I myself don't agree with that assessment.

Interviewer: How do you plot your novels, or should I ask, what's the germ?
Stone: I start with the situation and then I have the people. I believe that, in a novel, character is literally fate. Once you know who the people are, you know what's going to happen. I know the beginning in the situation, and I usually know the end. I don't always know the middle. I find out as I go along. It comes out of the people.

Interviewer: But you do have an end.
Stone: Usually have an end in mind, yeah.

Interviewer: That's very different.
Stone: I don't know. Maybe it is. I've never really asked other novelists how they do it. I can surprise myself sometimes. I didn't know, for example, that the quarrel between Dieter and Hicks was going to break out. The day I started writing that piece I didn't realize that was going to happen. It just developed as I wrote the dialogue and imagined myself into the situation. I'd have to say also that Dickens is a writer who I think had an enormous influence on me and who was, in a way, a *haluciné*, inasmuch as he could see his characters and his situations. He could really *see* them, and he makes the reader do the same. Dickens very much entertained himself and his readers with plot, and so do I.

Interviewer: Of course you're an extremely different writer from somebody like Henry James. But when you said that character is fate, that's what he thought, too. And you know the novel that he felt was his largest failure was *The American*, and that's what he said was wrong, that he started with an ending. He felt that there's a certain inevitability, but that things have to play themselves out and, by definition, if you start with an ending, you're going to come up violating the novel's sense of felt life.

Stone: You have to be flexible; you can't be rigid. You can find your way to a different ending. It's nice to have the ending there even if you don't use it, if you see what I mean.

Interviewer: But you started, for instance, with the idea that Holliwell in the boat at the end, and casting the jewel from Pablo's pocket—

Stone: No, not that precisely. I think I had a general sense of how things were going to end up, well for Justin, anyway.

Interviewer: That does seem inevitable.

Stone: Plotting this was quite different then than it would have been now, because when this was all mapped out, there was no revolution in Nicaragua, let alone in El Salvador. So this all precedes. It comes out of trips to Central America that I had made in the middle seventies.

Interviewer: *A Flag for Sunrise* preceded the facts of what's going on down there now?

Stone: But you didn't have to be incredibly prescient to see all this going on. The Church was already getting itself in trouble by organizing cooperatives and so forth. No American missionaries had been killed or anything like that, nor had the archbishop been killed. In fact, Duarte was a good guy back in the middle seventies. He had been denied the presidency after the election, and there were riots in El Salvador in his behalf at that point. So, it's true that it preceded all these—the headlines, considerably, and the revolutions. But I don't lay claim to any great prescience.

Interviewer: This is often true, in fiction, that fiction precedes reality. It happens a lot.

Stone: Yeah, it does.

Interviewer: Some critics feel that you lost control of the structure in both *A Hall of Mirrors* and *Dog Soldiers*. Do you think that's true, or are you satisfied with how they turned out structurally?

Stone: Yes, I guess I lost control of their structure. I'm pretty satisfied with the way they turned out. I didn't have a sense of being out of control.

Interviewer: What about the middle scene in *A Flag for Sunrise*? It's the only time we see the revolutionaries, other than glimpses of Godoy. Some readers have questions about that scene, the way it comes and goes, and you never see any of those people again.

Stone: It violates the traditional mode of the novel. I wanted a look at the revolutionaries. I wanted to put everything in the perspective of the revolution itself. I wanted to make it—I wanted to also employ what I knew about political forces in Central America. Certainly it is a violation of the traditional mode of the novel, but I figured I could get away with it and I think I did. I think it's worthwhile.

Interviewer: By traditional, you mean the organic expectations of—

Stone: Yes, it violates point of view. It violates the traditional consistent point of view. It violates the structure insomuch as we go from one central character to another and move along in time, and all of a sudden in the middle of this book we have these other characters planning a revolution. But I thought it necessary to get that perspective and to put them in, and so I did, without—well, I won't say without worrying about it too much, I worried about it a bit, but I thought if it was an effective scene, and had its element of verisimilitude, then I would put it there and keep it there.

Interviewer: What about the Mennonite boy? The same question has come up with the Mennonite. Some readers see him as being really only there to illuminate some central flaw or some central delusion in Egan's character at the end, and yet he runs all the way through. Did you feel you were taking a chance at all with him?

Stone: Yes, I did. I had him there, I think, to represent yet another manifestation of humanity in extremis, in delusion.

Interviewer: What about the fact that some eight years or so has come between the three novels? Does that mean that you work slowly, or does that mean other things have taken your time or that you rest for a while?

Stone: It's about seven years between them—biblical cycles. It means that I work very slowly and carefully, that I really have to spend a lot of time with plot, that I'm inefficient, my method of working is inefficient. It probably means that I'm lazy. I feel like I'm working all the time. I can't imagine how I can work so much, put out so much effort, and come up with only three novels. I do tend to put everything into the novel. I think I could've made more novels out of the material, if I wanted to write novels in a different style. But because I seem to be enslaved to the idea of the grand novel that I imprinted as an impressionable kid, it just takes me that long to do it.

Interviewer: How long has it taken?

Stone: Well, in fact, I did *Dog Soldiers* in about two and a half years. The expanse of time between publication is seven years, but I did that one in two and a half years. I really didn't know what I was going to do next. I was working as a freelance journalist and so forth. I *was* doing other things. But when I got down to it, it took me two and a half years. *A Flag for Sunrise* took me a long time, I don't know, four years or so—too long, longer than it should've taken. I'm not pleased with having this space of time between novels.

Interviewer: What is your routine? How do you work?

Stone: I get up in the morning. I get up really early, and I work as long as I can. I try to get as many pages done, either in rough or smooth. I do two versions. First I do it rough, then I do it smooth. Then I rewrite the whole thing. But I always start in the morning. I don't usually work at night.

Interviewer: Did you get a whole draft of *A Flag for Sunrise* before you went back and started retouching anything, or did you work in pieces of it?

Stone: I rewrite everything at least once. Then I'll leave a section that I think has some problems, and when I get some time I'll go back and work on it. I did that with the Naftali section in *A Flag for Sunrise.* I must've done that about six or seven times. Then when I have the whole thing done, I go through it and try to find what I think is wrong structurally or in terms of the writing in a given section and make myself a checklist and go through the whole book and do rewrites as I see them to be necessary.

Interviewer: Many of your book jackets refer to, and I'm quoting, your "heavy involvement in the counterculture of the '60s." Would you mind—what was your heavy involvement in the counterculture of the sixties?

Stone: I was a friend, and still am a friend, of Ken Kesey's and was around California when the Kesey gang was there. Many of my friends are from those days, who I sort of grew up with or grew old with or whatever. I was just another character with literary ambitions. Sometimes I feel like I went to a party one day in 1963 and the party spilled out and rolled down the street until it covered the whole country and changed the world.

Interviewer: How'd you come to meet those guys?
Stone: I had a fellowship at Stanford. I lived near Perry Lane where it was all going on, and Ken lived there. As I say, I went to a party one day, and that was the counterculture.

Interviewer: What's the story with you and the military?
Stone: I joined the Navy when I was seventeen. I was in the service until I was twenty-one.

Interviewer: Where'd you then go to school?
Stone: Started at NYU. I went there for less than a year and left and went south and worked a whole lot of crazy jobs and wanted to write and really didn't. I wrote a lot of poetry and read it to jazz in the days of poetry and jazz down in New Orleans. It was quite a while, I think, before I was able to get enough of the sense of life lived in time to begin a novel. But I finally did, about 1961, begin to write *A Hall of Mirrors*. Of course that was interrupted by my "heavy involvement in the counterculture." I was being involved in the counterculture when I should have been writing. So it took me kind of a while to finish that.

Interviewer: Going back to before that, what is your family background, and where are you from, and where did you go to school before you went to college?
Stone: I went to Catholic schools in New York. My mother's family had been in the tug business in Brooklyn for generations. My grandfather was fairly well known, a guy named Alex Grant, who was a legendary figure on the Brooklyn waterfront. He was a chief engineer and captain of a tugboat. A lot of his relatives and my relatives worked on tugs, worked on the New York waterfront.

Interviewer: When did you start to write? Or when did you have a sense of vocation? When did you receive the call?
Stone: Oh, I think fairly early on, although I wasn't in a position to recognize it. I always liked to write, but it took me years to decide that it was something I might be able to make my living doing. But as soon as I reached

the point that I saw that I had made no provisions for any kind of alternative career and had no academic credentials of any kind and was barely capable of delivering a day's work for a day's pay in any area other than making up stories or putting one word in front of another, then I had a vocation. I mean, I had a vocation or else. I had pretty much burned my bridges.

Interviewer: When did this happen?
Stone: Oh, I guess in my early twenties.

Interviewer: Was that when you began *A Hall of Mirrors*?
Stone: Yes. More toward my mid-twenties. But I was a would-be writer from the time I was out of the service, which was when I was twenty-one.

Interviewer: Are you a practicing religious person in the formal sense? Are you a Catholic?
Stone: Not in the formal sense. Sometimes it seems to me that I am some kind of Catholic. I hadn't made my Easter duty last year, so technically—I think you still have to do that. You're supposed to go to church, take Communion at least once a year, so I haven't done that. So I'm sort of a fellow traveler of Christianity.

Interviewer: One reviewer has pointed out that you write with a lot more care and regard for both women and children than is common of most men of your generation. How do you account for that?
Stone: I was raised pretty much by a woman. My mother was the parent who really raised me. I was a father fairly young. I don't know. I never found myself in any adversary relationship with women. I believe that a certain amount of tension between the sexes is not altogether a bad thing. But I think there is a surprising amount of woman-hating on the part of a great many men, and maybe a lot of man-hating on the part of lot of women. I was not caught up in that. I have not felt threatened by women as a group of people. On the contrary, I've always felt pretty good about women. I was real fond of my mother, who was a character. I never hesitated to write about women characters, and I hope I won't hesitate to do it. The human condition is universal.

Interviewer: Do you feel an affinity with any particular novelists or group of novelists among your contemporaries? How do you place yourself—with your friends such as Ken Kesey or with writers like Toni Morrison or the South American writers, the magical realists?

Stone: I don't have any sense of being part of a school. Most of us, of my generation, have read largely the same writers, were influenced by them in different ways, and then went off to do totally different things. I don't feel part of any party or group. I don't oppose one way of writing and advocate another. As I feel that I'm without political ideology—I also don't feel myself as belonging to any literary camp or opposing any literary camp. I don't mean to be sort of, you know, universally and superserviceably agreeable; I just don't feel that I'm part of a group or camp or school, one as opposed to another.

Interviewer: Do you enjoy the act of writing?
Stone: Yes, I do.

Interviewer: Is there an aspect of writing to slake off dread?
Stone: You do it because you need to do it. It's too hard to do if you don't need to do it. People who write are driven. Otherwise nobody would do it. I was warned when I began writing that it was very, very hard. I thought it was easy. I thought, well, you don't have to show up anywhere and go to work, and you can make up stories, and so forth. But I was warned, rightly, that is was very, very hard work. All writers who regularly write, I think, are driven.

"Keep the Levels of Consciousness Sharp"

Eric James Schroeder / 1984

From *Modern Fiction Studies*, 30: 1 (Spring 1984): 135–64. Included in *Vietnam, We've All Been There: Interviews with American Writers* (Westport, CT.: Praeger, 1992): 107–24. Reprinted by permission.

Schroeder: Can you start by giving me a bit of your background? What got you over to Vietnam, and how did you manage to get involved as a journalist?

Stone: I was living in London at that time—this was 1971. I was trying to begin a book, and I kept running into the Vietnam situation late in the war. I had been away from the United States for a couple of years. I couldn't get this book written. It seemed to me that these people—my characters—must have been in Vietnam, even though I didn't know quite who they were. I thought, "What is their relationship to this Vietnam situation that is filling everybody's life now, that is so much on everybody's mind?" It's all anybody could talk about when I was with other Americans. It was so present, looming large in everybody's consciousness. And I began to wonder suddenly if I couldn't get some work over there, go and have a look firsthand at what was going on, because it was such an attraction—the idea of Vietnam as a place and as more than a place.

At that time, an English publication called *Ink*, a London imitation of the *Village Voice*, was opening up. And they were ready to have someone go over there. They were started by Ed Victor, who had been an editor at Cape. They wrote me the form letter, and I got myself a cheap flight to Kuala Lumpur and from Kuala Lumpur to Bangkok and then on to Saigon. I spent something under two months there in May of 1971. Most of it in Saigon, looking into the drug trade. I had made some very, very far-out contacts in

Saigon.[1] I spent a large part of my time in Saigon itself. Sometimes I went out on Route One in the direction of Bien Ho. (I can't remember now the villages.) The part of the line I saw wasn't terribly active. Nineteen seventy-one was the year American forces were being withdrawn from the line in order to keep the casualty rate down. There wasn't a lot of fighting going on involving American troops, but there was quite a bit about thirty kilometers northeast of the city that involved Vietnamese troops. (At first I was only accredited to the Vietnamese government and not to JUSPAO.)

So I was in that area on a number of different occasions, for short periods. Most of the time I was in the city, and I wasn't there very long. It wasn't quite two months. While I was there, actually, *Ink* had folded, my putative employers were no more, so what I wrote was finally published in the *Guardian* (what was formerly the *Manchester Guardian*) sometime during the summer of 1971 on two different Saturdays. And that's the extent of my Vietnam career.

Schroeder: Didn't you publish a Vietnam piece in the *Atlantic*?
Stone: Yes, that's true. I had a piece in the *Atlantic*, too. It's been anthologized in a collection of Vietnam pieces. The book with that article is called *Who We Are*. The piece is about deserters, and it's boring. It is me trying to be a good supporter of the movement. It's boring and it's pretentious and (in my opinion) it's essentially false. I haven't read it in years, but that's the way I remember it; it seemed to be excruciating.

Schroeder: Your position seems to be analogous to Michael Herr's, who told me he originally went to Vietnam thinking to do something like a monthly column for *Esquire*. He got there and after only a week realized that the idea was futile. He called Harold Hayes and told him that. Hayes said, "Well, you're there; do what you like." Michael said that he had always had the idea of a book in the back of his mind, and that anyway the understanding with Hayes was that he was there to write a book. Hayes pretty much turned him loose and said to do what you like.
Stone: My position was a little different because I stayed a lot longer than I had intended. I was ready just to go and have a look around and then get back to work. I had also promised my wife that I wasn't going to stay there. So she was on my case to come back immediately. When I did finally go

---

1. In his essay, "There It Is," *Guardian* (17 July 1971) Stone stated, "Last month I went to Vietnam and stayed there for a couple of weeks," 9.

home, I felt guilty about leaving. I had a very strong feeling of guilt, which I continue to have about being there such a short time and then turning around and coming home. It was impossible not to feel guilty and flaky about such a lightning visit.

Schroeder: Did you go with the notion that you were going to be writing journalism, or did you always have the novel in the back of your mind?
Stone: I wasn't sure what I had in the back of my mind. I was ready to do journalistic pieces. I hadn't done much work lately. I had been freelancing in Europe. I wasn't getting a book written. I wasn't getting anything written. It was a dead time in my life. The trip turned out to be the right thing to do. I really was ready to work there as a journalist. I wasn't absolutely certain what the hell was on my mind. I just wanted to go there. That's more or less all the situation.

Schroeder: In that sense, when writing *Dog Soldiers*, did you feel that you yourself were a role model for Converse?
Stone: Yes, as a marginal journalist, sure, and to that degree. Not that Converse is me (I guess obviously). But yes, certainly.

Schroeder: Could you comment on marginal journalism in Vietnam?
Stone: There was just an enormous number of people who were accredited—there was even a high school paper represented. It was not particularly difficult for all sorts of adventurers and wanderers and hippies and whatnot of all sorts to blow into town, coming from Katmandu or from India. It wasn't that difficult to get in. Nineteen seventy-one was probably the baroque period of Saigon. You could run into anybody on the streets of Saigon. There was a whole antiwar contingent of people. And this was true on several levels. There were the Harvard lawyers, the Harvard Law Project people, who were basically antiwar movement types. There were Quakers, the American Friends Service Committee. Saigon was just full of Americans and Europeans of any possible description. It was a real carnival. There were a lot of people with marginal accreditations: stringers from quasi-papers, people with forged accreditation letters that they had written for themselves. A lot of people dealing dope. There were a lot of marginal people around, a lot of people only nominally press. There were reporters who allegedly dealt with the black market. There certainly were such reporters who dabbled in gold or cinnamon or dope—not reporters

from the major papers but marginal people, people with more secondary credentials.

Schroeder: I want to return to Converse for a moment. He is an interesting character for a number of reasons. Philip Roth wrote an article—I think in 1960 or 1961—in which he talked about the plight of American fiction. In it he claims the trouble with American fiction is that everything in our society is so wacky that when you try to write fiction it comes off as dull in comparison to journalism. Converse is interesting because in our age he is so believable; the whole plot to bring drugs back to the United States—all these things seem commonplace. He comes across as very convincing for this reason. It's easy to imagine him living in Saigon and doing what he does and then coming back here. I think that the horror of the book—and here I'd like to see if you agree or not—is that Vietnam appears to follow him back to the United States. Everyone always calls *Dog Soldiers* a great Vietnam book, but Vietnam is only sixty pages of *Dog Soldiers*. The remaining 280 pages are set in the United States. And yet I think Vietnam is the center of *Dog Soldiers*. To get to Vietnam you have to leave it.

Stone: I think that is right. I think I did absolutely the right thing to begin in Vietnam and then to take the story across the ocean. I am pretty well satisfied with the Vietnam scenes. They are more naturalistic than I am often given to. They follow the rhythm of events during my time in Saigon pretty closely. (Obviously I was not dealing or smuggling heroin, but I knew people who were involved with heroin. Certainly not on the international level, but there was a lot of heroin being used by people whom I was acquainted with while I was there.) I describe restaurants and make composites of people. Those people are like the people I knew; they are not individuals, but they resemble a number of types of people who were around. The streets of Saigon described are actual streets; the hotels and restaurants are actual hotels and restaurants. I did what I could to make that presence of Saigon, the presence of Vietnam, a recollection behind the events that unfold later in the book. You have that sense of Vietnam—the antipersonnel tactic which Converse remembers, those different things.

I wanted Vietnam almost literally in the background of the mind's eye while the rest of the story happened. I think that's quite right, that to approach the situation in Vietnam it's necessary to leave it, to get back and see what was happening in California at that particular time, which was, of course, the time of the dying dream of the sixties in California and also the dying dream of the Great Society—all sorts of little bills were coming up due for payment in the early seventies.

Schroeder: A literary analogue that comes to mind is Norman Mailer's *Why Are We in Vietnam?*, which many critics say has nothing to do with Vietnam; and yet, if you read the last page carefully, it has everything to do with Vietnam. His hero plans to enlist after coming back from the hunting expedition. John Sack has said much the opposite—that all good war stories begin in the United States and go back to Vietnam. But you start yours in Vietnam and bring it back to America. I think that in some ways the implications of this are more horrific for the American people because most Americans seem to think that Vietnam began and ended in Vietnam.

Stone: You're right; it didn't end over there. What it meant, its significance, didn't stop there. Vietnam is a terribly important thing for this country. It's like a wound covered with scar tissue or like a foreign body, a piece of shrapnel that the organism has built up a protective wall around, but it is embedded in our history; it is embedded in our definition of who we are. We will never get it out of there. I don't think it is a mortal wound for this society, but I think it is a very, very painful one. I would never write off the pliability of American society. America is really a very tough, endurable thing, and I would be very surprised if it was actually laid low by this kind of thing. We as Americans tend to be rather apocalyptic. Our history is short. You see a country like France, which has been totally destroyed, utterly discredited, has lost its soul eighteen times, and keeps coming back. When we use these terms like "America has betrayed its origin, lost its soul," and so forth, we forget that France does this every twenty years. It's complete with the idea of France—"the French nation is disgraced beyond redemption" and so forth; they lose entire generations, and they keep coming back. They probably always will. For all I know, we probably will too. But it was a very devastating and painful experience for us.

Schroeder: You went to Vietnam as a journalist, and you ended up contributing more significantly by your fiction. What do you see as the benefits of journalism as compared to fiction and vice versa?

Stone: I myself prefer fiction. The best fiction usually endures better than even the best journalism or even historiography. (It is true, for example, that what we know of the Napoleonic wars is what we know from Tolstoy.) I think that the function which fiction performs is that it refines reality and refracts it into something like a dream. It serves to mythologize in a positive way a series of facts which of themselves have no particular meaning. It is a deliberate, shameless, and open effort to make events mean something. When you use the mode of fiction, you are manipulating events deliberately in order to impose a meaning. Reality as a phenomenology, as a primary process, does not have any meaning. So you create a kind of artificial phenomenology. You create artificial events. You make up things that didn't happen about people who never were in order to render in a way more truly events that did happen to people who really did exist. Fiction performs the same function for history or for life that dreaming performs for the mind.

Schroeder: How would you comment, then, on the New Journalism and its impulse to do these types of things within a journalistic framework?

Stone: I think that all writing is ultimately justified by its quality and by its insight. If you have a good, insightful writer like Michael Herr, for example, or Tom Wolfe (who is also in his way, in his altogether different way, a good insightful writer—I don't think that he is as serious as Michael, and he certainly never paid his dues like Michael. But he is also a writer whose work I do not despise); I think that New Journalism in their hands and in the hands of some others works very well because they are as good and as perceptive as they are. It's not a form for me because I would rather have the freedom of being able to approach the "truth" without being bound by facts. In their situations they have an advantage in that their work has subjectivity. They have the freedom of the fiction writer and the authority of the journalist, which is a nice way to have it both ways. But that cuts the other way, too; they have responsibilities to what actually happened.

Schroeder: For you, then, fiction is the best way to convey this "truth." But when you look at Vietnam, it seems to me very curious that most of the books that have come out of the war, books which we would call literature (including the subdivisions of fiction and nonfiction), are in the fiction category, and yet it seems (to me, anyway) that most of the better books have been in the nonfiction category. Although fewer in number, the quality of nonfiction books has been better. It seems that there has been a real failure of realistic fiction to come to terms with Vietnam. I think that the two best works of fiction about Vietnam are *Dog Soldiers*—which as I say leaves Vietnam in order to get to it—and Tim O'Brien's *Going After Cacciato*, which is not cast in a realistic mode at all but is more like García Márquez's work.

Stone: Right. I think that, on the one hand, realistic fiction—a realism of sorts, obviously it's not the old style of realism—has been making an amazing comeback in America during the past fifteen or twenty years. It's almost as if that tradition which people were ready to write off in the fifties and sixties suddenly came back in a big way. Of course, strict realism, the realism of the thirties, is very difficult to apply to Vietnam. It's one of those situations where you have to extend. You're going to miss a great deal if you're bound by simple realism because in a way it's an instrument that has been played out. You just cannot get the effects that Hemingway got by his kind of stoic understatement. It just doesn't ring true anymore; it doesn't have the impact. Nor can you pile horror on horror in a kind of deadpan way because people are desensitized to that. You've got to be able to bring to bear other states of consciousness, even if only because so many people take so many drugs. Who knows, but that may be something subverting traditional realism. But yes, I do think it is true that the best writing about Vietnam, the best fiction, goes beyond the realistic mode. I think that is certainly the case.

Schroeder: Do you think that part of the reason for this is due to cultural factors which the media reinforced? Herr talks about this in his book: how people went to Vietnam with various preconceived ideas and fantasies that they then played out. Thus when these people came back and wrote books, they went through the same sort of things in their books that they went through in their minds. Even though they may have learned a different reality, they are unable to convey that because of the influence not only of other literary stereotypes that they may have encountered but of film and television as well.

Stone: Yes. I think that there is definitely something in that. If you want, it's kind of McLunanesque jargon to call it a nonlinear war; it sounds like Charles Reich. But there is a grain of truth in that. It's bullshit, but there's a grain of truth.

Schroeder: Maybe we could start talking about *Dog Soldiers* itself. Converse is interesting because he engages the reader's sympathy (at least initially) and throughout the course of the book commands more sympathy than Hicks does. He is certainly presented more sympathetically. And yet it is hard to feel sorry for a character who says something like, "I've been waiting my whole life to fuck up like this." It seems that he has an impression of himself as a loser, and in his own mind he sees himself as a victim of fate. Is there a danger within this characterization?

Stone: You always have a danger with a character who is not admirable. In a way, for self-preservation, the reader has to deny the Converse within him, just as I have to deny the Converse within me in order to be Stone the writer. I can hardly be Converse, nor can any reader be Converse. Yes, you run great risk with a character who is so spiritually slovenly and so unsympathetic in so many different ways. Certainly you risk alienating your reader, but if you can bring the reader into a certain degree of sympathy or identification with Converse, you gain much more. It is one of those risks that if you get away with it, you have a richer engagement with the reader. You have a greater commitment from the reader.

Schroeder: Hicks seems to be just the opposite. You start out hating Hicks, but you end up admiring many things about him.
Stone: That's the intention. I want to bring a reader into that very situation. You have to be able to see that Hicks is really disturbed in very deep ways. He is almost a psychopath—the term that Converse is always using about him. Yet he is not anything totally alien to people of principle. He is in his own way a person of principle. He isn't a monster at all, but in fact a kind of fellow traveler, another human being. I hope that I can bring people to that realization. I'm taking a risk there, too, with a quirky character like Hicks. I'm unsympathetic. I'm brutal, brutal to the point of being murderous, although I didn't really mean him to kill Gerald. Gerald, the writer who ODs, is not supposed to die. I didn't make that clear enough. I left it open. I should have been more specific. In my mind, anyway, Gerald doesn't die.

Schroeder: I think that Marge is certainly convinced that he is dead.
Stone: Yes, she thinks he's dead.

Schroeder: I think that even Hicks seemed to think that he's dead. Hicks says that he got what he deserved. There's a wonderful quote from Hicks where he says, "I'm a Christian American who fought for my flag. I don't take shit from Martians." This is his view of Gerald. Gerald does come across that way. I find an interesting parallel in Michael Herr's book. The two characters Converse and Hicks—the soldier and the journalist—are mirrored in an early scene in *Dispatches* where Herr recounts a conversation he has with a young grunt who says, "All the propaganda is just a load, man; we're here to kill gooks. Period." Herr then editorializes, saying, "Which was not at all true about me; I was there to watch." There's a similar scene in *Dog Soldiers* where Hicks has just alluded to the fact that Converse has called him a psychopath. Hicks responds by asking, "What does that make you?" And Converse replies, "I'm a writer; and I'm here to watch." You're obviously conscious of this dichotomy between the two viewpoints here.

Stone: You ran into people—it happened more than once; it happened more than once to everybody—who said, "I hope you get killed, you fucking asshole. You don't have to be here. What are you doing here? You guys are really sick. You have homes to live in. You don't have to fuckin' be here. You like this shit? I hope you get killed." It didn't happen once; it happened a lot. You do get very aware of it.

Schroeder: Hicks finally does come across a bit better because it seems that at least he has a clearer view of what he is doing—not only at the end but throughout his life. He has been trying to live his life by principles. You may not always agree with those principles, but you feel that he has some sort of order in his life, whereas just about everyone else in the novel—except the really bad guys—is floating. Hicks is interesting for another reason. In some ways he seems larger than himself, and that feeling is reinforced by Pablo in *A Flag for Sunrise*. Both of them emerge as warrior figures. Are you conscious of this sort of mythic structuring in creating these figures?

Stone: Yes, though in Pablo I'm after something different than in Hicks. There are ways in which they resemble each other, but Hicks and Pablo are not really alike. I think Hicks is really extending—he is actually having a shot at greatness, at power, at true virtue, the old Roman *virtus*. He really is trying for that. He thinks of it as being a samurai because that's his Kurosawa-conditioned Marine Corps orientalism. But he is really after this classic *virtus*, this classic male virtue. Pablo is coming from the opposite direction. Pablo is a real little rat who is almost ennobled by his addled mysticism. I want people finally to feel sorry for the guy. Yet I don't want to fudge on how awful he really is. The guy is complete bad news. Ideally, you should be able to understand why Holliwell kills him, to understand that and not to condemn Holliwell too much. At the same time, you should feel sorry for Pablo.

Schroeder: We wait throughout the whole book for their two tracks to intersect. When they finally do, it's wonderful—the two end up in a boat together. You know that one of them has to go; it's a question of which one. And just as Pablo seems to be a spin-off of Hicks, so, too, does Holliwell seem to derive his literary being from Converse. Holliwell is another figure who seems to be a bit of a bumbler; he's not really clear where his moral and ethical priorities lie.

Stone: Not so much, perhaps, because I think he really regards himself as an honest person. He worries. He's much more securely located. He abstains from the vote by the American Association of Anthropologists and doesn't cooperate with the Intelligence Committee because he's done it in the past. He does this as an act of honesty. He has every reason to think of himself as a humane and decent person. He is more securely located. He's not as wild and crazy. He's not as young as Converse. He's not as much of a Bohemian. He is in some ways a more conventional, a more solid figure. He comes a bit unstuck under the pressures of Tecan, but Converse starts out unstuck. Converse is really all over the place. Maybe it is that Holliwell is simply older, but I mean it to be other things beyond that.

Schroeder: Do you, though, see Hicks and Pablo on one hand and Converse and Holliwell on the other as being representative of certain American "types"?

Stone: That's one way of saying it. But I mean them above all to be individuals. I also mean them to be recognizable. There isn't really a Hicks type. I haven't met many people that good. If you meet one Hicks in your life, that's enough. And if you meet one Pablo in your life, that's more than enough. You couldn't say they are types because they are too special in their individual makeups.

Schroeder: Children play an interesting role in all of your books. They seem to be not only symbols of innocence but also victims of the world around them, of forces larger than they.

Stone: One of the reasons that they are in there is to make the action of the book represent the larger world, which has a lot of children in it. Getting the kids out of the way so that all the bad stuff can happen is unrealistic. There are children in the world. They do also represent, I think, innocence. They represent an aspect of the human condition in that they are people who are in the world, a world they haven't made, a world they dimly comprehend, and their situation stands for the situation of the adult characters, too. I think that comes out in the area of my own mind, in my own sensibility, that I'm not in complete control of. I know roughly what the kids are doing there, but my putting them in was not total premeditation—I know what they're doing there after the fact, after I put them in. First I think, "Well, there should be a kid here because in real life there would be," and then the kid takes on that dimension that you were referring to, which I believe is really there, but it is not something that I had control of. It's something that I'm doing and am not altogether conscious of.

Schroeder: What's disturbing about the children in the books is that they all seem so helpless. You talk about how they mirror the adults in the book, and I suppose it is true of the mirrored adults as well—Converse in particular is certainly helpless in that way.

Stone: That's true. The people in these books do a lot of things. They're always performing acts—they perform more acts to determine their own situation than most people do—but they're still helpless in spite of all the acts they perform. As you say, look at Converse. They do things like decide to sell heroin. Go to Vietnam. Escape with other people's dope across deserts. They perform a lot of actions, but they are still finally helpless in spite of all the actions that determine the actions that they are able to perform.

Schroeder: The whole question of action in the books is pertinent because of the structures of your books, especially *Dog Soldiers* and *A Flag for Sunrise*: their structure is really that of a thriller. You have two or three strands of action that converge and finally intersect toward the end of the book. The denouement of both of these books reflects the thriller's structure. Are you consciously using this formula and manipulating it?

Stone: Yes. I want to exploit what there is of the mythic in that kind of popular melodramatic form. When I started doing *Dog Soldiers*, I vaguely had the *Ramayana* in my mind, which must sound totally blasphemous to Hindus. I soon cast off from it, but the *Ramayana* is about the theft of Rama's bride by a demigod. At the center of the story is the pursuit of the demigod and the bride by Rama through all these worlds that are peopled by monkeys and elephants and strange beings and creatures. I vaguely have that kind of form in mind—*Dog Soldiers* is, of course, full of great battles and ends in great battle. I got into that—the sort of shopworn thriller form—as a kind of irreverent echo of the epic. But it also created the necessity to make the thriller work as a thriller, which is rather fun but also a pain in the neck because I'm not very turned on by plot. I don't believe in it, and yet I do have lots of plotting in my books.

Schroeder: Most publishers would argue that it is plot that sells books.

Stone: [laughing] It doesn't seem to sell mine!

Schroeder: But your publisher doesn't market your books as thrillers. You seem to be doing two very different, almost mutually exclusive things. You seem to be writing this thriller, and at the same time you are writing a very serious book as well. I think that your publisher's choice to have your book marketed as serious is a compliment to you, but, on the other hand, do you resent the loss of a larger reading audience?

Stone: I think that if I had started out commanding a large audience and had somehow been deprived of it, it would bother me more than it does. I'm getting larger audiences than I really had expected. I've always thought of myself as a serious writer, and I have never expected large sales. I'm at the stage where I'm not in the position of a really massively selling writer, where if I don't sell fifteen million copies in the first month, I'm in big trouble. Everything from my point of view is gravy. I never know how the book is going to sell. But, no, I certainly don't resent my publisher offering the book that way. I think they are being straight with the reading public.

Schroeder: I want to ask a question that ties in with what we were talking about earlier, the notion of fiction versus nonfiction. You talked about how we remember the lessons of history through literature. Is this part of your intention in your writing, to lay down the lessons of history?

Stone: Absolutely. I've no modesty as a writer. I'm ready to interpret history if I can get away with it.

Schroeder: What does fiction have to teach that television, traditional journalism, and films can't teach?

Stone: You are not bound by the structure of events. You can get at the nature of events and the nature of humankind in a very direct way because you can manipulate events so that patterns of causality are made clearer. These patterns of motive can be examined more thoroughly than they can in a real-life situation, something that is bound by the circumstances of its actual occurrence. You can present ambiguities of motive in a fiction which correspond to the ambiguities of motive in life. But if you are writing about a situation that actually happened, you cannot present the reader with this much ambiguity of motive—you've got to pretend to detect the real motive, give the reader the sense of why they did that, why they made the expedition, why they killed a person, why they did whatever they did.

Schroeder: It seems to me that another thing you are able to do is to take other types of experience and to plug them into different situations. What

I'm referring to specifically here happens in *Dog Soldiers*. In rereading *Dog Soldiers* it occurred to me that the last section of the book was a rewriting of Ken Kesey's and the Merry Pranksters' experiences at La Honda.

Stone: Sort of, yes. Absolutely. You can conveniently mix different experiences, take the experience in one context and move it into a totally different one. There's a way in which that whole mountain situation obviously resembles La Honda.

Schroeder: Is there a danger, then, of the reader who is familiar with Tom Wolfe's version of La Honda picking up your book, reading it, and saying, "Isn't there a parallel here; isn't this character supposed to be Ken Kesey dressed up?"

Stone: I would hope not because Dieter is so totally un-Kesey. That is, whatever Kesey is, he is not a Central European intellectual. Perhaps there is a danger. I don't really paint from life. My tendency is the opposite. If I base something on actuality, it will be recognizable, or nearly so by that time. I don't try to render; there're no *romans à clef* in me. I just don't work that way.

Schroeder: I interpret the point of view in the novel as being that the experience on the hill is a failed experience whose time has come and gone. I wonder if you feel that way about the real-life analogue; is your view of the La Honda experience nearly as cynical as *Dog Soldiers*'s rendering of the situation on the hill?

Stone: It's a lost paradise, in a way, but a paradise that was something of a false paradise, too. I don't know if one can speak of being cynical about the events at La Honda because one was never really reverent about them. I don't think that anybody felt reverently. As far as I'm concerned, what was going on was a lot of extremely pleasant goofing. It was just a crazy time.

Schroeder: "Goofing" was one of the words used in *The Electric Kool-Aid Acid Test*.

Stone: It probably was. That's basically what it was. I wouldn't have missed it for the world, but it isn't something you want to spend your whole life doing. When I look at the old movies of those days, the fact is that what it looks like now is a Stanford fraternity party. There are all these very young people—people in their twenties—carrying on. They're loaded, and they're carrying on. If you look a little closer, maybe they would look a few years older—Beta members at Stanford—but not that much older. Just a bunch of kids carrying on. If we were all behaving like that in our forties, we'd be cases of arrested development. It was fine; we were just young and partying all the time.

Schroeder: The other thing of interest here is that while this was going on at La Honda, we were just getting involved in Vietnam. Where did those two experiences intersect?

Stone: The funny place where they intersect in La Honda is in the person of Ken Babbs, who in 1962 or 1963 returned from Vietnam, where he had been a helicopter pilot. There he was, returning in what was a literal intersection of those two. If you read Richard Tregaskis's book, *Vietnam Diary*, which was written about 1961 or '62 (it's Tregaskis who wrote *Guadalcanal Diary*, one of the great books about World War II), you'll find him quoting this Marine pilot, Ken Babbs, as saying what we really ought to do is get in there and win it. Let's take over the war from the ARVN and get in there and straighten things out ourselves. Ken Babbs said that. You can't hold him responsible twenty years later. But strangely enough it's Babbs, this merry prankster. This guy is going to appear later—not a merry prankster who went and became a Marine but a Marine who went and became a merry prankster, reversing all logic, the logic of life. So there's a real intersection.

Schroeder: In the novel, do these two worlds come together on the hill?

Stone: They do.

Schroeder: We seem to see an extreme version of La Honda in *Dog Soldiers*; we get the drug experience pushed to an extreme and then gone sour.

Stone: The drug experience didn't particularly go sour for us. There comes a time when you just don't want to take any more acid. I think it goes sour for everybody to that degree. Some people lost their minds over it, and I think it went sour for the country and for that generation generally and for my friends individually. With one exception—there's one person I know who still takes acid, and he's a judge. He's the only person I know out of that whole bunch I knew in those days who still takes acid. Everybody else has quit because finally you figure, "I'm just not up to eight or nine hours of that craziness. I don't have the physical energy; I don't have the emotional energy. I think I'll just listen to a few Beethoven quartets and have a couple of brandies. I'm not going to take one of those pills and go nuts for nine hours."

Schroeder: Along the same lines, one of the phrases I found haunting me in *Dog Soldiers* was the notion of "those who are." It's one of the mysteries in the book. You get the feeling that it's something tied in to the hilltop experience, although it is never articulated. It seems like the same sort of fraternity as "those who are" that I suppose existed at La Honda (you certainly get that impression from Tom Wolfe), except that on the hill we sense a more dangerous aspect of this fellowship. What is the reader supposed to infer from that?

Stone: The presence of wheels within wheels in a secret society. It's the kind of thing that in drug investigations on a large scale you do run into—the Church of Naturalness or the Brotherhood of Eternal Life or whatever. People call themselves different things at different times. Basically it's been about dope. So you could say that "those who are" is one of those weird organizations that has to do with dope. And it also relates to the Greek *esthlos*, which Hicks has tattooed on his arm. It was an old form of the verb "to be," a Homeric form which signaled "the aristocracy."

Schroeder: This is one of the loose ends in the book. *Dog Soldiers* breaks away from the traditional format of the thriller or mystery in which everything is tied up neatly at the end. *A Flag for Sunrise* displays the same sort of thing with "the deep"—what Holliwell sees in "the deep."

Stone: I certainly don't want to pin that down at the end, but what is down there we don't really know. It could be (probably is) that right over the reef where he is diving is where Egan dumped the body in the beginning. More than this, though, just what's down there is awful. It's unknown. It's things themselves.

Schroeder: What's down there seems to be tied in with what's on the surface in Tecan itself. Later we meet the operative who is lounging by the swimming pool.

Stone: Yes, he says he's the shark at the bottom of the lagoon. Aside from any metaphorical meaning these scenes may have, there's a very practical reason for their presence in the book. Somebody once wrote a paper called "The Undersea World of Robert Stone." That was even before I wrote *A Flag for Sunrise*. I have apparently always included those images because I'm a diver. *A Hall of Mirrors* actually had a lot of stuff about fish and the bottom of the ocean. I apparently have a thing about doing this.

Schroeder: Certainly this layering effect is something unique to literature, especially fiction. I know, for instance, that you aren't very pleased with the film versions of either *Dog Soldiers* or *A Hall of Mirrors*. In fact, you disassociated yourself from the latter project. What happens when you turn books into films?

Stone: It's like a book in translation, but much worse because it is in a different medium. It's a fish out of water. If you rely on the power you associate with levels of language, you build your structure basically with language, with sound, and pictures aren't the same as sound. So that it flattens out rather badly. All your possibilities are swept away with tremendous precision. You have one face, one actor. You don't have this blurry space between events where people move through the murk of the mind's eye, charged with all sorts of dimensions. When images are out there upon the screen in good color and good clear outlines, your structure loses an awful lot of magic. It flattens out. Motive flattens out; characters flatten out; dialogue flattens out.

Schroeder: Do you think it is possible for a film to do justice to Vietnam?

Stone: A feature film would be difficult. You just look at those pictures, and you see the kind of thing you would have to do. A documentary might do it.

Schroeder: Returning to literature, I think it is quite easy to read *Dog Soldiers* as an antiwar novel because of the things that happen to the people in the novel. Most of the characters lose. The fact that they are alive at the end of the book means something, yet they have lost an awful lot by the time we get there, and I'm not sure what they gain is worth the losses. *A Flag for Sunrise* is a cautionary tale. This is a book that is really written before the fact. Do you think that books like this can have any influence on what we as a people are going to decide to do?

Stone: I hope so. I don't know how seriously I should take my own hopes. But I'm preaching in a way. I'm not ashamed to say that. I mean, the secretary of state isn't going to read it and say, "Okay, I'm not going to do whatever nasty thing I was going to do." That's not going to happen. But you have to be given something. You have to begin the assaults. You have to keep the levels of consciousness sharp. Somebody has got to do it. It's a small thing, but we're small people in a big world. So I'm writing a piece of fiction that a couple of thousand people read. It's no big thing, but it's worth doing.

Schroeder: Have we learned anything from Vietnam?

Stone: I hope so. It's hard to learn. It's hard for a society to absorb an experience. I don't know whether we have. I sure hope so.

Schroeder: When will we know?

Stone: I think if we could ask somebody in fifty years, "What's America like? What's it like to be an American?" then we might know. At this point we don't know. Maybe by the turn of the century we will. Not much before that, I'm afraid.

Robert Stone: The Art of Fiction No. 90

William C. Woods / 1985

Originally published in *The Paris Review* Issue 98 (Winter 1985): 26–57. Copyright © 1985 by The Paris Review, used by permission of The Wylie Agency LLC.

Robert Stone lives in a small frame house on the Connecticut coast. Inside, a long white living room with curving walls suggests Oriental calm, and a pocket kitchen like a ship's galley offers the comic sight of tame ducks feeding on the water just below. The hesitant phrases of the Modern Jazz Quartet chime from a battered stereo flanked by bookshelves filled with fiction, philosophy, and church history. Over a built-in sofa hangs an unframed poster for *Who'll Stop the Rain?*, the film Stone coauthored from his second novel, *Dog Soldiers*. Stone and his wife Janice moved into this house in the fall of 1981; they have a son and daughter, grown and gone.

The novelist works in an attic room crowded with cardboard boxes and manuscripts and decorated with several brightly colored samples of Spanish religious art. At one end of the long room, a wide window affords a view of a gray October sea; another looks down on the gravel parking lot of a clam bar. Stone writes at a table only a little larger than the word processor it supports. When his office phone rings, it may be an editor on the line begging him to cover a story, a director seeking to interest him in a new part (in the summer of 1982, Stone played Kent in a professional production of *King Lear* in California), or an interviewer plaguing him with yet another question that he will answer with care and unfailing courtesy.

Although the Stones have lived in many parts of the country, and for four years in London, changes in locale have rarely altered the writer's routine: "I get up very early, drink a pot of tea, and go for as long as I can." Stone says he stops only when he has left himself a clear starting point for the following day. For weeks on end he will take few days off if his work is going well. "My imagination will still be functioning," he says with a laugh, "twelve hours after my brain is dead."

He lives more quietly now than in his years in the California countercul-ture as one of Ken Kesey's Merry Pranksters; his free time is given over to milder pleasures, such as the exploration by canoe of the salt lagoon behind his house. But even this quiet coast has its threat; the past summer, Stone told me, a large shark was spotted in the lagoon, just off the docks, import-ing a frisson of fear into the neighborhood.

Stone is in his late forties, a trim man whose thinning hair and well-bar-bered beard frame a ruddy, pensive face yet to be done justice by his book jacket photos. His voice, branded by years of Scotch and smoke, was deep and serene as we began our two days of talk.

Interviewer: Was there one book that started you writing?

Stone: It was a rereading of *The Great Gatsby* that made me think about writing a novel. I was living on St. Mark's Place in New York; it was a differ-ent world in those days. I was in my twenties. I decided I knew a few mean-ings; I understood patterns in life. I figured, I can't sell this understanding, or smoke it, so I will write a novel. I then started to write *A Hall of Mirrors*. It must have taken me six years, a dreadful amount of time. I really began work on the novel during my Stegner Fellowship at Stanford, which brought me out to California just about the time that everything was going slightly crazy. So I spent a lot of my time, when I should have been writing, experi-encing death and transformation and rebirth on LSD in Palo Alto. It wasn't an atmosphere that was conducive to getting a whole lot of work done.

Interviewer: You once described writing your first novel as a process that paralleled your life.

Stone: *A Hall of Mirrors* was something I shattered my youth against. All my youth went into it. I put everything I knew into that book. It was writ-ten through years of dramatic change, not only for me, but for the country. It covers the sixties from the Kennedy assassination through the civil rights movement to the beginning of acid, the hippies, the war . . .

Interviewer: Does that mean you changed your conception of the book as you were writing it, that you tried to respond to those changes?

Stone: Yes. And to things that were happening with me. One way or another, it all went into the book. And of course it all went very slowly because once my Stegner Fellowship was over, my wife, Janice, and I had to take turns working. I'd work for twenty weeks and then be on unemployment for twenty weeks and so on. So it took me a long, long time to finish it.

Interviewer: You mention responding to national as well as personal change. Do you consciously try to write about America?

Stone: Yes, I do. That is my subject. America and Americans.

Interviewer: You have been cited as a writer who addresses larger social issues. Do you start with those in mind, or do you simply start out with the characters and because you have political concerns these issues naturally come out?

Stone: It is very natural. You construct characters and set them going in their own interior landscape, and what they find to talk about and what confronts them are, of course, things that concern you most.

Interviewer: Is writing easy for you? Does it flow smoothly?

Stone: It's goddamn hard. Nobody really cares whether you do it or not. You have to make yourself do it. I'm very lazy, and I suffer as a result. Of course, when it's going well there's nothing in the world like it. But it's also very lonely. If you do something you're really pleased with, you're in the crazy position of being exhilarated all by yourself. I remember finishing one section of *Dog Soldiers*—the end of Hicks's walk—in the basement of a college library, working at night, while the rest of the place was closed down, and I staggered out in tears, talking to myself, and ran into a security guard. It's hard to come down from a high in your work—it's one of the reasons writers drink. The exhilaration of your work turns into the daily depression of the aftermath. But if you heal that with a lot of Scotch you're not fit for duty the next day. When I was younger I was able to use hangovers, but now I have to go to bed early.

Interviewer: You really think of yourself as lazy?

Stone: Well, my books aren't lazy books, but I have a lazy way of working. I do a very rough first draft and then a second and sometimes I have to do a third because I didn't take the trouble to really organize the first. And I take breaks between drafts. And I do altogether too much traveling.

Interviewer: You have gone for relatively long periods of time between books. Seven years between *A Hall of Mirrors* and *Dog Soldiers*, and then another seven before *A Flag for Sunrise*. Are you writing all that time?

Stone: It seems to me that I am. I was working all those years on *A Flag for Sunrise*. I could probably have gotten six books out of my three if I'd wanted to do smaller themes. Twice as many books, and they would have been half as good. Six so-so books. I don't need that. I like big novels; I really admire the grand slam.

Interviewer: Do you have any special requirements, conditions necessary for your working environment?

Stone: Well, of course, I find ways to delay the day as much as possible, but there are no particular rituals connected with that for me, like having a special coffee cup or sharpening six pencils. I do need physical order, because I'm addressing the insubstantiality of structures—that's where the blank page starts. No top, no bottom, no sides. I find it hard to sit still. I pace a lot. I've got to have a pen in my hand when I'm not actually typing.

Interviewer: You mostly type?

Stone: Yes, until something becomes elusive. Then I write in longhand in order to be precise. On a typewriter or word processor you can rush something that shouldn't be rushed—you can lose nuance, richness, lucidity. The pen compels lucidity.

Interviewer: Do you read your work aloud to yourself?

Stone: No. My inner ear is very accurate. I know what the writing sounds like.

Interviewer: Your prose is very rich in sensual detail—imagery intensified by the cadence of the sentence.

Stone: I use the white space. I'm interested in precise meaning and in reverberation, in associative levels. What you're trying to do when you write is to crowd the reader out of his own space and occupy it with yours, in a good cause. You're trying to take over his sensibility and deliver an experience that moves from mere information.

Interviewer: I see that. But one of the things I respond to most in your writing is the tremendous particularity, your way of relating language to reality. It seems to me that there's a danger, if language takes the reader too far into cosmic preoccupations, of losing that immediacy.

Stone: The object is to make a connection between your characters and the contour of things as they are. The danger is of becoming pretentious. And yet it's necessary that a given dramatized scene have a richness of reference. Take a basic philosophical question: why is there something rather than nothing? Two people in love, two people in a battle to the death, refer to that question. To say so directly is preposterous; you have to get there along the path of art. How do you relate events to that basic question? You choose words that open up deeper and deeper levels of existence by sustaining a sound which perfectly serves the narrative and which at the same time relates through a series of associations to the large questions.

Interviewer: That would account for the shifting levels of your rhetoric, which plays the colloquial against high ornamentation. The effect is a constant tone of irony.
Stone: Irony is my friend and brother. "To know true things by what their mockeries be." There's only one subject for fiction or poetry or even a joke: *how it is.* In all the arts, the payoff is always the same: recognition. If it works, you say that's real; that's truth; that's the way things are. "There it is."

Interviewer: The classic aphorism of the Vietnam War.
Stone: Exactly.

Interviewer: I understand one article you filed from Vietnam was about a Saigon rock festival. That certainly puts two worlds of the time together.
Stone: That was a funny scene. Stoned rear-echelon GIs and a Vietnamese band that was a phonocopy of the Grateful Dead. Meanwhile, a light plane was circling overhead streaming a Christian banner attacking rock as the devil's music. There was an oncoming monsoon, and the banner kept threatening to foul the guy's propeller. Finally he fell out of sight, and everybody waited for the crash, which didn't come. I remember one very stoned GI saying to another, "There it is."

Interviewer: You were a correspondent in Vietnam in 1971 . . .
Stone: Well, I was there less than two months, but every day was different. It was the kind of place where anything could have happened. There's nothing that couldn't have happened there. If you encountered choirs of seraphim up the river or if somebody said he's just seen a vision of St. George on Hill 51, you'd just say, "There it is . . ." I was in Saigon a lot of the time. I did get deeper into I Corps, and I was in Cam Rahn Bay. But in Saigon I picked up with a guy who was involved in the dope trade there and in a very short time I found out more than I really wanted to know. It was very frightening. I should also say that this period—1971—was a time when, in the line, there was not a lot of combat involving American troops. There was rocketing up around Phu Bai; there were some bombs going off in Saigon; but nobody was quite sure who was responsible for them. American troops were not

heavily engaged. It was the time of Vietnamization. The talks were going on in Paris, and American troops were being kept out of the line to keep the casualty rates down.

Interviewer: Was Vietnam your first experience of war?

Stone: No, I first saw war when I was in the Navy in the Mediterranean in 1956. I saw the French air attack on Port Said—jets from the carrier *Lafayette* coming in right on top of our radar mast and shelling. Those multicolored tracers in the night that I saw again in Vietnam I saw with something like nostalgia. But it was quite horrible. You could look through the glasses and see donkeys and people flying through the air, chewed up by 7.62s and rockets. It was a slaughter of civilians. But it always is.

Interviewer: Are you interested in observing future wars, or have you had enough?

Stone: I don't know. There was a wonderful expression soldiers had in the American Civil War that captures the strangeness of combat, the charm—they called it "going to see the elephant." There are times when I feel that once you've seen war, you want to see it again.

Interviewer: It seems to me that your work is in the tradition of twentieth-century fiction that takes war as its principal metaphor for our lives. Would you say that war is the most complete description of our situation?

Stone: It's literally true that the world is seen by the superpowers as a grid of specific targets. We're all on military maps. There happens to be no action in those zones at present, but they're there. And then there are the wars we fight with ourselves in our own cities. It is the simple truth, wherever you are, there is an armed enemy present, not far away.

Interviewer: I'd like to ask a little about your evolution as a writer.

Stone: My early life was strange. I was a solitary; radio fashioned my imagination. Radio narrative always has to embody a full account of both action and scene. I began to do that myself. When I was seven or eight, I'd walk through Central Park like Sam Spade, describing aloud what I was doing, becoming both the actor and the writer setting him into this scene. That was where I developed an inner ear.

Interviewer: So you grew up in New York?

Stone: For the most part we were in New York, my mother and I. It was just the two of us. My mother was, I now realize, schizophrenic, and sometimes she was better than at other times. She lost a job as a schoolteacher in New York for medical reasons; she had a very small pension, and when she was very ill, there was really no place for me to go. Except this place that was, well, it functioned partly as a day school. My mother was in and out of hospitals. I was in an orphanage run by the Marist brothers from the age of six until just before I was ten.

Interviewer: I wonder how the schizophrenia influenced your imagination.
Stone: I wonder that too. I am not really sure. One thing I know is that I usually can recognize schizophrenics when I see them. There is a certain way of speaking. I am talking about functioning schizophrenics, professional people; there are a lot of them around. It is very hard to talk about it in the abstract. In California, years ago, I had a doctor who would tell me these rather askew anecdotes that didn't seem to have any point. What it reminded me of was my mother's disconnection. Their associative patterns seemed to be similar. I finally realized what the problem was. He was about halfway into another kind of reality, but at the same time he was a doctor, functioning as a GP.

Interviewer: Lu Anne, the heroine of *Children of Light*, is schizophrenic.
Stone: Lu Anne's condition is based on what I have experienced with people. There are people who have delusional systems they are really quite aware of and treat as nemeses. That is Lu Anne's condition; she has a lot of insight into her own delusional systems. Actually, many people have that, and I have been waiting a long time to write about it. It seems to me part of how I see things. I think that is partly because of my mother, whom I liked very much, but who was very difficult for me to understand. When she was my contact person for reality, for information about the world, I got some confusing signals.

Interviewer: Have you ever written about your childhood?
Stone: I don't write about my childhood or New York; I have hardly any reference to it at all. In a way, that's because I always used my imagination as a kind of alternative life when I wanted to be in another place than the one I was in. I just didn't want to write about that stuff. I wanted to enjoy myself. I wasn't ready to write about it; perhaps I'm not ready to write about it yet.

Interviewer: Did you read in the Navy?
Stone: Yes. Everybody on a ship reads, whether it's comic books or Westerns

or the Bible or whatever. They always read a lot. I was reading *Moby-Dick*, which sounds terribly precious, but I thought if you can't read *Moby-Dick* in the roaring fifties, you'll never read *Moby-Dick*. So I brought it along. I also read *Ulysses* on the same trip. I seem to have imprinted the ocean in a very strong way because I end up with all these marine images that just seem so readily at hand for me.

Interviewer: Many people think of you as having a considerable grasp on the major shift in American culture from the Beats in the fifties to the sixties' counterculture.

Stone: I was in the right place at the right time to see that. It started out with Jack Kerouac's *On the Road* while I was still in the Navy. My mother recommended the book to me. I am probably the only person who had *On the Road* recommended to him by his mother. It is very hard to go back and think about what *On the Road* was saying to me. I pick it up now and all I can see is Neal Cassady. I got to know him. It was a wonderful rendering of him, but I don't see much else in it. Now it just reminds me of somebody writing on speed. That may be uncharitable, but frankly I find it very sentimental. As I say, I am not sure what it was that moved me. I suppose there was that tradition of the American road. I can almost remember what that was like. Thinking about the great continent out there and the city intersections, that myth of the roadside traveler. It reminded me of how every once in a while my mother and I would take off on some migration to where things were going to be better, like Chicago or wherever. We went all the way to New Mexico. I can't remember what we were in quest of. We were in quest of something though. We usually ended up on welfare, then trying to get out of wherever we were. One time we went to Chicago and ended up in a Salvation Army shelter on the North Side before we ran out of money. We stayed for as long as the Salvation Army would keep us, and then somehow my mother scraped together money to get back to New York. When we got back, we spent two nights sleeping on a roof. It was wild, you know. It was useful. On the one hand, it gave me a fear of chaos, and on the other hand, it was a romance with the world and bus stations and things like that.

Interviewer: You didn't finish college, did you?

Stone: No, I started at New York University and hung on for about a year, but I couldn't stay with it. I was working at the *Daily News* at night and trying to go to classes in the daytime. I just couldn't do it, so I dropped out. In Greenwich Village, a lot of stuff was happening then. Janice worked in the Figaro, and she also worked at the Seven Arts on Forty-third and Ninth Avenue. The Seven Arts, of course, was where Kerouac and Allan Ginsberg and Ray Bremser and all those other guys with droopy expressions were regulars. I kind of hung out smoking lots of cigarettes, looking very cool, listening to Coltrane. Janice and I were both at NYU until I quit. She had another job as a guidette in the RCA Building. We both got out about one o'clock, I from the *Daily News*. She took off her guidette uniform and put on her black stockings and was a waitress in the Seven Arts where I'd go to hang out.

Interviewer: Were you writing poetry at that time?
Stone: Yes, I was writing it and reading and hanging out, though I didn't have too much time to hang out. I had to assume a languid posture in a hurry because I had to be up early in the morning. I really felt that hanging out was the price I had to pay, whether I wrote anything or not; these were the people who were more like me or what I wanted to be. One had the sense in those days that it was a relatively small thing, not mass bohemia like you had in the sixties. There was a lot of marijuana, and you could really go to jail for years; we all thought it was very decadent and terrific of us. There was an expresso place on Sixth Street between First and Second avenues run by a guy named Baron, who was a follower of Ayn Rand—he had a dollar sign outside his café: Baron sold peyote buttons. It was very hard to eat peyote; you had to put it into a Waring blender and do all sorts of things to get enough down. I remember being on peyote and seeing a wrestling match for the *Daily News* in Madison Square Garden; seeing this on peyote may have changed my life. Once I got my Stegner and got out to California, I happened to collide with Ken Kesey; he lived just a couple of streets away. That whole scene was just ready to take off. And I thought I knew all about peyote and drugs and such. It didn't bother me to experiment. Kesey had a job as an orderly in the Veteran's Hospital and he was involved in the first experiments that were being conducted in psychedelic drugs. He was a volunteer and so was his friend Vic Lovell, who is a psychologist now. They were doing all these crazy drugs on an experimental basis. Some of them worked; some of them did not. I can remember really off-the-wall things called IT290s; they didn't have names they were so arcane. Whatever IT290 was, I remember walking through the woods and suddenly encountering this huge locomotive, a green locomotive with gold trim, a very detailed hallucination which I remember particularly well. I still have a lot of friends out there, people who I went through that stuff with.

Interviewer: Were your friends important to your work at that point?

Stone: The whole scene probably set me back a year or two, but my friends were certainly important in my life. California in the early sixties was really quite wonderful. It seemed so civilized and so easygoing; really it was fun when the strangest thing around was us, and we were pretty harmless.

Interviewer: *A Hall of Mirrors* is a cohesive book, considering the conditions under which it was written and the long span of time . . .

Stone: It was necessary that it be cohesive. I was looking for a vision of America, for a statement about the American condition. I was after a book that would be as ambitious as possible. I wanted to be an American Gogol if I could; I wanted to write *Dead Souls*. All of the characters represent ideas about America, about an American period of extraordinary, vivid transition.

Interviewer: In a way, it seems to me that the novel is a kind of counterpart to *On the Road.*

Stone: *On the Road* twenty years after. In a way. Yes.

Interviewer: Certainly Ray Hicks in *Dog Soldiers* has some biographical touches drawn from the same Neal Cassady who appeared as Dean Moriarty in *On the Road.* Did you know Kerouac when you were hanging out with Kesey—"on the bus"?

Stone: I didn't know him well. And I didn't travel on the bus. I saw the bus off and greeted the bus when it arrived on Riverside Drive. We went to a party where Kerouac and Ginsberg and Orlovsky and those guys were, and Kerouac was at his drunken worst. He was also very jealous of Neal, who had shifted his allegiances to Kesey. But Neal was pretty exhausted, too. I saw some films taken on the bus—Neal looked like he was tired from trying to keep up with the limitless energy of all those kids. Anyway . . . Kerouac at that party was drunk and pissed off, a situation I understood very well. The first thing I ever said to him was, "Hey, Jack, have you got a cigarette?" And he said, "I ain't gonna give you no fucking cigarette, man. There's a drugstore on the corner; you can go down there and buy a fucking pack of cigarettes. Don't ask me for a cigarette." That's my Kerouac story.

Interviewer: That's a sad story. The passing of the torch. Is Tom Wolfe's book on Kesey, *The Electric Kool-Aid Acid Test,* a pretty good picture of that whole scene?

Stone: It's amazingly good. It also forces a coherence on that scene that it didn't necessarily have. I mean that stuff was all so ephemeral, there was no philosophical core to it, particularly; it was all just goofiness.

Interviewer: Well, the Wolfe book on Kesey does convey—or impose—the notion of religious quest.
Stone: It's hard to stay away from religion when you mess with acid.

Interviewer: Neal Cassady as a figure on that scene does more than form a historical link between the Beat Generation and the counterculture. He also carries on the image of the affectless sociopath as a major American cultural type, a figure of particular interest to you in your fiction.
Stone: Cassady was a benign version of that figure. Gary Gilmore may be closer to what I mean, a vicious drifter of the kind America seems to produce in greater quantity than does any other country, probably because there is no moral center to our middle class. The society is so fractured. It never really had that period of high bourgeois cultural development that most European countries had. The American underclass has never had the tradition and stability of a European peasantry so it could never develop feudal loyalties. Instead we get these institutionalized personalities whose arrested emotions oblige them to mimic mood, feeling, love. This is the origin of their violence.

Interviewer: Such people will always constitute the night side of a counterculture. Charles Manson. Gilmore. Figures like Kesey and Kerouac draw forth its princes and saints.
Stone: I think cultural undergrounds develop in the void left by the abdication of the official culture. During the sixties, so many august institutions seemed to have no self-confidence. The universities, corporations, the very fabric of the state. Everything you pushed just seemed to fall over. Everything was up for grabs. For me, the counterculture was like a party that spilled out into the world until one had the odd feeling in society that one was walking around looking at the results of a party that had ended a few years before—a big experiment. But there was no program, everybody wanted different things. I think Kesey wanted a cultural revolution, the nature of which was uncertain. He was just making it up as he went along. Other people were into political reform. Others thought drugs would fix it all. Peace and love and dope.

Interviewer: There's a lot of dope, and an epic amount of drinking in your books—

Stone: I can't stop from doing it. I just can't. It's getting ridiculous. I get laughed at for the volume of chemicals that gets consumed, the amount of dope and booze. And now this guy's doing it again in my new book [*Children of Light*].

Interviewer: Whom do you consider your literary forebears?

Stone: My "forebears" are unsurprising—the great masters, the late Victorians, more Hemingway and Fitzgerald than Faulkner. I like Céline and Nathaniel West and Dos Passos. I can't really begin to characterize my own style beyond saying that it closely reflects my thinking, my world view. But in my first novel, I felt pretty free—I was all over the lot. And I did try as forcefully as I could to invent a voice. It's filled with influences and echoes, but it's mine, as nearly as I can make it so. I began *A Hall of Mirrors* as a realistic novel, but my life changed and the world changed and when I thought about it I realized that "realism" was a fallacy. It's simply not tenable. You have to write a poem about what you're describing. You can't render; you can't dissect. Zola was deluded.

Interviewer: Those remarks suggest an affinity with writers like John Barth and William Gass and Donald Barthelme. But I don't really see you in that camp.

Stone: My difference with those writers is that they take realism too seriously and so have to react against it. I don't feel the necessity of reacting against it. I don't believe in it to start with. Realism as a theory of literature is meaningless. I can start with it as a mode precisely because I don't believe in it. I *know* it's all a world of words—what else could it be? I had this curious luck to be raised by a schizophrenic, which gives one a tremendous advantage in understanding the relationship of language to reality. I had to develop a model of reality in the face of being conditioned to a schizophrenic world. I had to sort out causality for myself. My mother's world was pure magic. And because I had no father I eventually went into a sort of orphanage when my mother could no longer cope. So at the age of six I went into an institution, which taught me to be a listener. I had to deal with all the ways people were coming on to me, had to listen to all their trips and sort them out. Realism wasn't an issue because there wasn't any. I always had a vaguely dreamlike sense of things. There was no strong distinction for me between objective and imaginative worlds.

Interviewer: Life was failing to provide you with coherent narrative.

Stone: That's right. Life wasn't providing narrative so I had to. I had very little personal mythology of my own.

Interviewer: All this suggests some intricate connections among living and writing and acting. Many of your characters seem preoccupied with the shifting roles in their lives: who am I here?

Stone: Yes. And my becoming a writer was my answer to that question. It was an absolute necessity. I had to create somebody significant, or I would have been swept away. I've been known to say, not altogether facetiously, that life is a means of extracting fiction. If I start out with the claim that I tell stories to serve life, it's easy enough to reverse the terms.

Interviewer: The characters in your books are often writers, but of forms other than fiction. Can you speak a bit about your own work in other forms?

Stone: I intend to write a play. I'd direct a film if the chance came my way. But with those forms too many other people get their hands on your work. The joy of fiction is its autonomy. You take the risks, you take the rap.

Interviewer: Has your work as a screenwriter taught you anything about writing novels?

Stone: No. My screenplays have had no influence on my own fiction. But many writers of my generation, which was spared television in its youth, grew up with their sense of narrative influenced by the structure of film. And you can go back much earlier to see that in Joyce, for example. Interestingly, Dickens seems to have anticipated the shape of the movies—look at the first few pages of *Great Expectations*.

Interviewer: When you think of the writers of your generation, do you find a special constellation of contemporaries where you locate yourself?

Stone: Not really. I think more of generations of readers—for me, people who had some intense experience of the sixties. That's a generation I address. I share their concerns, their history. I get a certain amount of mail that reflects that. But there are no writers I'm aware of who are doing the same sort of thing I'm doing because I take seriously the questions that the culture has largely obviated. In a sense, I'm a theologian. And so far as I know I'm the only one.

Interviewer: Does this connect in a way to what you've called the fractured state of American letters?

Stone: You have famous writers, but there's no center. There are the best-seller writers, who are anonymous, almost industrial figures. You have writers who write primarily for other writers. And you have writers with their separate and different constituencies. But American fiction is not in a state of high health. This has something to do with the economic exigencies of publishing, of course. There's a lot of pressure on the noncommercial novel, on what publishers call marginal fiction. Fewer first novels are published, fewer books of any real quality that don't seem immediately bankable. This has to show itself in a kind of reduced, duller national literature, at least for the near future.

Interviewer: As far as best-selling fiction is concerned—

Stone: The best-seller list has always for the most part been the work of hacks, but in the past there seems to have been more space for serious writers. The pressure that's squeezing them out is dangerous and worrying. At the same time there's all these academic writing programs turning out the new second lieutenants of literature, and some of them somehow do manage to get published.

Interviewer: All of your books offer the same general structure: multiple characters, introduced at disparate points woven slowly together until the principals collide. How is that done in the writing? Is one figure followed nearly to the end, or is each scene treated in what will be its final sequence?

Stone: The latter. To run all those lines out one at a time would quickly turn stale. You have to be able to surprise yourself. In *Dog Soldiers*, for example, I didn't know Hicks was going to shoot Dieter until the day I wrote it. I just began writing their dialogue until it became inevitable. I was always attracted to the idea of bringing different elements together. One of my favorite radio programs was *Tell Me A Story*, in which people were presented with three things to weave into one.

Interviewer: As material emerges, do you control it with an outline? Charts, notebooks, things like that?

Stone: The only thing I do is make a short list that indicates sequence, very loosely. And then I sometimes jumble the stuff once I've got it written.

Interviewer: You juxtapose sequences in ways you hadn't planned on?

Stone: Yes. Literally juggle them. But I don't use charts or notes.

Interviewer: You don't plot through to a conclusion?

Stone: I know the beginning and usually the end. My problem is the middle—the second act, so to speak.

Interviewer: At what point in the process of a book is your consciousness of technique strongest, as opposed to times when the sheer energy of invention carries you along?

Stone: There are always certain metaphorical events that have to carry special weight. My stress on technique will be strongest when I encounter them. But there's no point at which the pleasure of invention justifies you in self-indulgence. You can never give yourself a break; you always have to make the hardest decisions. That means, for example, writing a brilliant passage and then throwing it away if there's no use for it in terms of the total design. It means scorning to find a clever way around problems that must be grappled with. There are times you have to take the chance that you may derail the structure of your book.

Interviewer: Can you give an example?

Stone: Well, the meeting of the revolutionaries in *A Flag for Sunrise* broke some rules of structure. They invaded the order of the book—for good reason—and then were never seen again. That scene was tough, I had to rewrite it a lot. The scene of Naftali's suicide—I must have rewritten that eight times. And cut it to the bone. In the book, it's only a fourth as long as it was in earlier drafts. All kinds of great lines—they had to go. It took forever. I couldn't get it right for the longest time. And when I reread it in the finished book, I thought it was awful. I was desolate. But Janice persuaded me that the scene was good. I always feel desolate when I finish a book. I thought that *A Flag for Sunrise* had some good scenes, but it troubled me overall. I fell into a deep depression.

Interviewer: Has there ever been a negative criticism of your work that you found useful?

Stone: I've seen negative positions I could respect. But I don't know that I learned anything from them. Negative criticism of my work tends to be very vitriolic.

Interviewer: The religious element in your work often asserts itself in classic existential form—for example, Hicks's ideal of ideas embodied in action, or Holliwell's remark in *A Flag for Sunrise*, "There's always a place for God—there's some question as to whether he's in it." This seems a near reflection of Heidegger's assertion that he is neither theistic nor atheistic but adrift in a world where God is absent.

Stone: I feel a very deep connection to the existentialist tradition of God as an absence—not a meaningless void, but a negative presence we live in terms of. I do have the sense of a transcendent plane from which I'm barred and I want to play off of it. If it's there, I'll get one sound. If it's not, I'll get a different sound.

Interviewer: Was the Catholic orphanage the start of your religious opinions?

Stone: Yes. I felt very rebellious. Every once in a while I would get very angry at the whole structure, although I guess I believed in it. I was in that very difficult position you get in when you really believe in God, and at the same time you are very angry: God is this huge creature who we must know, love, and serve, though actually you feel like you want to kick the son of a bitch. The effect on me was I felt I was just doing things wrong.

Interviewer: Do you have a fully articulated theory of fiction? In the sense, say, that Conrad framed his in the preface to *The Nigger of the Narcissus*?

Stone: "Fiction must justify itself in every line." Yes, I'm beginning to frame one—and along rather Conradian lines. Prose fiction must first of all perform the traditional functions of storytelling. We *need* stories. We can't identify ourselves without them. We're always telling ourselves stories about who we are: that's what history is, what the idea of a nation or an individual is. The purpose of fiction is to help us answer the question we must constantly be asking ourselves: who do we think we are and what do we think we're doing?

Interviewer: This quest can, on the part of some of your characters, particularly the more blighted or thwarted, take very brutal forms. Think of Rheinhardt, in *A Hall of Mirrors*, who can't seem to make America deliver on the American dream.

Stone: What I'm always trying to do is define that process in American life that puts people in a state of anomie, of frustration. The national promise is so great that a tremendous bitterness is evoked by its elusiveness. That was Fitzgerald's subject, and it's mine. So many people go bonkers in this country—they're doing all the right things, and they're still not getting off.

Interviewer: Do you think those expectations will be changed by the economic fact that most Americans will probably live in somewhat more straitened circumstances for some years to come?

Stone: I'm not sure. I think even the poorest people, partly for purely commercial reasons, are still encouraged to think of themselves as candidates for participation in the big American payoff. And of course the nature of the payoff has changed—no more white picket fences. The mass media has taught everybody the glamour of crime. When you're a crook, you're on the side of the chaos; how can you lose? If you're the guy that walks home from the felt factory after twenty years on the job and gets blown away by a freak on angel dust for the pay in your pockets, you're a chump.

Interviewer: This touches on a contradiction central to your work—what you've called everybody's "diminishing margin of protection." Thus in *Dog Soldiers* you replay Vietnam in Southern California. And in the other books people are always falling prey to some form of planned or random violence—

Stone: We live in a time of ongoing war, and the threat of violence is very close to all of us. It's not an exotic thing. You have to be pretty lucky to get through a year without witnessing it.

Interviewer: If a writer explores violence at length in his work, is there a sense in which he inevitably celebrates it?

Stone: I would call it a coming to terms. There is a catharsis. For me, it's a way of dealing with the violence in myself. I think it can do that for the reader as well. Violence *is* a preoccupation of mine. It occurs in my books perhaps disproportionately. But it's been my fortune to see rather a lot of it and to have to think about it. I try to curb my fears in what I write. There's a sense in which I use my characters as scapegoats to pay my dues for me, to ward with their flesh danger away from mine. You know, when some drama intrudes on your life your first impulse is to recount it—to turn disaster into anecdote or art. I deal with much that's negative and gruesome, but I don't write to dispirit people. I write to give them courage, to make them confront things as they are in a more courageous way.

Interviewer: Let me return to Conrad, with whom you've claimed some affinity. I've seen it suggested that Freud and Conrad provide polar notions of reality and thus suggest a continuum along which we may locate ourselves. In Freud there's the faith that psychic reality is knowable, once we strip away the skins of neurotic fiction that conceal it. In Conrad, we find reality numinous, and indeed composed of all our fictions about it.

Stone: Freud created a mythology out of nineteenth-century scientific optimism; he said that the glow in the haunted house was just phosphorescence from the swamp—a comforting high bourgeois myth. Conrad was a man of the world and a skeptic who worked not on the basis of ideology but of common sense. He saw things as they are without wanting to reduce them to theory. In that respect he's closer to the temper of our time and certainly closer to my own ideas about reality and about how to explore it in fiction.

Interviewer: Conrad provided you with a powerful epigraph for *Dog Soldiers* and Robert Lowell, one for *A Hall of Mirrors*. There's no epigraph for *A Flag for Sunrise*.

Stone: It's in the book. The Emily Dickinson poem Justin quotes. "A wife—at daybreak—shall I be—"

Interviewer: Of course. "Sunrise, hast thou a flag for me?" That throws a lot of the weight of the book on Justin.

Stone: It gives many of her scenes the quality of metaphorical event I mentioned. It links religious themes with erotic encounter. But it also summarizes a larger idea, the question of what awaits us all on the morning after the battle, so to speak. What will be there to claim our allegiance—the red banner of revolution, or some emblem we can't recognize but that we've somehow created? And of course I intend an ironic reference to the American flag.

Interviewer: Do you have your own ways, like Hicks, of "endeavoring to lead a spiritual life"? I mean, distinct from your work.

Stone: I attempt to. I'm always looking for a spiritual discipline I can live with. When I stopped being religious, being a Catholic, it was—as I did not realize at the time, but have come to since—devastating to me. It was a spiritual and moral devastation—shattering. And yet there was no trauma at the time; it seemed painless. It felt like ordinary maturation, but it left a great hunger.

Interviewer: Is Catholicism still important to you?

Stone: Somebody has said that it's almost as hard to stop being a Catholic as it is to stop being a black. But I greatly admire the Protestant spirit, the Protestant heroes—Luther, Kierkegaard. And I admire the great skeptics—Erasmus and Montaigne, that cast of mind. It's very valuable. And, ironically, it's built into the kind of rigorous training in language and logic that I received.

Interviewer: Catholic reason enabled you to cast off Catholic faith?
Stone: Well, it surely wasn't intended to. But I did learn the lucid analysis of rhetorical argument and thus became more immune to propaganda. And yet the skepticism that led me out of religious belief also leads me out of secular complacency.

Interviewer: Aside from that childhood training in rhetoric, did you learn anything about writing in other academic programs? Anything useful or valuable about creative writing?
Stone: Not really. But a creative writing class can at least be good for morale. When I teach writing, I do things like take classes to bars and race tracks to listen to dialogue. But that kind of thing has limited usefulness. There's no body of technology to impart. But that doesn't mean classes can't help. The idea that young writers ought to be out slinging hash or covering the fights or whatever is bullshit. There's a point where a class can do you a lot of good. You know, you throw the rock and you get the splash.

Interviewer: Your own experience in a way represents a synthesis of available models for American novelists: some academic background and connection and an active life in a varied world.
Stone: I think writers at present can pass fairly easily between these worlds. I have no academic credentials aside from my work. But I've been able to teach, and I sometimes enjoy it.

Interviewer: Do you have any interest in writers' conferences and colonies, that kind of thing?
Stone: I've been several times to a wonderful conference in Alaska that's filled with trappers and fishermen and people who spend a lot of time alone. Every year, on the winter solstice, they get together to talk books and writing and party.

Interviewer: You've been accorded from the beginning a handsome ration of prizes, awards, literary recognition of that kind. Has that had an effect on your work—given you an image you had to live in terms of?
Stone: I've kept my edge, stayed hungry, I think. I never sold so many copies

that I got overfed. It's less things like prizes than the simple fact of your first publication that changes everything forever. The minute you appear in print you lose some freedom and innocence and accept a degree of responsibility.

Interviewer: Are there things you'd like to attempt in fiction that you haven't done yet?
Stone: I'd like to write more comic stuff. There's always some humor in all the awfulness I write about, but sometimes I think of writing—well, I don't know that I could write a purely humorous book that wouldn't have some sort of ghastliness in it. It would have to be a weird kind of humor.

Interviewer: Are there areas of weakness in your work so far that you can identify, things that dissatisfy you?
Stone: Ken Kesey once told me I use too many commas.

Interviewer: Do you ever have writer's block?
Stone: I have a lot of depressed periods during which I'm incapable of working. But I'm not blocked by material or anything when I'm actually writing. I turn up more stuff I want to do than I have room or time to do it in.

Interviewer: That must be in part because you don't stay in your study numbed by an inward gaze, but return repeatedly to the world of experience—to Central America, for example. It's that fact that gives your work its political dimension and lets your readers encounter realized characters in a recognizable world. Incidentally, I'm interested in a remark of yours I encountered somewhere to the effect that Central America is a "due bill coming up for payment."
Stone: No mystery there. That's been a sphere of influence we've exploited economically and dominated politically and militarily very much the way the French, with a bit more success, continue to dominate their former colonies in Africa. We've run that part of the world without a lot of respect for the people who live down there; we've looked down on them as racial inferiors. I have a copy of the *Navy Times* from around 1913 that carries an ad for Shinola shoe polish that says, "Whether you're going on the beach for a party or storming ashore to teach the greasers a lesson, you want to look sharp!" We saw these places as banana republics peopled by gooks who somehow were not quite real people. Nobody thought it compromised American virtue to kick their ass if they got out of line. It was, you know, the white man's burden. And we have to remember that when Kipling passed

that duty on to the United States there was no cynicism or irony intended. I don't believe this country has simply been some horror story of racism and murder. But we have incurred a blood debt, and it *is* coming up for payment. The end of empire comes for everybody and it's coming for us. So now we're faced with this area close to our southern sea frontier where people have it in for us and are only too eager to collaborate with our enemies. I mean, if there is an invasion of the United States and whoever it was wanted to have a Central American legion, they'd get plenty of volunteers.

Interviewer: You've remarked in your own voice, as has Holliwell in *A Flag for Sunrise*, that we've exported what's worst in our culture, while what's best doesn't export. What is best? What have we got at home that keeps us going?
Stone: Idealism. A tradition of rectitude that genuinely does exist in American society and that sometimes has been translated into government. Enlightenment ideas written into the Constitution. Emerson and Thoreau. The whole tradition so wonderfully mythologized in John Ford's Westerns— the Boston schoolmarm seeking service on the frontier. We've tried to export that in the form of, say, missions to China, but it hasn't really worked because we were more a commercial than a military or cultural empire, so it was our appetites that we exported, along with the relevant parts of our popular culture. The French at least attempted to include their artistic traditions in their *mission civiliatríce*; they and the British, to a lesser extent, did have something to offer their colonials. All we wanted was to do business. The point is that so much that is best in America is a state of mind that you can't export.

Interviewer: But, as you say, we do export shoddy aspects of our culture along with our commerce. Holliwell argues this in his speech in Compostella.
Stone: Low-level pop culture, yes. Because America has managed to create a working class with the leisure and money to command the resources of the society but without the taste to enhance those resources. From that derived the pop culture we've exported. Now that isn't evil, but it is a form of pollution. It's why you get Central American Indians with transistor radios glued to their skulls. I don't mean to make a reactionary argument about the purity of the noble savage. But there is such a thing as authenticity. You'll recall that Holliwell's speech attacks American culture but also America's enemies. He sees, as I see, contradictions that simply have to be faced and

that possibly cannot be solved. There's a shared Marxist and American attitude that where there's a problem there must be a solution. What about the problem that doesn't have a solution?

Interviewer: There it is.
Stone: There it is. That aphorism may not be the least significant link between Central America and Vietnam.

Interviewer: You've raised the specter that haunts all of your work—as an aspect of American culture that fuels Rheinhardt's spite in *A Hall of Mirrors*, as the heart of darkness of *Dog Soldiers*, and as dreadful nostalgia in *A Flag for Sunrise*. Do you think the war will persist as a background for your work for some time?
Stone: I'm constantly drawn back to it. I had to keep myself from doing that in my new book, *Children of Light*, which is about the personal lives of some fucked-up people, unhappy writers and actors in the movie business. But even here I try to refer those lives to the American condition, my usual subject. And the war, as you say, continues to haunt us.

An Interview with Robert Stone

Robert Solotaroff / 1991

From the *South Carolina Review* (Fall 1993): 27–49. Reprinted by permission of Robert Solotaroff.

Line for line, perhaps the best criticism published on Robert Stone's work is A. Alvarez's 1986 review of the fourth novel, *Children of Light*. Alvarez begins: "In just four novels in almost twenty years Robert Stone has established a world and style and tone of voice of great originality and authority. It is a world without grace or comfort, bleak, dangerous, and continually threatening." With his triumphant fifth novel, *Outerbridge Reach*, which came out in February, Stone cemented his position as one of our very best living novelists.

My own exposure to his writing came belatedly in 1977 when I read the section of *A Flag for Sunrise* which introduces Pablo Tabor, and which was published in *American Review 26* as "A Hunter in the Morning." If memory serves, my initial response to Stone's fiction was something like Mailer's comment about the quality of the prose in Ellison's *Invisible Man*: "It's like holding a live wire in your hand." When, late in 1988, I was offered the opportunity to do the book on Stone for the Twayne United States Authors Series I jumped at it. Although I knew that an interview would be helpful, I kept putting off asking for one because I wanted to find out, through writing, the questions I needed answered. Finally, in early October 1991, I wrote to Stone. He called back promptly, and I arrived at his house in Westport, Connecticut, a bit before 11 a.m. on Sunday, October 27, a lovely autumn day.

There had been some confusion about the time the interview was to begin, and Stone was out on a walk. Janice Stone, the author's attractive, intelligent, and obviously large-spirited wife of thirty-one years, offered to field what questions she could until Bob returned, which he did, at about 12:30.

We talked for a bit more than three hours, pausing for lunch. But our conversation quickly turned back to the sorts of things I needed to know, and so I turned the tape recorder back on while we ate. While Stone was unfailingly gracious, he was almost always professionally detached, calmly matter-of-fact. Save for his repeating Hick's "I hope you got off on the fish," there was none of the grim playfulness that so often helps to charge his writing. A bit of anger did come into his voice when he spoke of how, as a boy, he wanted no part of his schizophrenic mother's delusional systems. Although he had clearly been hurt by the relatively unfriendly critical response to *Children of Light*, one would not have known it from the tone of his voice. As I was leaving, I half-jokingly commented on how unfair were the descriptions of his paranoia. Stone smiled and said, "It comes and goes."

Stone was kind enough to grant a follow-up, telephone interview, which occurred on January 26, 1992. Some of the interchange, which lasted about a half hour, concerned my introductory, biographical chapter which I had mailed to him a month earlier, for I wanted to be sure that I had the facts right. A few more questions had occurred to me, both as I went over the October interview and with the writing I had done since we'd met. Again, Stone was as helpful as he could have been. In what follows, I wove into the transcript of the first interview some clarifying sentences from the second one. I also edited out my occasional interruptions (which Stone bore patiently) and his occasional repetitions as he sought for just the right phrase he wanted. Several times, a question came to me which I should have asked earlier. Below, I placed the question and response in what seemed to me the most effective place. It was only at the end of the telephone interview that I mustered the boldness to ask the question that begins what follows.

Solotaroff: Did the perception that you were an illegitimate child at all bother you as you grew up?
Stone: It really took me a long time to figure out that that was what I was, but all in all, no.

Solotaroff: Of course the absence of a father in the home heightened the importance of your mother's schizophrenia. Would she at times occupy anything like the continuous alternative terrain that Lu Anne occupies with the Long Friends in *Children of Light*?
Stone: Yes, but she was kind of reticent about it with me. It was something she didn't really want me getting into, and she would get kind of cryptic. There was a sense of something, an ongoing reality I was not supposed to

know about, at least not yet. I didn't like it and didn't want to get any sense of the details.

Solotaroff: When your mother was hospitalized for three-and-a-half years, between the time you were six and the time you were almost ten, you became a boarder at St. Ann's School in Manhattan. In the 1987 story, "Absence of Mercy," the protagonist, Mackey, puts in the same amount of time at St. Michael's, a place where "a good beating was forever at hand," a locale with "the social dynamic of a coral reef," where the school disciplinarian, "implacable as a shark or a hurricane," would lash the palms of boys as young as six who had waited in terror at night outside his room. Was St. Ann's really as bad as this?

Stone: I'm afraid so. This is the one time I've written fiction that followed my experience so closely. I started with the incident, which is in the story and which is true, about the hassle in the subway the grown-up Mackay gets into. I told the story so many times to friends that I decided I've got to stop telling it and write it. I found myself getting back into St. Ann's, and the more I thought about St. Ann's, the more angry I got. That's a story written in anger, and it doesn't look at the up side of the place.

Solotaroff: So there was even the disciplinarian who told the kids, "You'll come to my room."

Stone: "You'll stand by my room." I don't think he understood the dimensions of it. When I look back I can hardly think that such small children were subject to that degree of terror. You were six or eight, and you were standing there waiting to get smacked on the hand with a leather strap. When I look back on it I can hardly believe it, but it was true all right. I think they believed in it, thought it was good for you.

Solotaroff: Did the beatings continue after you moved back in with your mother and became a day student again?

Stone: You just got slapped around in the classroom.

Solotaroff: When Mackay is in boot camp in the Navy he learns that he's developed an instinctive cringe. Did you also have one?

Stone: I did. When I got into the Navy, when I was being subjected to their stuff, I really shocked them. I don't normally write *roman à clef*. That story's an attempt to make fiction out of several elements in my life more directly than anything else I've written.

Solotaroff: When did you have the scuffle in the subway station that led to the writing of "Absence of Mercy"?

Stone: I would guess that this was 1964 or '65. It happened in the Seventy-Second Street station of the IRT subway. What happened was this kind of well dressed man was haranguing a very small, elderly black woman. Against my better judgment and everything I had been conditioned to do, I interfered, and he really came at me.

Solotaroff: The danger of getting pushed in front of the in-coming train must have been something else.

Stone: It's a very narrow platform. What happened was that I started to get the better of him and he started to yell for help. The train pulled in and my contacts left, including the lady I imagined myself assisting, and everyone else on the platform who had seen what had happened got on the local that I had been waiting for and disappeared. So I was left with the guy, and when I started getting the better of him, he started to yell "help." I had a peajacket on, I had a beard, and my hair was long—it was the mid-sixties—and what people coming down the steps were seeing was a young longhaired guy who was slamming around an older, fiftyish man who was yelling "Help" and "Police!" up the stairs. It suddenly occurred to me that I had better get out of there and I fled. That was it.

Solotaroff: What emerges in the story is the way this event reinforced Mackay's sense of the ultimate unfairness of things. Was this more or less the case with you?

Stone: I guess so.

Solotaroff: What's also interesting is that this happened before you finished *A Hall of Mirrors,* so you were a much more marginal person than you became.

Stone: I was. I was working at the tabloid, the *National Mirror,* so I was even more marginal than that.

Solotaroff: Getting back to your schooling, I've read that you went to Archbishop Manning High School after St. Ann's.

Stone: No, the school was still called St. Ann's the last year I was there. They changed the name of the school when it moved from Manhattan to Queens. I think the school changed in the sixties; they got some lay teachers and got into therapy and encounter groups.

Solotaroff: I understand that you were thrown out of high school for trying to convert your classmates to atheism. Could you say something about that?
Stone: The specific classmate I got in trouble over became a novelist. He was known to me as Freddy [Marco], his last name was Vassi. He became a novelist too, wrote a book called *The Stoned Apocalypse*. He got me into trouble because he refused to go to mass with his parents. They asked him who he'd been talking with, and he confessed to having talked to me. His parents called the school, and the school called me on the carpet.

Solotaroff: How did you take all this?
Stone: I felt pretty good when they called me on the carpet and they were accusing me. I felt like Martin Luther.

Solotaroff: So this was in May of 1955?
Stone: That's about right. I had just won a Regent's Scholarship for college. Occasionally the school finds me and writes to me for money. They always have the names of my books wrong.

Solotaroff: You told one interviewer that your drinking began to affect your performance in high school. Could you say something about this?
Stone: One of my party tricks to amaze my friends I did a number of times when I was about sixteen was to drink four or five cans of beer and show up for class drunk, completely plastered, to show that nobody was more crazy or out to lunch than I was. That was my way of demonstrating my self-destructiveness and willingness to do any crazy shit.

Solotaroff: I've gotten the sense that when you moved back in with your mother after she got out of the hospital, you and her situation was much different than before the hospitalization.
Stone: It was. Before the hospitalization she had her job as a teacher, and we lived in apartments that were quite comfortable and middle class, including finally one in Yorkville on Lexington and Eighty-Fifth. With the hospitalization, she lost her job and since she was no longer a teacher, she couldn't get any leases. From then on we lived in furnished rooms, but before that life was very comfortable and middle class, which figured for me as a kind of lost paradise.

Solotaroff: I know that you went on a number of trips with your mother, looking for a new life. Did any of them occur before the hospitalization, and how many of them were there?

Stone: There were four of them—two to Chicago, one to New Mexico, and one to Montreal. All occurred after my mother got out of the hospital.

Solotaroff: In one of the Chicago trips you ended up in the same sort of Salvation Army hospital that Hicks of *Dog Soldiers* remembers.
Stone: That trip was the longest one, about four months, and we probably spent a bit more than three of it in the shelter. I think it was called a Booth Shelter, and it made a tremendous impression on me. I always go back to it in my mind. It was basically for women who didn't have any men, and the kids there were gypsy kids in a way that I was sometimes but not always. I went in and out of that life. In a way there was a lot of stability in mine. This was a taste of what happened when there weren't any systems, and what you can end up with. Those kids were interesting, from all over. This place was interracial, black kids, black families there at a time—this was about 1948—when this was relatively uncommon. Chicago in 1948 was a relatively segregated city. To be associated with that shelter was to be of not very high status, and the fact that there were black kids in there made it all the more troublesome.

I always held on to that. When I was writing *Dog Soldiers*, when I was thinking about Hicks, I was thinking in terms of that shelter, of going to that priest to get money out of the poor box, also getting in trouble for playing cards. I had a deck of cards and was teaching other kids "Go Fish," and the Salvation Army types were against the cards and came down on me for that. The last trip was when I was about twelve; after that I just refused to go on those expeditions. Of course, I'd participated in these fantasies of a better life. My mother did them partly to please me. She'd come up with something, and I'd say, "Yeah, we've got to do that." I would kind of talk her into it.

Solotaroff: In interviews, what comes through from these trips is the romance of the road, but of course in the beginning of *A Hall of Mirrors* we're made conscious of the exhaustion, the depression that went with traveling. Were both states aspects of these trips?
Stone: Yes, they were.

Solotaroff: How old were you when you started writing stories?
Stone: Around ten.

Solotaroff: Did you write more or less steadily?
Stone: Just occasionally. Sometimes I'd get a notion and write a story, and

of course I was writing compositions. The only thing I did at school that got me favorable attention was my compositions.

Solotaroff: You've spoken of the opposition that you felt blocked the way to your becoming a writer. Was it primarily from your mother?

Stone: There was no cultural opposition from my mother. She was kind of a maverick in this blue collar milieu I was in. I really think that with a few exceptions the teachers and friends I had really didn't look at the life of the arts except as an excuse for not working. This was not the case with my mother, who always liked, looked favorably, on bohemians and eccentrics.

Solotaroff: Did you have a sense that you'd like to be a writer but that it was just not possible?

Stone: I didn't think it was possible. I'd come to share from somewhere, not from my mother, the sense you had to make a living in a more solid way. It was unstable, and one thing I was really after on some level was stability. I really wanted to be something absolutely solid, something un-eccentric, perfectly acceptable and secure that didn't have a lot of surprises. I thought that was what I wanted.

Solotaroff: You said in one interview that you won a story contest in high school. Could you be specific about the winning story?

Stone: I won the story writing contest in my junior year, and it was probably written a couple of weeks after I finished reading *The Catcher in the Rye*. I have the feeling that if I read it now I would find it intensely Salinger-esque. I used to have a copy of it. It was collected in something called *Good Themes*. I don't know who sponsored the contest, maybe *Scholastic Magazine*. Actually, I won a couple of contests when I was in high school. There was a drama contest on the subject of cancer sponsored by the Cancer Society. I wrote a little one-act play, a really corny play. It had Napoleon, who died of cancer, in it, and I had Napoleon talking to some guy looking for a cure for cancer.

Solotaroff: You've talked about being a member of that West Side gang, the Saxons, and of getting out when knives were taken out in a scrape in Central Park. But Wallace Stegner wrote in 1967 that you contemplated joining "some Brooklyn survival of the Christian Front." Could you comment about this? How relevant was the experience toward the conception of Bingamon's operation in *A Hall of Mirrors*?

Stone: The truth of that was I had this bunch of friends who were kind of right wing. What I contemplated joining was an essentially Italian neo-fascist youth outfit operating out of East Harlem, where Freddy Vassi lived. A lot of guys I hung with were remnants of that area in Harlem around 116th Street and Pioneer Avenue. They used to do things like paint "Viva Il Duce" on walls, more on bust balls than anything else. It was idiocy, but it was also a reaction to the pressure of the general black and Puerto Rican takeover of the park. So there was a kind of a falling back upon powerful symbols. It was no survival of the Christian Front, just a bunch of kids playing with the symbols of Italian fascism. We used to give each other Italian fascist salutes. Still, I knew about rightwing feelings and rightwing numbers from very close up, not entirely from the outside.

Solotaroff: Did you try to enlist in the Navy right away?
Stone: Yes, I did but there was a waiting list. I couldn't get in until August 9.

Solotaroff: Where was boot camp and what was it like for you?
Stone: Bainbridge, Maryland, and it was absolute hell. It was summer and so uniform was whites. The only way you could wash your clothes was with a scrub brush and Ivory Soap. My mother was an old lady. I wasn't very handy at keeping my gear together, and I was also kind of dreamy and unfocused, not ideal Navy material at all. It was really traumatic for me. The up side was that though they terrorized me, they didn't hit me. And I was in boot camp from August until November. I got sent back and had to do part of it over again.

Solotaroff: What was next?
Stone: I went to a technical air patrol squadron at Norfolk Naval Air Station, and from there I went to radio school in Norfolk. From there I went aboard the *USS Muliphen*, during September of 1956. The ship was an AKA that looked like one of those ships off Normandy: big A frames and landing boats stacked up on the hull.

Solotaroff: I understand that when you saw combat at the Suez Canal in the next month you were aboard the *USS Chilton*.
Stone: We were moored at Rapallo and had liberty; we had gone to Rome. Suddenly the Sixth Fleet was called to go to the Suez Canal and get civilians out of there. I was put on the *Mount McKinley* and transferred to the *Chilton*.

Solotaroff: Why the Navy?
Stone: My fascination with the sea, with water.

Solotaroff: How many Mediterranean tours did you have?
Stone: Two, that lasted about ten months; they ended up being extended through the spring of 1957.

Solotaroff: Then you passed a competitive test and became a Navy journalist and third-class petty officer?
Stone: Right. I was a correspondent for almost all of my last year-and-a-half in the Navy. The big trip was Operation Deep Freeze. We started in Davisville, Rhode Island, in November, and we went around the world by way of the canal to Port Littleton, New Zealand, then down to Antarctica, then to Sydney, to Durban, South Africa, then Montevideo. We got back in the spring of '58. We were in Antarctica for two periods: the first at Cape Hallot on the Pacific side for almost two months, then to Sydney for a liberty, then back down for a couple of more months. The ship's mission was taking off old Seabees, putting new Seabees on, giving them new equipment. Also we had scientists aboard; we were tracing cosmic rays. We had these receptor instruments. The University of Chicago had apparently supplied a course for us to follow, and we were tracking cosmic rays. I think that there was also some kind of secret military function, but I can't remember what it was.

Solotaroff: It would have been summer when you were in Antarctica.
Stone: The ship was divided into two work parties, twelve hours each because it never got dark. Sometimes we'd have these shore parties where we'd go in and hang out, drink a couple of cans of beer and look at the penguins. The weather often didn't get much colder than a winter day in New York.

Solotaroff: So most of your correspondence was about the Antarctic expedition?
Stone: That's right. I did do a story on the Marine residence station in Beirut but that was when I was in the Mediterranean.

Solotaroff: Did you do much writing in the Navy?
Stone: I started writing poetry and wrote a story that I sent to *Esquire* that they refused. It was a kind of neighborhood thing, a boy-girl story, kind of

an idealized version of my girlfriend and me at the time. I think I kind of repressed it. Oh yes, my mother sent the story that won the contest to the *New Yorker*, and I got a rejection which said to try us again. It certainly set me up. It was nice to get.

Solotaroff: Could you say a little bit about the quality of your two-and-a-half years in the Navy after boot camp?
Stone: I had a lot of sea duty, and I really had a pretty good time of it. I was fairly lucky in getting to travel a lot. I got to the Mediterranean. In the fifties, especially, the eastern Mediterranean was a pretty exotic location. People in the mid-fifties didn't often get to Greece, for example. It was interesting. And certainly, Operation Deep Freeze III was wonderful. I felt fairly successful. I got rated, got a badge of junior petty officer. It gave me a certain sense of attainment, of being productive.

Solotaroff: So after boot camp you didn't find the authoritarianism of the Navy particularly oppressive?
Stone: Not really. Boot camp in those days was really quite strict, so it was tough because I wasn't handy. I wasn't good at that sort of stuff. But once I was out of boot camp it was quite different.

Solotaroff: In a way it was authoritative, not authoritarian. It wasn't irrational?
Stone: Well, the military has an irrational side. I managed to stay out of trouble. Certainly there were arbitrary situations, and the irrational stuff is always there in the military.

Solotaroff: So my surmise that you shed the self-destructive ways of high school is more or less accurate?
Stone: The Navy did not engage my tendency to fuck up. They didn't bring that out in me.

Solotaroff: You obviously met a great many people among your shipmates. Do you feel that this enriched the writing you were going to do?
Stone: Oh, absolutely. Being thrown together with a whole lot of people from all over the country, especially since this was at a time in the mid-fifties when the country was less homogeneous, when for example the South was still the South and all that it entailed, and people from Appalachia were much more distinct, regional types, when there was much more contrast

between New York and kids from West Virginia. It was very interesting and tremendously helpful.

Solotaroff: When did you get out of the Navy?
Stone: Bastille Day, July 14, 1958.

Solotaroff: So you started at NYU in the fall semester then?
Stone: Yes.

Solotaroff: Do you remember what you took?
Stone: Spanish, economics, composition, and I think some kind of course in communication arts. I really felt school was a drag. I didn't have a history of making connections through formal education. It was not something that I had easily overcome. I was much more interested in what was going on at the *Daily News* and at the Seven Arts, where I'd hang out after I got off work.

Solotaroff: Janice said that she met you in a writing course M. L. Rosenthal taught in the second semester.
Stone: Yes, that was the only course I took. I only wrote a couple of stories, one long one about a guard in a naval prison. It was based on a brief experience I had just before I got out of the Navy. I was technically a prisoner chaser for about a week. I'd go to the brig at Camp Allen where the Marines had the court-martialed prisoners. I had to march them along the military highway to breakfast. We'd have ours and see that they had theirs. They'd relax and get out of hand, and I was always afraid they'd pull some dangerous thing on us when we were bringing them back to the Marines. Admirals would be going to work, and we wanted to make it look good. We had these .45s we were passing around. It was stressful to eat with these .45s with these guys who were fighting with us. It was no way to have breakfast.

Solotaroff: An anticipation of Converse at the Yokasuka brig.
Stone: I guess so.

Solotaroff: So that was it for your formal education?
Stone: I think I might have sat in on a second course with Rosenthal for the fall semester of the next year.

Solotaroff: Could you talk a bit about your stint with the *Daily News*? What did you do? When did you start?

Stone: I started just a bit after I got out of the Navy. The *Daily News* was the last of the old time newspapers. They still had these superannuated reporters of Damon Runyan's generation. Gene McCabe had covered the Legs Diamond trial; two other reporters disguised themselves as a doctor and nurse and got a picture of Ruth Snyder in the electric chair.

Solotaroff: So as a copyboy you ran copy from one desk to another?
Stone: Yes, but there was more. I did get to judge a poetry contest. The idea with the copyboys was that they were also a kind of talent reserve; some people did features for the big thick Sunday section. Sometimes they would send you out as a kind of substitute reporter. They would send you to places they didn't want to go, the morgue for instance. I did a lot of sports. I wrote some sports captions.

Solotaroff: Had you thought of becoming a newspaperman when you got out of the Navy?
Stone: I think I was fortunate in that what I met with at the *News* was the same thing I met in high school with a not altogether dissimilar type of person. There was a kind of New York, working class authoritarianism that I don't seem to get on with. That was the prevailing ethos. The *Daily News* in those days was like an extension of a police department. One of the things about the *News* which in those days made it special was its paranoid and vicious political position. It has no politics any more but in those days it was a rabid rightwing affair with some of the most wicked and devious editorials ever written. Some critic commenting on the contents of TV provoked an angry editorial: "We're all for culture, my dear." "My dear" implying the limp-wristed aesthete. If they had a choice of coming out for life or coming out for death, they'd come out for death.

Solotaroff: You've talked in other interviews about the gaggle of jobs you had in New Orleans: working in a coffee factory, selling encyclopedias, working for the 1960 census, reading poetry to jazz accompaniment. Did you, like Rheinhardt in *Hall*, work in a soap factory?
Stone: Well, I worked in a coffee factory for a few weeks, and I did work in a soap factory. One of the things I did was to serve on the labeler. What that gave me a look at was the American assembly line, and no tour of American life in the twentieth century would be complete without a little time on the assembly line. You had to see one of those to know what the system was about.

Solotaroff: You've written about how, when you were selling encyclopedias in towns outside New Orleans, you were arrested by local police who confused you with the northern civil rights workers who were organizing Louisiana at the time. I've gone through histories of Louisiana at the time, of CORE and SNCC, and I don't think organization by outsiders was to occur for a few years.

Stone: It's possible that I've been projecting history backwards. The way I remember it, when we were picked up there was always a suggestion that that's who we were. They'd ask us if we were selling encyclopedias to blacks; they seemed to doubt whether we were really selling encyclopedias. They seemed to question what we were up to, kept asking us how and in what way it might concern blacks. I could be grafting a different history onto my recollection.

Solotaroff: What precisely were the grounds they gave for the arrest?

Stone: We were getting arrested for peddling without a license, for violating an ordinance against selling from door to door.

Solotaroff: How often and where were you arrested?

Stone: We were arrested twice, once in Covington, once in Bogalusa.

Solotaroff: You use the August 1960 striking of a good many black children from the welfare rolls in *A Hall of Mirrors*. Do you remember your response at the time?

Stone: It was probably something like "This is terrible." The people who were speaking for that were so obviously corrupt and demagogic and in the wrong that you couldn't much get around it. It was plainly traditional, racial demagoguery.

Solotaroff: I gather that your sympathy for blacks grew considerably during your nine months in New Orleans.

Stone: What had also been going on was that we had been taking the census in the black parts of town and were increasingly fascinated and charmed by the blacks in New Orleans. They had a certain something that we found tremendously sympathetic and appealing. We had this experience in black Louisiana. Now all those sections of New Orleans are terribly dangerous and frightening, and it's interesting to think that in those days they weren't at all. I think this made a difference. We were really seeing the horrid side of white Louisiana, the sweet side of black Louisiana.

Solotaroff: Did you write any fiction during your New Orleans stay?

Stone: I think I went through a time of thinking that I wanted to write plays. I can't really remember; everything was so day to day. I don't know if I had a long-range plan. I finally just wanted to get the hell out of there because there was no money to be made.

Solotaroff: According to Janice you were working as a copywriter for low-end furniture stores when you decided to write a novel.

Stone: Right. We were living on St. Marks Place in Manhattan late in 1961. I had read *The Great Gatsby* for the second time and felt "That's what I want to do. I want to write novels."

Solotaroff: Janice said you got on a bus and went off to Pennsylvania for a weekend to get started. Could you talk about that?

Stone: I just took a bus out to the Delaware Water Gap. I stayed at an old inn in East Stroudsburg and walked around and went out by the river and thought about the book I might write.

Solotaroff: Do you remember what it was you sent to Stanford that got you the Stegner writing fellowship?

Stone: The first section with Rheinhardt, the first with Geraldine, and I think I had some pages on Rainey, around thirty odd pages.

Solotaroff: Do you have any reason for not giving Rheinhardt a first name?

Stone: That now looks rather like a dramatic posture. I think it was to make him even more alienated. The same reason I gave him those extra letters at the end of his name: to make him a more substantial character.

Solotaroff: I had a sense of you and Janice pretty much hanging out with sweet beatnik types like Bogdanovich. Did you meet any of the con-artist types who surface in *Hall*?

Stone: I did hang out with beatniks like that, but one of the things I did was to work in a telephone [company] boiler room. Some guys there and some of the guys who sold encyclopedias were true con artists, and I knew a guy who hung out with [Robert] Maestri's daughter. He was kind of a bad guy. I knew a whole range of guys. I knew a kind of psychopathic hustler, a part time actor. I knew some sweet people, but there was a mix.

Solotaroff: Did any of the later drug experiments in California translate into Rheinhardt's hallucinations?

Stone: I don't think I would have had any trouble imagining my way into alcoholic hallucinations even if I had never taken drugs, but I definitely think my taking acid affected the book. It kind of liberated me from my addiction to realism. I felt released from the restrictions of the realist mode. But this might have come more from reading Céline.

Solotaroff: Between the similarity between the names of your protagonist and the shapeshifter in Ellison's *Invisible Man*, and the way in which both books close with the surrealistic rendering of a riot deliberately fomented by whites, I was wondering about Ellison's influence.

Stone: I read *Invisible Man* about two years into the writing of *Hall*.

Solotaroff: I was impressed by the erudition of the discussion of the Mozart Clarinet Quintet in *Hall*. Did you have much formal musical training?

Stone: When I was in St. Ann's they had musical instruction. I learned to read the F and G clefs. I learned pretty quickly to read music, but then they discontinued it. I never got back to it. I never really studied again. Sometimes I think that I should just study music, just to come to terms with musical theory. I've always loved it. There was a certain point in my life when everything I loved about music got subsumed by rock and roll. When I was at Stanford I was really very interested at that time in musical theory. I was even trying to teach myself at that time how to read. I don't know; I'd blow hot and cold. It made a lot of difference in my life to get that scholarship because suddenly I had Stanford and all its facilities, and I really went crazy using it, going to the music library.

Solotaroff: Was the story "Aquarius Obscured" originally in *Dog Soldiers*? Marge tells Hicks that she'd been to the aquarium when there was no time for her to do so and here's this story about a stoned woman at the aquarium.

Stone: And Hicks says "I hope you got off on the fish." "Aquarius Obscured" wasn't meant to be in *Dog Soldiers*. I meant for there to be an aquarium scene but not that story.

Solotaroff: Were there any false starts with *Dog Soldiers*?

Stone: No.

Solotaroff: You say somewhere that the narcs in *Dog Soldiers* are not really in the government; surely Antheil was a government employee. Is there such a thing as a "regulator," or is this part of the fiction?

Stone: Antheil works for a regulatory agency. I conceived him as an agent of the Federal Bureau of Narcotics, which doesn't exist anymore, and which technically speaking was a regulatory agency. It was abolished because it was getting increasingly corrupted and highhanded, a real loose cannon. Antheil was my attack on the Federal Bureau of Narcotics.

Solotaroff: Of all your well-done minor characters I find Danskin the most overwhelming. The mix of the 170 IQ, the tire iron, the ways his anger and playfulness work are just wonderful. Could you offer a few words on how you hit on him?

Stone: Danskin came from someone we had in the Saxons, an educated Jewish kid from Central Park West, a big hulking kid who had trouble breathing. He was really crazy. He would give people these looks, these hot-eyed stares; he was completely demented. He could talk about books, but when he was loose he was like Frankenstein's monster.

Solotaroff: That's fascinating. At just this time, around 1953, there was this bunch of Jewish kids in Brooklyn, one of them an honors student at NYU, another a brute named Melvin Mitnick, built more or less like Danskin, and the bunch went around Prospect Park beating up and sometimes killing bums.

Stone: Well, Stuey was Jewish; Danskin was basically him and a couple of other guys like him, a fairly familiar type in the great morphology of New York characters.

Solotaroff: In the shootout toward the end of *Dog Soldiers*, Hicks tells Converse that he killed one and Antheil killed another. Are we to feel then that Danskin and Smitty have been killed?

Stone: I think I leave it a little obscure about who's killed out there.

Solotaroff: Some critics have placed the shootout in California, which has got to be off because everyone drives east for at least thirty hours to get from L.A. to Dieter's. Even at 50 mph. this would put the locale east of El Paso, which is not possible. Did you have eastern New Mexico in mind, or are we to regard it as a kind of dream terrain, even though you render it with such precision?

Stone: It's really a dream terrain, like northern New Mexico but on the border. Then there was the presence of Kesey's house in La Honda.

Solotaroff: Early on, Marge lets us know that it's eight years after the big Berkeley Vietnam Day. Since that would place the novel in 1973, and the treaty was in January of that year and all our troops were out by March, was that a slip?
Stone: I meant it to be in 1971.

Solotaroff: Was Guatemala the model for Compostela in *A Flag for Sunrise*?
Stone: I really meant Mexico with its leftist rhetoric and rightest political behavior.

Solotaroff: Of Honduras, Nicaragua, and Costa Rica, the three countries you travelled in during the 1976 trip that got you thinking of writing the novel that became *A Flag for Sunrise*, you've said that, geographically, Tecan is modeled after Honduras. But there are so many problems with this. For one thing, the capital of Nicaragua is on a huge lake, as is the capital of Tecan. For another, the coasts of Nicaragua are to the east and west. In Honduras they're to the north and south.
Stone: The average person will think of the coasts of any Central American country as being east and west. That's what made it easy to make that change. Most are not aware that one is north and one is south. Geographically I was thinking of Honduras in terms of what places look like. Honduras is the place I travelled in most, got the closest to the ground, knew what the people were like, got the feel of the place. Honduras really did not have the air of repression that Nicaragua did. Honduras, though very poor, was a rather cheerful place. Partly because it's rather underpopulated, it has a kind of *dolce far niente*, exactly what you don't have in El Salvador and Guatemala. In Honduras you don't have this terrible desperation of where is the next meal coming from? There is a kind of poverty, but a more tolerable poverty, not a desperate situation. Honduras is a somewhat less violent country in every way because the population pressure is less. On the other hand, that was the Central American country I knew most closely. I went back several times over the years because I liked it, and that's what I mean by geographically: not the shape.

Solotaroff: Did you start *Flag* right after your return in 1976?

Stone: I might not have really started writing until early '77, but it might still have been '76.

Solotaroff: Did you do a lot of background reading for it?
Stone: Not really. At that time not a lot was going on, things were just beginning to break. When I started writing things were quiet there.

Solotaroff: I've read that you put down a historical novel to write *Flag*.
Stone: I was trying to write about the Munster Anabaptists in 1545, a kind of scatological sect of apocalyptic Proto-Mennonites who took over the city of Munster. Meyerbeer wrote an opera about them, called *The Prophet*.

Solotaroff: About how much did you get done?
Stone: I probably got about thirty pages done. I just couldn't handle the diction. How am I going to get these sixteenth-century Germans to talk? I had no idea.

Solotaroff: Were we to believe that Heath would have kept his promise to Holliwell to protect Justin?
Stone: I meant him to have intended to keep his promise.

Solotaroff: But he just disappears?
Stone: Heath disappears in the confusion of the day; he can't keep his promise.

Solotaroff: In *Flag*, you have these three, very attractive, blond women: Justin, Deedee Callahan, and Mariclara Obregón. I thought it a fine touch that Obregón has honey-colored hair, and this is one of the very few physical details we get about Justin so that we can see Holliwell's drunken lurch after Obregón is just a prelude for the pursuit of Justin. I must say that it is fascinating to see someone who went through a Catholic school contemplating the sexual life of a nun. You're so explicit about Deedee Callahan's body and her sexual behavior, but you're so discreet with Justin. All we learn about her body is that she has smooth skin. The description of the intercourse with Holliwell is just as discreet.
Stone: I think that was natural and was the result of Catholic conditioning regarding the body of a dedicated virgin, but I think it's also appropriate to the book. When I say a dedicated virgin I mean a virgin dedicated to sacrifice. I think it's important that Holliwell does not succeed in reaching her when they do have that sexual encounter because she isn't really available

in temporal terms. She remains a sort of semi-sacred figure; she belongs to God in a way, as she discovers. I think my not defining her in immediate sensual terms is the result of superstitious dread to some degree, but constructive because I think it suits the purpose of the novel, the function of the character. She's really just frightened and confused. She doesn't turn to Holliwell with any great sense of liberation. Her renunciation of religion is essentially intellectual and philosophical. She was not terribly constrained by physical vows; it was not a big problem with her. She was kind of in love with this priest, but what she really misses in terms of physicality is just the opportunity to be able to turn to a person. She's not exactly brimming with repressed carnal desire. She just isn't, so her sexuality is really less important. What Holliwell sees in her, he says he wants to wear her skin. It's a spiritual seduction. He's not really after her body; it's her soul.

Solotaroff: Holliwell's ruminations are so extensive, so garrulous. Did you worry about his sometimes costing you the usual trenchancy you have in your novels?

Stone: There's a level on which you have to give a character his head. You want to strike a balance. You want to keep control, but I think you ought to take out the parts when you're just reminding yourself who the character is. I tried to keep a tight rein on the character.

Solotaroff: Did you ever have a more explicit description of Campos's torturing of Justin?

Stone: I thought it an absolute necessity to put that on the level of her from the inside. I wanted to make it plain that the violence was intense and terribly painful. What is important to her is not what is physically happening. Any explicitness is not serving the purpose I want, which is her being surprised by, in Graham Greene's phrase, "the appalling strangeness of the mercy of God." It's not about a woman being tortured by a sadistic animal. What was going on was the infliction of sexual sadism, the destruction of a woman by a sexual sadist. To do that from the outside is to just sort of join in, to be in some kind of complicity. That is not what I was about. As a woman, as a religious person, she's subject to the forces of brutality and evil, and that's what I was writing about. I didn't want to get into where the cattle prod was going.

Solotaroff: Gnostic thought is so important in *Flag*. I think of that famous line of Yeats's, about how his wife gave him the automatic writing so that he might have metaphors for his poetry. Does Gnosticism give you metaphors for experience, or is there a part of you that takes it literally?

Stone: I think there is truth in it. I always found it sublime and on a certain level true.

Solotaroff: The Gnostic doctrine of the diffusion of the primal light of God, of our need to return the light within us to God and help reconstitute Him, of His being outside the world, which is only a distraction—do you see this as a real experiential alternative, an alternative to canonical Christianity?

Stone: It has a great aesthetic attraction and it also has a degree of truth. There is a way in which life, like a dome of multicolored glass, stains the white radiance of eternity. It is true. It is a metaphor that has a lot of truth.

Solotaroff: How long have you been reading the Gnostics?

Stone: I've been reading about the Gnostics for a long time, going back to when I was in high school when I must have come across a religious pamphlet refuting every imaginable heresy. The Gnostic vision struck me as rather sublime; it always has. I went through a period of reading about the same time I was writing the book. Above all, I read the Hans Jonas book and the Elaine Pagels, *The Gnostic Gospels*, which I'm afraid I don't really buy.

Solotaroff: Why?

Stone: Because whenever someone comes up with a thesis, in which they go back to historical documents and find that the documents somehow dovetail neatly, dovetail with a progressive, trendy attitude of the moment, I think that you can question the scholarship. I just find it altogether coincidental that the Gnostic gospels should emerge being so antipatriarchal and nonsexist. It just seemed to me a little too good to be true.

Solotaroff: I realize that the emphasis on the political developments in Tecan is increasingly upon the American principals and not on the country, but I still have a sense that I missed what you intended the reader to pick up on concerning the prospects of the country. On the one hand, Tecanese history would seem to suggest that no good can come to the country in the foreseeable future; on the other hand, Emilio Ortega Curtis, who assumes the presidency, seems to be as well qualified as anyone could be to initiate a process to bring some good to the country. Did you have any sense of the future of Tecan, or is that just a different novel?

Stone: I have to put myself back into a world in which there was no Sandinista revolution, no civil war in El Salvador—for example, Duarte was a good guy—things were so different. Castro had just stopped trying to export revolution. But I think that what I was suggesting was that the process was tainted.

Solotaroff: So many critics talk about the bleakness of the novel's vision but not one of them seizes upon what an admirable man Ortega seems to be.
Stone: I mean him to be admirable in many ways, but he's got historical baggage: the conditions, the contradictions of Marxism-Leninism.

Solotaroff: Would you be good enough to talk about the origins of *Children of Light*?
Stone: I did a screenplay a long time ago about a bunch of people who went to the Baja for a weekend, and I kept thinking about that trip and various things. Then of course I'd been down on location a couple of times for the making of *Who'll Stop the Rain?*, and I knew a couple of things about the movie business. Above all, I got into the notion of a relationship between two people who know that nothing good can happen to them from each other and who know that they have nothing but trouble and even potential destruction to give to each other. but one of them more willfully than the other—out of nostalgia, out of weakness, out of perversity, out of a desire for generalized destruction, for his own destruction, out of a combination of self-destructiveness and selfishness—makes this pilgrimage. I thought once of calling this *Death and the Lover*. I always felt that this was a knight on a pilgrimage to bring death. I had the image of a skeleton in armor, death as a knight errant, going after this enchanted princess and bringing her nothing but destruction. The fascination between two people who present each other with nothing but the abyss.

Solotaroff: I understand schizophrenia as a kind of leaking of unconscious structures into waking life. In the case of someone like Lu Anne, her substitution of drugs and alcohol for her medication accelerates the leakage. The Long Friends, who leak the most, seem to function as a kind of superego structure. They admonish Lu Anne for her sudden interest in Lowndes. She consigns her children to their care. They're very traditional, conservative. What gets very interesting to me is how powerfully the Long Friends are drawn to Lowndes. Now are they drawn to him because he's somebody

who, like Rheinhardt, couldn't wrangle his talent and is exhibiting a kind of a living death?
Stone: Yes.

Solotaroff: Now with Lu Anne, everything is sort of exponential. . . . she calls Lowndes a bone god.
Stone: He's like a zombie.

Solotaroff: But she says, "he's one of what I am." She feels that a part of herself is sort of ghoulish.
Stone: She has this sense of having picked up something from the cemetery, of having breathed something in. Lowndes is in real trouble. She identifies him as connected with the cemetery, as part skeleton, whether it's a bone god or a knuckle deity, a thing of death and corruption. Everything about him is awful to her: she calls him the shit between her toes, calls his eyes fecal. She is subjecting him to the most dreadful psychological terrorism.

Solotaroff: He has some endearing features; you gave him some very sympathetic lines.
Stone: I meant him to be just a poor guy; he's having a miserable time. He's not the nicest guy in the world because he's very unhappy.

Solotaroff: Some of his lines, like "You're a long way from home, little sister," show a real lyric sympathy.
Stone: He's getting in on their fellow Southernness in a way which is exactly the wrong way. Her savagery toward him is so demented that if he feels half of what's in her mind it's terrible for him.

Solotaroff: She says she breathed in the Long Friends in the cemetery. Is this her attempt to give an experiential explanation to a genetic condition? Or are we to feel that she might have played with a skeleton's bones as a child?
Stone: Well she might have; something happened in Louisiana that rings a bell to me. Somebody being told not to get a Snoball because he would be exposed to something. Maybe there was a flood and the bones were exposed. Maybe that really happened; maybe it just happened once.

Solotaroff: Her secret eyes—is this like an aspect of her as sacrificing priestess, some aspect of the White Goddess?

Stone: Yes, it's also something that she as an actress would do. Actors will sometimes try to use this. It's a kind of prepping device, to look a whole lot of different ways. Kind of like, "I'm going to show you my glossies, my eight-by-ten glossies." It is her secret power.

Solotaroff: But it always seems to be her absolutely dangerous power play. Walker dozes a bit, and she's standing over him naked. He feels his life is in danger, and he tries to scamper back to safety.

Stone: No, that's real. It's like Diana bathing, and the guy sees her and goes blind. It's an aspect of her that must never be seen. Or it's like Medusa. She can reveal this. Most of the time she does not reveal this, but if she decides to she can use this to destroy somebody.

Solotaroff: One gets the sense that she's going to work through all of her grievances during the Mt. Carmel scene. Like when she says, "I am your sister Eve, borne of your body." Is she complaining of being unjustly sub-ordinated to the screenwriter? I'm just trying to get a hold on the different structures that bubble up in her. For example when she suddenly sees Christ as a scorched cat, or she changes Rosalind from a deer to a hind to a cat—I know it's very dangerous when schizophrenics begin drawing pictures of jungle cats—were you trying to catch a killer aspect of her?

Stone: One of the things that was on my mind was that way in which, as she says, you can kill an animal by looking at it a certain way. It's mutual preda-tion. It really floors me to go back through this and to realize, to remember, that I put all that stuff in there, that I actually did that. I didn't know why the world didn't beat a path to my door. There's a lot of great stuff there. Just kidding, just kidding.

Solotaroff: I'm baffled by Lu Anne's statement about how there is only one love.

Stone: By that she means a great sort of space. What I'm thinking of is a great space to fall through. What's on her mind is the phrase "to *fall* in love," which is an abyss, which is that one kind of space of love and destruction, Eros and Thanatos. There's just one love. It's close to saying it's death. It's destruction. It's darkness. It's just one big void. There aren't all these indi-vidual things, these individual emotional attachments. That's just an illusion.

Solotaroff: The great continuum of the liebestod?

Stone: It is a liebestod, but it's a liebestod seen by people who know what

Tristan and Isolde don't know, that this is all a much bloodier business. I find myself very moved to come back and think about what was on my mind when I was doing this. I wish others would have read the book as closely as you did.

Solotaroff: By the way, this is the first novel that doesn't have a line of Hopkins in it. You said somewhere that you got some Hopkins in each novel.
Stone: No, I don't remember any.

Solotaroff: Of course there's a lot of Shakespeare in it.
Stone: Oh, yes.

Solotaroff: One thing I particularly enjoyed in *Hall* was that great line of Rheinhardt's: "Defend me friends; I am but hurt." That's Claudius; he's identifying with Claudius! That's wonderful. But getting back to *Children of Light*, to Lu Anne, on the one hand, initiating the pig shit fight with Walker; on the other, her attempt to scrub off the blood and pig shit. Are these her attempts to get back to Yeats's foul rag and bone shop of the heart where all poetry begins—her wanting out of this human mire?
Stone: Yes. Another Yeats line that crossed my mind was "Love has pitched his mansion in [/ the place of] excrement." ["Crazy Jane Talks with the Bishop"]

Solotaroff: Could you say a bit about your acting career?
Stone: It was never much. I studied acting for a while at Hagen and Berghoff when I first got out of the Navy. I did a few shows. I never really had much time for it. The last thing I did was to go with some acting friends to the Santa Cruz Shakespeare Festival, and the director asked me if I would read, if I had any experience. I said yes, and he asked me if I would read for Kent.

Solotaroff: When was this?
Stone: 1983, I guess.

Solotaroff: And how long did it last?
Stone: All summer. So I was in *Lear*, and of course was on stage so much since Kent is. That was a very strange production because it had actors from all over—classically trained actors, soap opera actors from television, people who had to have it explained to them what the lines meant. But *Lear* is bottomless, bottomless. To have all these people take on Shakespeare whose

educational backgrounds were altogether different, to have everybody subjected to trodding on the crust of the abyss with Lear was really very interesting. It just subsumes everybody's life. It goes on and on, and the more you do it the more it begins to kind of dwarf you. It becomes your alternative life. This seemed to apply to everybody no matter how distant their past was from Shakespeare. By the time the show was over nobody knew what to do with themselves at that hour, at eight o'clock at night. People were just gathered together and thinking, "What will become of us?"

What seems to me to be the absolute center of Shakespeare and of the English language, is when Edgar playing Tom comes up to Lear, and Lear is hallucinating. Lear says, "Thou art the thing itself. Unaccommodated man is no man is no more than such a poor, bare, forked creature as thou art." The thing itself; that to me is the center of all English literature, that confrontation of man with man. The moment when man in his self-revelation becomes more tragic and more noble than God because of that self-confrontation and recognition, of men by men. It's like a great moment of enlightenment. In all literature, it stands like this electric discovery.

Solotaroff: You review fairly consistently. Could you say something about how you feel about that string in your bow?

Stone: I don't think I always do a good job. Sometimes I think I'm good when I write about a very established writer whose reputation I don't think I can affect. I like what I've written about Graham Greene. Did you read that review?

Solotaroff: Yes, that was really written with a pen of fire.

Stone: I have a great hatred for Greene's work. I did a review of Bruce Chatwin's last novel I feel good about.

Solotaroff: You mean the attack upon the aestheticism of *Utz*?

Stone: Yes. Otherwise I think I tend to overpraise, get enthusiastic, and end up somewhat displeased with the results. There are a number of things I respond to in my teaching; what I believe about basic rhetoric and writing. I don't always apply them consciously when I'm writing a review. I tend to take a kind of nondirectional approach which might not necessarily be the best approach.

Solotaroff: Could you say just a little bit about the origins of *Outerbridge Reach*?

Stone: One of the origins is that one of the incidents occurred in an around-the-world solo race in the 1960s, where a guy was going to fake his position and not sail around the world and say he did. You can't do that anymore because of the satellites, but what I have happen here is the satellites break down. There's a phrase in *Job* where one of Job's comforters says to him, "The spheres are set round about; the abundance of waters covers thee. Thou sayest, 'How shalt God know? The clouds are a covering to him that seeth not as he walketh the circuit of heaven.'" The satellite is down; nobody sees what's going on. That incident always stayed with me. It struck me as an amazing existential incident. But that was in England, and this is in America. And, as you will see, this is another triad, two guys and a woman.

Solotaroff: As of now I can't see how Strickland and Browne can be in the same book—this sleazebag and this apparently austere fellow.
Stone: You will see; you will see. I hope you like it.

Solotaroff: I'm sure I will. Finally, just a few things about your movie work. Was it the case that after writing the screenplay for *A Hall of Mirrors* (which became *WUSA*) you became progressively appalled by what was being done to it?
Stone: Yes, I was progressively appalled, and when I saw the rough cut I really knew it was all over.

Solotaroff: The same sort of thing happened with what was done with your screenplay for *Dog Soldiers*, which became *Who'll Stop the Rain?*
Stone: No, *Who'll Stop the Rain?* was quite a different experience because I'd been burned the first time, and I was very wary. Karel Reisz is an extremely able and intelligent man, a man whom I really like and who really tried to do something special. Certainly we were fighting an uphill struggle. There were changes that had to be made; and then I started separating myself from the project. But I really liked the performances, and I especially liked Nick Nolte, who is a reader. I just sent him *Giants in the Earth*. A friend of mine wrote a script of it, and he hadn't read the book. Nolte sat down and read *Dog Soldiers*. He's a reader, which is quite uncommon among film actors. I saw his copy, which was underlined; he really got into his character. His performance, I think, is really good, and there are other good performances too. So I don't feel the same way, even though they changed the title.

Solotaroff: To support the dopey song.
Stone: I know. Hollywood dopeyness.

Solotaroff: Of course the movie lost a lot of social resonance, much of *Dog Soldiers*' critique of the counterculture, because when Hicks and Marge get to Dieter's, there's nobody there. Did you originally have Dieter and his son in the screenplay?
Stone: They were there, all right.

Solotaroff: Well, Osric has spent all his golden coins.

Talking Sense

Steven Benson and Robert Solotaroff / 1992

KUOM, Minneapolis, radio interview on 1 May 1992. Reprinted by permission of Robert Solotaroff.

Robert Solotaroff graciously sent me a tape, a rough transcript of the interview, and corrected my draft. Almost all the interview was preserved.

Benson: Steve Benson back with *Talking Sense* with regular guest Dr. Robert Solotaroff, professor of English, here at the University of Minnesota.

Solotaroff: Following the lead you gave in that piece by Bruce Weber in the October *New York Times Magazine*, you referred to the English sailor, Donald Crowhurst, who had actually done what the protagonist of *Outerbridge Reach* does, that is try to hide out between the coasts of South American and Africa and pretend that he's sailing around the world in this circumnavigation race and not do it. Do you think a book at all close to *Outerbridge Reach* could have been written had you not come across Ron Hall's and Nicholas Tomalin's *The Strange Last Voyage of Donald Crowhurst*?
Stone: Yes, I think it could have, but that situation just seemed so right. When I read it originally in the London *Times* twenty years ago or more now, twenty-five years ago, it just seemed like such a wonderful example of the connection between heroism and folly which are never too far separated. Often the line between them is very fine.

Solotaroff: Crowhurst of course was this wildly extroverted life of the party type, a kind of roaring boy of the pubs, who was reportedly drummed out of the Royal Air Force for driving a motorcycle through his mates' sleeping quarters. Could you talk a bit about how and why in your version you hit upon Browne, whose only public manner is that of the naval officer, who is such an introverted type?

Stone: Well, because I wasn't all that taken with who Crowhurst himself was or Crowhurst's individual circumstances. The human dimension of the story is wonderful, but it was more the universal aspect than the particular world of Crowhurst that interested me. It seemed to me that the points I wanted to make are not necessarily the same points that are brought to the fore by the people who handled the Crowhurst story. I wanted to illustrate a theme of mine, which is how difficult it is for people to behave well and how even a good person in certain circumstances can trap himself in something like a lie. In a way he ends up being undone by his own honesty, and he makes the discovery at one point; he actually says, "the truth is my bride." Of course he has to find this out the hard way. So I had my own agenda, very much my own agenda, but I really loved the idea of someone reducing their circumstances to the ocean and the sky and the boat and of course their own mind, and having to live it out to the most intense degree.

Benson: You've talked about finding the soundings or getting the soundings of a character. Major characters in the novel are Ron Strickland, a documentary filmmaker, his prostitute friend Pamela, Owen Browne, Anne his wife, and Maggie. Could you talk a little bit about soundings?

Stone: I think you have to discover something about your character as you go along. You start with a situation and a handle on the principle characters. I think there are three things necessary for me to undertake a novel: one is the situation the people are in; another is the characters themselves, what they're like; and then usually I have a scene in mind toward the end. Once I get a fix on the characters, it's then time for me to bring them to some kind of life, psychic and verbal existence. This is a process, what I call soundings, the discovery of the dimensions of the character, is something like an impersonation. It's less like being possessed by a spirit than it's like acting. It's as though you do the voice, you impersonate the character, you take on the character's psychology and mentality. You speak with the character's voice. And as you do this you discover leitmotifs and your prose will take on a certain quality of sensibility. The savor of the prose will reflect what the person is like and this is an ongoing discovery, and so that's what I meant when I talked about soundings. Some characters are a lot harder than others.

Benson: Who are the hard ones in this book?

Stone: Without question, Owen Browne, who is an introvert, who is not given to storytelling; he's not a raconteur; he's a man who in a way disguises the intensity of his inner life to the world. His dialogue is not particularly individually colorful; he's not a master of words in the way Strickland is. He's a quiet, introverted man who's been raised in a way to keep his own confidence. Also, he's a difficult guy, with rough edges; he's the kind of guy who even though he's conventionally good looking and has a beautiful wife, he doesn't get a good table at a New York restaurant. He's a guy who at first glance looks okay but there's something of the wrongo about him. He's very complicated, and it was hard to get him into the book and also to keep all the other characters from using up the oxygen.

Solotaroff: Between the Gnostic struggles and the sea lore, the radical questions of *Outerbridge Reach*, I'm sure a fair number of critics have been referring to this book as Melvillean in different ways. I think of Melville's essential plot, in a way, as if someone's skating along, just skating along, and then falls through into a different, very terrifying world. Now of course as soon as Browne imitates someone headed further to the east when he's already turned west, things are happening, but I was wondering if you meant the place for him to fall through. If you did, it was when he's holed up on the island and goes into that house and mistakes a chair with some clothes on it for a woman, then crabs come crawling down from it, and then as he looks through the window: "Finally, broken-willed, he consented to turn, dreading the thing that might confront him in the window. There, in place of the declining sun, he saw innumerable misshapen discs stretched in limitless perspective to an expanded horizon. It was a parody of the honest mariner's sighting. Each warped ball was the reflection of another in an index glass, each one hung suspended, half submerged in a frozen sea. They extended forever, to infinity, in a universe of infinite singularities. In the ocean they suggested, there could be no measure and no reason. There could be neither direction nor horizon. It was an ocean without morning, without sanity or light." And on you go with this doctrine of particularities.
Stone: This is what he's looking at, what he's stood against all his life, and also what has always threatened him. He thought by trying to deceive the world about his precise location, in such a precise way, by trying to hide himself on the grid of the world, he's performed an act against all measure, and against all proportion. There's something almost blasphemous for him about pretending to locate the sun at an angle that it isn't at. It's as though he's creating a universe with this deception which is utterly without order, which consists of singularities—in other words, where things happen that have no relationship to each other, where anything can happen and there

are no laws, not even physical laws. Everything that happens is a singularity. Nothing is predictable. Nothing can be defended against. It's the world with a vengeance, an absolutely arbitrary, godless, meaningless, unfathomable world in which he has located himself.

Benson: And created this individual. Back to Ron Strickland, who is the filmmaker, and the idea of film as control, creating reality and putting it on celluloid.
Stone: Strickland ends up in the ironic position of being the person who understands all this better than anyone. He begins with his usual attitude, which is to expose the difference between what people say they're doing and what they're really doing. He, too, sees himself as a disciple of truth in a way. This is his squared-up way of defending what he does. He likes to quote Raleigh and say that he who follows truth too close by the heels shall strike out his teeth—which he has reason to reconsider later. He also has his own obsessions. He has his claim on authenticity.

Benson: And part of what he has to do is to worm his way into Browne's family—into his wife, his daughter.
Stone: Yes, this is what he's often done with the subjects of his documentaries. He presents himself as a sympathetic observer and makes himself agreeable in order to trap people into relaxing their guard so that he can expose them as poseurs and absurdities.

Solotaroff: One of your great strengths as a novelist is your control of your dialogue. I'm struck by the practical problems of a writer with a protagonist alone in a boat. Thus, for example, Hemingway will have Santiago have his right hand talk to his left hand; he'll talk to the birds, talk to the fish. One of the things you do is to bring aboard that wonderful missionary [radio] station from Africa to provide different voices coming in, and to have Browne, of course, responding, sometimes unwillingly sobbing, cursing. Have you ever heard a station like that?
Stone: There is such a station. It transmits from various places. It used to originate on the island of Bonaire in the Dutch West Indies, and it covers just about the entire earth. They broadcast to a large extent to seamen, and they broadcast in Tagalog and Cantonese and English. They do these dramatizations, and the actors who do it are not professional actors. They're a very mixed lot. And the English speakers are various Africans, British,

Canadians, Americans. You get this mixture of accents of spoken English from all over the English-speaking world, and it's quite fascinating to listen to this woman of whom we have been speaking. It's geared really for people in the Third World. I mean, they're speaking to people in Africa. This sometimes makes the Biblical situation tremendously relevant when they're talking about goats and sheep and camels. They're addressing a situation that is close to the one that people are living in—tribe against tribe, stuff in the Old Testament. It's something that is right there in the lives of the people they're broadcasting to. So it's sometimes very moving.

Benson: I want to talk a little bit more about that fascination that almost anyone who's been in an oceangoing ship—the idea of going in swimming and then watching that sheet rush by and whether to grab it or not.

Stone: It's funny; a lot of people who haven't sailed really find it difficult to believe that somebody sailing alone would do such a thing. Just trail a line and go swimming around at the risk of missing the boat. The fact is that in the Doldrums, where the forward motion is minimal, people do it all the time. It's very commonly done.

Solotaroff: This image of Browne afloat in the water . . . at different times, as I read *Outerbridge Reach*—is it in *Fear and Trembling*? one book by Kierkegaard—where he speaks of faith as being afloat in 25,000 leagues of water, I wondered if you thought of this at all as you were writing this because of course if Browne could be a good party believer in the missionary station and believe in God, then the particularities would all be interconnected.

Stone: I did think about that. There are so many references to religious literature, the literature of religion that feature analogies to a boat. That's why boats and the ocean get you into big questions right away. I really have him deliberate on religious matters. I could have gone farther with this, but I wanted to leave it where it was. He's a resolute nonbeliever, but he's also inclined toward belief. This is one of the things that's going on with him. When he hears his father's voice, when he's thinking about his father, when his father teases him: " . . . are you going over to religion?" and he sort of resists that. But of course this is what's on his mind. The solitude is talking to him. The difficulties of his situation are driving him in search for answers.

Solotaroff: One line I missed, when you had Browne think of his father's "black, unlucky face."

Stone: "Smiling, unlucky face."

Benson: Because you referred to that wonderful, nineteenth century poem, "Invictus."

Stone: Yes, yes, yes. "Out of the night that covers me / Black as the pit." I think that I say something about the black pit. Something like the pit that he was in was so black that he ceased to be a man at all. He says that he remembered his "unlucky, smiling face."

Benson: There's that reference, too, to the shark shadow. In other novels you've written about that, how suddenly the whole sea seems to be aware of this terror.

Stone: I'm a scuba diver too. I used to do quite a lot of that, and in *A Flag for Sunrise* there's a place where he senses this happening on the reef. Something's out there.

Benson: You have a wonderful taste for absurdity, and you quote at one point the opening lines of *The Midshipman's Book*.

Stone: Yes, *The Bluejacket's Manual*: "The sea is not inherently dangerous but it is extremely unforgiving." That's a paraphrase. That's so true—the unforgivingness, the not getting a second chance.

Solotaroff: A while ago I came across a big picture synthesis of your career. I've been struck with the profound impression that St. Ann's orphanage had, with its terribly unjust authority with five to nine year olds pitted against it. It occurred to me that in the first three of your novels, one character after another in each book is pitted against unfairly powerful, often sadistic authority. Then in your fourth book, *Children of Light*, no malign, external force is needed. The two characters do each other in all by themselves. By the fifth book the character will be undone, Browne will. Although he has his troubles, he's not damaged to the degree that earlier protagonists were. It's almost as if you worked your way free, throughout your career, from that reshaping of St. Ann's. Is that totally around the bend?

Stone: One tries to get a handle; one tries to get in control. If you spent some of your childhood feeling completely out of control and pitted against forces at whose mercy you were. . . . I'm still tremendously angry. I've never been able to get away from that. I just never stopped being angry about that, I now realize.

Solotaroff: Bob's referring to the Catholic orphanage—actually a day school which took boarders, which he attended between the time he was six and almost ten.

Benson: There's a section in your book, a wonderful sense of dialogue, Robert, that talks about Strickland's childhood, during which his mother supposedly worked in a circus. If you'd just read a couple of paragraphs. [Stone reads dialogue in which Strickland talks about theatrical hotels.] Was that part of your childhood?

Stone: Yes, I lived with my mother in SROs, in various cities, mostly New York. In those days they weren't such buckets of blood as they later became. There was a wide range of people living there. There were some addicts and down-and-outers, but there were also a lot of old people on pensions who didn't have much money and then sort of out-of-work marginal, theatrical people and old vaudevillians and people like that. It was really kind of interesting. It wasn't a great hardship if you were used to it. The bathroom was always down the hall. I never had my own bathroom until I got married. Between St. Ann's and the hotels I lived in and the Navy, the bathroom was always down the hall somewhere or down the passageway. I was about to say maybe that's why I got married, but I'd be in big trouble with my wife if I say that.

Benson: That sense of the child who is a little out of sync, and the mother who is out of sync, where the child is helping to take care of the mother, trying to come to grips with the world, comes across in that passage.

Stone: I borrowed some. There is a way in which Strickland's childhood has resemblances to mine.

Solotaroff: One thing that struck me was that once again in *Outerbridge Reach*, as with your second and third novels, the protagonists have been powerfully affected by serving in Vietnam for a while, and I wondered if you felt that Browne's attempt to justify his participation in Vietnam was a sort of prelude to his imaginatively living a lie, faking his position.

Stone: One thing that he had to do in Vietnam, and it was one of the novel's ironies, was that while he'd been serving with the tactical air squadron what he'd be doing there is coordinating carrier strikes. He'd be really as close as he possibly could to the target, and he'd be sort of talking the strikes in, which is dangerous and demanding work. It calls for coolness and so forth. And he'd be proud of what he did, though he could never talk about it because it was all very classified. They picked him because, although in a way some people spot him as a wrongo, he's presentable and well-spoken, so they made him a briefing officer in Saigon. So it became his task to conduct what were called in Saigon "the Friday Night Follies," which was the press briefing. They were often conducted by officers who were well groomed and well spoken, and Browne, my character, becomes one of these officers. Of course very often he had to misrepresent things, and their attempt to misrepresent things was extremely transparent—they weren't kidding anybody. And very often the officers didn't really know how much truth there was, especially when they got into statistics like body counts, which irritated everyone. Everyone knew that lurking behind the statistics was, first of all, the ineffectiveness of the military effort and then a lot of needless killing of civilians, for you couldn't tell combatants from noncombatants in that situation. So it was a really uncomfortable lie for everybody concerned. Of course he was drafted into the situation.

Benson: In other interviews you talked about your own stint in Vietnam and realizing that things were terribly, terribly wrong.
Stone: Yes, to somebody of my generation who was a child during the Second World War and in the postwar world that America dominated, to see this enormous mistake, ten thousand miles long; all these people, all these personnel, all this equipment—all of it—being thrown into an effort that at the point that I was there everybody knew was unavailing. It was shocking.

Solotaroff: So Browne, for example, might have been ten miles from a bombing target?
Stone: Well, he might have been even closer than that in certain circumstances, and he's also working with a whole lot of sensors, a whole lot of electronic stuff. He's supervising a bunch of technicians. In a way he's a kind of intelligence officer. He could be working very close to the target. He'll have one guy come in and drop yellow smoke, and then he'll direct guys toward the smoke. This was often done after the local Vietnamese authorities had certified an area as not having any civilians but being entirely the province of the enemy. Of course these okays from the Vietnamese became a kind of alibi. The ARVIN, the South Vietnamese officer, who was saying it, he hadn't been there; he didn't know who was there. Maybe his brother-in-law whom he hated was there, but this finally became good enough for the American military authorities. "Okay," they'd say, "its' a free fire zone. So we can consider anything in it a legitimate target."

Solotaroff: So the rigidity that Browne shows dealing with that woodworker—the man who was making the cabinets for his boat, where he tells the guy he has no right to say a word about Vietnam and angers him so—did you mean this to be a kind of fatal rigidity which was not going to serve him well?

Stone: He was unable to not say that. I really got on both sides of the argument, but I was probably more looking at it through Browne's eyes because in a way it's the woodworker who's the most rigid person. He's an absolutely convinced believer, and he drives Browne to being in his most overbearing mode, his most moralizing and overbearing mode. The two of these guys get into this impossible confrontation where they're both very rigid. They're both convinced they're right. It's the immovable object and the irresistible force, and of course it costs Browne a great deal.

Solotaroff: The title particularly fascinated me because I was born in Elizabeth, New Jersey, about four miles from the southeast corner of Staten Island, so I am particularly interested in *Outerbridge Reach*. Apart from the iceberg looking like one of the tugs that Browne's father-in-law would have there, I couldn't figure out why you chose that title. It's a wonderful name, but why did you choose that as a title?

Stone: It really meant a lot to me. I was going down the Arthur Kill, doing a travel piece for the *New York Times* on the harbor. There was a supplement called "The World of New York." Everybody did one aspect of New York, and I did the harbor. And when I saw on the chart . . . it was a late November afternoon, almost sundown, there was this old yard called Woody's, full of skeletons of all these old steam tugs piled on each other so that the proportion was lost, and because the shape they were in, the old straight, instead of raked stacks, and straight up and down cabin—they looked like little kids' bathtub toys. They were all piled on each other. And on the other side was a tank farm, oil storage tanks, almost as far as you could see. Then in the middle of the reach these blue herons were feeding. It was on one hand a kind of marine landscape, and it was a blighted landscape at the same time. And I thought, "Outerbridge Reach," it just to me suggested so many different things. It suggested a crossing; it suggested extending, stretching, trying for something, trying to get across something. All the weight of the name came with me. It was coming on that chart that made me decide to put down what I was working on and write this.

[Stone reads of how the sight of returning salmon brings Browne to tears, "They had won out over time and the ocean. They had survived everything and come home."]

Solotaroff: This is a recurrent theme of yours. Browne at one point weeps at the thought of a blessedly awaited return. And I remember how moved Geraldine is in your first novel—that line from the *Ancient Mariner*.

Stone: "Like stars that are certainly expected, yet there is a silent joy in their arrival."

Solotaroff: That sanctuary or harbor that is denied. In the opening two pages of the book, Browne tries to escape from his winter doldrums by going on a one-man sail from New York Harbor to Annapolis, Maryland. But he is using a new boat of his company—the Altan Marine Corporation, it's a Highlander Forty-Five—and it turns out there's shoddy workmanship, and he has to turn it in. Now of course he will be undone in his round-the-world sail by the fact that they have used just—what?—steel wire instead of stainless steel tie-rods, and the boat is breaking up. He has to turn back and so on. Many other people say, "Well, stock boat, who knows how it's built?" Was it just his crazy ambition to do something like this which made him not question the reliability of the boat?

Stone: The problem for him was that he's in the business of praising these boats, and he really talks himself into the position where he believes the boat's a good boat, in a way that a good salesman sometimes does this. Even though he has his doubts, he represses his doubts. He's been writing up these boats in the catalog, and the fact is he doesn't know as much about boats as he thinks he does. Like a lot of people who sail something for a living, he can talk a good game, but he doesn't know that much about it. And of course the particular boat he gets is a knockoff. The worst thing about it is that if you don't keep a crew on twenty-four hours and the laminate cools on the fiberglass, it just doesn't get the suitable laminations, and it isn't going to hold up to extreme conditions. You have to keep the laminate hot; you can't let it cool. And what they'll do in the Orient sometimes, they'll keep one crew on, and the guys will work sixteen hours. But then they'll have to go home, and they won't come back. In the meantime the laminate will cool. The way to do it right is to keep adding the laminate around the clock. It stays hot. It isn't allowed to cool between the layers of fiberglass.

Benson: I'd like to ask you to talk just a little about the dilemma of Anne, caught between these two rather extraordinary individuals.

Stone: She's taken by surprise at the intensity of her own feelings. Like a lot of people who have made their own accommodation with life and never question their own assumptions and their own situation, she's just astonished at what happens—the way she finds herself drawn to Strickland and the outcome of it. She has not guarded against this in any way because she hasn't been aware that it was happening to her, that she was falling for this guy, and it had not occurred to her that she would do this. She in a way is in the same position that Browne is in. She finds all of a sudden that it is much more difficult for her to behave in a right way, in what she believes to be the right way, than she would have expected. She finds it much easier than she would have imagined to violate her own moral principles. It is a situation which illustrates my doctrine of the difficulty of behaving well and the readiness with which we find ourselves falling through and doing things we would not have believed that we might do.

Solotaroff: Yet in this book you have an empowered person who consistently behaves well with Harry Thorne. I've never seen anything like it in your earlier books: someone who has power and who uses it well or as well as he can and is intelligent and sensitive—amazing.

Stone: He has a certain function here. There's a level on which he's kind of like Shakespeare's Shylock. What Shylock represents in *The Merchant of Venice*—being a hermetic play, it's full of hermetics—and it isn't Shakespeare trying to be anti-Semitic because Shakespeare just didn't know any individual Jews—there were none in England. What Shylock really represents is the law without charity, the Christian take on the pre-redeemed world. Shylock stands for the law, and the law without mercy. In a way, Harry is financing this argosy. Harry at a certain point refers to the argosies of the characters whose voyages he's financing, so he's like Shylock in a way, but not like Shakespeare's Shylock but like Boris Tomashevsky's Shylock. This is how I see him. I see him as a figure of rectitude, of embattled rectitude. I see him also when he says, "Well, I was always a sucker for the old white shoe routine." His situation is a little bit like Shylock's with the Venetian aristocrats. And this is kind of what we see. I see him as a kind of religious man although I don't go into this. I see Harry Thorne as being religious.

Solotaroff: So this street toughness, putting his finger on Strickland as "That stuttering prick"—very funny.

Benson: The figure of Pamela is fascinating to me. She's a person who has street smarts but she's blown her mind on drugs. You presumably knew lots of people like that.

Stone: Yes, I've known a few.

Benson: When you look back in your biography, people always refer to the time you spent with Ken Kesey.

Stone: Yes, there weren't too many literary reverberations to that experience, but I think I learned a few things about relativity and the varieties of experience and the qualities of reality. Above all, it was lots of fun, and I wouldn't have missed it.

Benson: You said in one interview that you learned that time is the only commodity that an author has.

Stone: I think you learn that every day in a way, and it's certainly true. That's your capital.

Benson: Your three different homes are three different ways of looking at the sea.

Stone: Down in the Keys you're looking at this beautifully colored aquamarine water which is very often unruffled because it's protected by a coral reef and then Block Island where you're looking at the open ocean and the waves crashing in and then along the shore of Long Island Sound where that also is different—that's protected water.

Solotaroff: Again I'm fascinated with the different ways in which you're using dual concealment—the relationship between God and man and concealment. In *Flag*, there's Father Egan, lamenting why do you hide your face with me, *eli sabactani*, but here you're playing with that thing from the Book of Job with the human being trying to conceal himself from God; as I remember in Job, which you quoted, it's as if God cannot see through the clouds.

Stone: In that passage of Job, this is what the wicked say, "the clouds are a covering to him, he seeth not." But this is a mistake. This is the reasoning of the wicked. They're wrong about that. I happened to be reading Aquinas; there's one Aquinas argument where he cites this text in Job. Okay, what is Aquinas looking at Job for? This is the passage: "sudden fear troubleth thee or darkness, that thou canst not see; an abundance of water covers thee. Is not God in the height of heaven? And behold the height of the stars, how high they are, and thou sayest how doth God know? Can he judge through the dark cloud? The clouds are a covering to him that he seeth not, and he walketh in the circuit of heaven. So this is what thou sayest?" This is one of Job's comforters telling him why he's in trouble, or why he might be in trouble is because he's reasoned this way, though of course he hasn't. But I mean Browne is very much like Job. If Strickland is the Satan figure in the Job story—he comes in and in a way he's saying, "Well, Browne is a man of rectitude, but give his life over to me; the man of rectitude with a faithful wife, deliver these people into my hands for a while. I'll show you that they're not so great." So he's a tempter. He's the tempter in Job. He's the tempter of Genesis.

Solotaroff: As Browne heads into outer insanity, he's listing all these human sins and says God's only sin is hiding Himself. It's very moving.
Stone: Concealment.

Benson: There's that one terrifying moment for Strickland, though, when he feels that he's about to lose Anne. He's controlled this entire situation. He's the filmmaker. He's the controller, and yet there's this one appalling moment when he realizes he may lose her.
Stone: He really doesn't want this to happen. Then he's bought into this barrel of fun that's no fun. Then he's stuck. They're all finally chained together in this thing.

Benson: Presumably this is the kind of book lots of filmmakers would like to get their hands on, depending on how much control they would have.
Stone: That's right. This would very likely be a director's picture. These days, books tend to be snapped up by actors who see themselves in a given role. We'll just see what happens. There is certainly some interest in the picture business about *Outerbridge Reach*. We'll wait and see.

Solotaroff: You said before that some names had been mentioned for castings.
Stone: William Hurt and Harrison Ford were a couple of actors who were having a look at it. Jonathan Demme and Karel Reisz were among the directors.

Solotaroff: Those are fine directors.
Stone: Those *are* fine directors. We'll just see.

Benson: In the past, you didn't have that much control over it. Is there any way that you and your agent can work to control this, or is it that when the rights are gone, they're gone?

Stone: Well, it's like selling a horse. When you sell the horse they can do what they want with it. If they want to shoot it, they can shoot it.
Solotaroff: Take your book to the knackers.

Benson: You just finished editing a book of short stories. What are some of the criteria you use for short stories? What are some of the things you look for?
Stone: A good short story speaks for itself. I look for intensity with economy, felicity of language, memorable characters, a situation that involves the reader—all these things that short stories can provide when they're well done.

Solotaroff: I know someone who has edited one of those said that he found himself restricted by the selection he got from the woman who continually oversees them. Was that the case with you, that you had to step outside?
Stone: I did go outside. I didn't restrict myself to the hundred and twenty that were sent to me. I think all my final selections were from that lot.

Interview with Robert Stone

Michael Silverblatt / 1992

Reprinted by permission of Bookworm, KCRW-FM, and Michael Silverblatt.

Silverblatt: My guest today is Robert Stone, the author most recently of *Outerbridge Reach* published by Tickner & Fields, as well as *Children of Light*, *A Flag for Sunrise*, *Dog Soldiers*, and *A Hall of Mirrors*. I want to leap into the fray right away. It seems as if the subject of heroism passed over a generation of American writers, that when American writing was dominated, say, by Nabokov et. al. certain kinds of what used to be called the larger themes were escaping fiction, and those seem to be your dominant concerns. The argument back then was that fiction couldn't really solve these problems, and therefore could only patrol its own territories. Could you speak a little bit about heroism?

Stone: Heroism and the idea of it in America are full of ambiguities. I think there's a way in which the United States from its founding has resisted the idea of heroism. The military ideal in this country is very different from the military ideal abroad. For example, the great model was Cincinnatus. The idea was of someone who was a peaceable man who would put his plough aside and be a hero on the field of battle. In fact, there is a very, very strong resistance to the heroic mode, to acting out heroic postures. I think this is partly because of the origins of the country in sensibleness. Its foundation by merchants and mechanics and farmers. The traditional heroic mode is, on a certain level, despised here. It's one of the reasons why people in Latin America and Europe profess such distress with us.

Silverblatt: It is an interesting thing to me because in your fiction there is a paring that I don't find elsewhere. You may be the only writer I know who creates cerebral and violent men. Cerebral violence: it's almost as if by the time you're getting to your novel this man who lays down his plough and goes out onto the field of battle is someone who doesn't quite remember how to work the plough and doesn't know where the field of battle is. There's a kind of haziness of idealism. I wondered who these figures are now in contemporary life.

Stone: I don't know how much this ideal of Cincinnatus the part-time hero corresponds to reality. I think there's great resistance to the heroic mode because in a way, regardless of what we say, we've made a virtue of mediocrity to a large extent. There is great pressure on Americans not to distinguish themselves. This is reflected on the absurd and vulgar level of George Bush pretending to like pork rinds. This reflects something real. If we look for heroes today, certainly I don't think you're likely to find them in politics, and that's been true for a long time. We really do everything we can to eliminate people of any distinction on the level of public life. It's an impulse toward mediocrity which is not *wholly* a bad thing. Mediocrity has its positive side. Whatever we may say, we really try to diminish our public figures.

Silverblatt: From its earliest pages *Outerbridge Reach* seems to be about the disappearance of recognizable boundaries. In its very first pages winter has given way to a warmth that people attribute to the greenhouse effect. A boat starts to leak, one of the best boats, and friends say to one another as if it were a routine, or a commercial they were reciting, "Nothing works anymore." They all agree and seem to like saying this. It's about a world in which expected qualities have disappeared and been replaced by public relations and other kinds of similitudes.

Stone: That's true, and it is for that reason in the beginning of the book we have this sense of something wrong even with the weather. I really mean it to be a story of the nineties, and what my view of America in the nineties is keeps coming up in it. And my central character, one of my three major characters, Browne, is a man who has heroic longings. He feels as though there are circumstances which if he were matched with them he could prevail. He could satisfy himself and his dreams about himself, his own youthful dreams.

Silverblatt: In a funny way I think the question becomes where is the field of battle. And if a man wants to distinguish himself today, at least this man Owen Browne, he has to go out and face not an enemy but the void, the emptiness of the world ocean. It seems almost as if in his hallucinations and visions he's repopulating the world with islands, with terras incognitas so that he can almost reinvent a possible world for heroism before he parts from it.

Stone: I think that's what he's doing. He's a dreamer on one level who was raised on stories of late nineteenth century heroism. He thinks of [Sir Ernest] Shackleton and people of that mold. One of the phrases that we see coming up a lot is the old phrase of William James, "the moral equivalent of war." Browne is a man who saw some combat in Vietnam, and this awoke in him complicated impulses. He's not a war lover, but he really welcomed the opportunity to live as part of a larger cause. In a way, I think that phrase, "the moral equivalent of war," is an interesting one because it gets trotted out by politicians from time to time, but I don't think they realize what they're saying when they use it. What James said in the work that's called "The Moral Equivalent of War" was that if we are against war, which we must be if we want the world to continue to be a civilized place, then we don't want to see wars breaking out. But on the other hand, James said war does nevertheless bring out certain positive things—community, bravery, self-sacrifice, courage—all these things which are positive human attributes. Then William James suggested that if we as responsible people want to end wars we must somehow find something that is, as he said, the moral equivalent of war. Something that will not subject the world to the horrors of war, but at the same time will bring forth community and courage and things like that. In a way what Browne is looking for in this book is the moral equivalent of war.

Silverblatt: It's an interesting idea. I want to go back a little bit. The last time you and I met each other was at the time *Children of Light* had come out, and I had told you that I thought that in a very dark way it was a dispirited book, that the characters were engaged on a battleground of their own invention, their engagement was with their own fictions, and not with the world. I think in your own interest in reflecting America that was very much a time when people were inventing their own stories, unpropelled, unmotivated, unattached to any ostensible reality. It was a movie book, and genuinely so, with the hero and heroine—she fighting her own inner demons and hallucinations, he becoming Othello, becoming Hamlet, fighting through a series of roles, most notably Lear, that were never his own. What brought you back in the years between that book and this one is this engagement with the physical world. This is a man and the sea novel. It felt at least at that time like you might sink entirely into that internalized universe.

Stone: No, I don't think I was going to be condemned to stay there. I really wanted to do that book, *Children of Light*. I really wanted to do a work reflecting people who make enormous trouble for themselves. There was a time when I wanted to call that book *Death and the Maiden.* I mean the idea of the principle character, Gordon Walker, as a kind of questing knight who brought nothing but trouble with him, who came basically as a destroyer of this woman, whom he thought he loved—around whom he had constructed fantasies as she had to a degree constructed fantasies about herself. And their relationship to each other, their relationship to the movies that they both worked in, all these things were very much on my mind. But it was a book I needed to do at that time. Really I'm happy with it. I know that it was not universally well received, even by people who follow my work and like it, but I'm proud of it. I think it was a good book, but it was an excursion into mere interiority that did not address very much the concerns of the larger world. I would not have stayed with that subject. I really am too much interested in all the things you're not supposed to talk about like politics and religion to spend more than one book with people whose troubles were so discrete, so special to themselves.

Silverblatt: In the process of turning to this book was there a turning away from the other?

Stone: I don't think so, because this was a book where the difficulties of the individuals came very quickly to reflect all the big questions. For one thing it's a sea story, and sea stories by their very nature bring you into the big picture. They bring you up against elemental questions. Because the ocean is this enormous, unforgiving force, things that are true about the ocean, I think, tend to be true about life itself. With these people having to deal with the ocean, with a man reducing his life to a diagram of sky and sea and boat, I think automatically one is speaking in universals.

Silverblatt: Well, it's very interesting to me when I was reading in this book I remembered that story years ago in *American Review*, "Aquarius Obscured," in which the porpoise speaks and reveals universals to one of its watchers. I think it took this long for the sea to have its message given to one of your characters.

Stone: I always had a fascination with the sea, and that was my dealing with the whole thing on the level of the absurd. I think I have a mantra recited in the course of that story that goes "surrender to the notion of the motion of the ocean."

Silverblatt: That's right.

Stone: I was clowning around with that one, but I spent a lot of my young life at sea. It meant a lot to me, and I have a good time invoking it, writing about it, and thinking about it.

Silverblatt: I found myself thinking a lot about *Lord Jim* in the course of reading this book, especially toward its conclusion, and you've always had a deep relation to Joseph Conrad's work. What's your favorite Conrad? Mine is *The Secret Agent*. You seem more affiliated with the earlier, the Marlow stuff.

Stone: My favorite of them all is *Victory*. I really like Axel Heyst, and the storytelling process. I love *The Secret Agent*, too—that really is one of his very best—and at least the beginning of *Under Western Eyes*. I learned a great deal reading Conrad. I think anybody would learn a great deal. Of course you don't learn stylistic lessons from Conrad because his style is literally inimitable. You would have to have English as your third language to write like Conrad. But one of the things that he was interested in, one of the things that his life led him to was the state of an empire at the height of its power, that perhaps was going into some decline. This is something that he had intimate and first hand and upfront knowledge of as a sea captain. In a way my subject might be said to be the American imperium at the height of its powers, perhaps at the beginning of the waning of its relative power. I spent a lot of time at sea, so he really was the master to whom I went for notions of what the novel was supposed to be about. I think I learned a great deal.

Silverblatt: Conrad seems to me, after George Eliot, to be the great embodier of moral questions of what defines humanity and of the relationship of action to thought, which seem to me to be peculiarly your themes and themes that seem, in the wake of that nineteenth century novel we were speaking of and its heroism, to have disappeared. Some people would think of these themes as being wholly ambiguous, and in these days unembodiable in the action of a novel. That's why I always think primarily of Conrad. Hemingway, a bit, in that question of what is the morality of style, but Conrad principally.

Stone: Conrad was very concerned, really in a practical and fairly simply way, with heroism, and his notions of heroism were fairly conventional. They were certainly imperial virtues. In *The Secret Sharer*, of course, he has his captain, his character, defending another sea captain. He prevents the prosecution of another sea captain who killed a man who behaved in a cowardly way during a storm. So he really had a very hard code. He was

MICHAEL SILVERBLATT / 1992 **165**

not a particularly merciful sea captain. I don't think I would have liked to have shipped aboard one of his ships. I may admire his novels, but I don't think I'd want him to be captain over me. His sense of the heroic was fairly uncomplicated, and I suppose in a way it is an uncomplicated thing. I find myself certainly in this book speculating on physical courage, on its relationship to moral courage. I have a character say that while you can have moral cowardice along with physical courage you cannot really have moral courage without physical courage. I have a character maintaining this. I'm kind of inclined to think that that is a melancholy fact. I suspect from what I've seen it may be true. It's very hard for people to bring moral courage to bear if they don't have physical courage. I don't know why that should be true, but I suspect it might be.

Silverblatt: There are these characters in your work like Strickland in this book who take charge not of actuality but of representation and who are aware that things can be made to seem much more malignant and humiliating than they are. But the people who are at the mercy of characters like this eventually seem to become humiliated and weak. Do you take it then that representation, the whole media carnival that goes on in the misrepresentation of this boat and the misrepresentation of the race, of diaries and logs, actually physically corrupts the characters?

Stone: There's a way in which characters can be made to act in terms of what's expected of them. People who are aware of low expectations of themselves often fulfill the low expectations. I think that's something that does go on, and there is an obsessive ruthlessness about Strickland in his belief that everybody is on the con, that what anybody claims to be doing is not what they're really doing. I think with this character he sometimes hopes on some level that this might not prove to be true, but he really for the most part sees it as his job to expose this. He puts the people that he makes documentary films about in an impossible position because of course he controls not only what he films but also the way it's cut. So there is a way in which media attention can be corrupting. I don't think it's quite as simple as that, but there is a grain of truth in that, that there is a kind of media curse, a media whammy, that can be put on people who are trying to perform. I have someone in this book say, "you know there are two sorts of people: there are people who do things and then there are the people who follow them around trying to find out why they are imposters, why they're not really doing what they're claiming to do."

Silverblatt: You know what I miss after *A Hall of Mirrors*? I was thinking about it last night because people are comparing you again, I think for obvious reasons, with Melville. In *A Hall of Mirrors* you had a kind of cosmic vaudeville like *The Confidence Man* going on, but in the subsequent books there's been a harrowing naturalism that tries intentionally to stay away from the absurdo-comic. Hallucination enters only when the character hallucinates. The world is no longer hallucinatory in these books. How come? I miss the Grand Guignol.

Stone: Well I know what you mean. I think I moved toward it to some degree in this one. I have that level of hallucination, a level where the world threatens to become completely antirational and threatens to dissolve. There's a moment where whatever sense it makes threatens to disappear completely. But never since *A Hall of Mirrors* have I used a completely disintegrating world as I did in that book. There are characters in *A Hall of Mirrors* who for all we know may well be supernatural beings. There's a lot of nonrealism in it, and I've always seen myself not as a strict realist. I think there are sections in *Outerbridge Reach* that are also of questionable . . .

Silverblatt: Oh absolutely, but they accompany the disintegration of Owen's mind. There are reports of what he thinks he sees, whereas in *A Hall of Mirrors* the objective world had become a kind of shell game.

Stone: I may get back to that because you know there's a level on which that very much attracts me. I believe it's a true thing. You know the world sometimes does deconstruct itself in a way. I do this in my short stories. I go back to the mode of *A Hall of Mirrors* more in some of my short stories.

Silverblatt: The cover of this book—although I notice it's called "Hail and Farewell" and is from a print by Rockwell Kent—it does make me think of *Billy Budd*, a book to which it's been compared. Did you choose the cover?

Stone: I didn't choose it. It was chosen by John Herman, the editor. I had in mind a [Gustave] Doré drawing of the Ancient Mariner, which of course is very striking, but I have to say that I like this cover tremendously. It just seems as though it were made for this particular book. It just knocks me out.

Silverblatt: It is haunting.

Stone: Who knows exactly what it means, but there does seem to be an image of a man up in the shrouds of a boat and off in the distance there's a town. The narrative here moves between our main character at sea and his family back home.

Silverblatt: The figure cruciform as well, his eyes somewhat hooded, attired in what seems to be a shaft of celestial light, in the midst of moonlight, and the callipygian shapeliness that reminds me of Billy Budd, and in a novel that also has a stutterer, so I wondered if you'd talk about *Billy Budd* a bit.

Stone: *Billy Budd* is a great novel. In fact I do have somebody refer to Browne; Strickland, his rival for the affections of the principal female character, refers to Browne as the handsome sailor. So there are certainly echoes of *Billy Budd. Billy Budd* is a great work, and I've always been a great admirer of Melville, as is all the world I guess.

Silverblatt: It's a funny kind of question, and I've never had anyone to ask, the books that you write, do they begin in your mind as important novels? You and William Styron seem to be similar as novelists in that the importance of the subjects taken on and the seriousness with which they are engaged almost ensures a certain sobriety in the response to them as well. I wonder whether this is there at the inception of the book—I can't treat this, this is not important enough, its theme is not central enough.

Stone: I don't think I begin it with a sense of its being "important." I really start with the people. There are two things that I need to begin, and one is a sense of who the people are and usually then also the ending. But I try to do the voices, and I really enjoy philosophical and psychological complications. I put them in there because I enjoy them, and because one of the great pleasures of creating characters in writing a novel is putting people up against life. But I don't do it with any kind of premeditation that this is going to be an important book. With any book I'm writing, what I'm writing at the time, I take my pleasures where I find them, when I'm writing it. But I don't set out to write "important" books.

Silverblatt: And yet you manage to.

Stone: Well, I have a weakness for big questions.

Robert Stone on *Damascus Gate*

Robert Birnbaum / 1998

Reprinted by permission of Robert Birnbaum/Our Man In Boston.

It's highly unlikely that if you are reading this you are unaware (or unappreciative) of American novelist Robert Stone. For what it's worth, I rank Stone among a handful of living great American writers and have hungrily seized opportunities to chat with him—with the publication of *Outerbridge Reach*, *Damascus Gate*, *Bear and His Daughter* (his one story collection), and *Bay of Souls* (published in 2003). Rooting around various computer backup storage devices, I noted the conversation that follows, done around the time (Spring 1998) of his great Middle Eastern novel, *Damascus Gate*, and realized it has had only very limited circulation. A situation I am pleased to correct for Stone readers and admirers the world over.

Regarding *Damascus Gate*, the contemporaneous *New York Times* cover opined: "Reviewers have long praised Mr. Stone's ability to create richly detailed settings of hallucinatory or surrealistic sharpness, along with gritty verismo dialogue. *Damascus Gate*, in particular, many said, hauntingly conveyed the strange volatility of millennial Jerusalem, a considerable feat for an outsider. . . . How did Mr. Stone achieve it?

'I don't take a lot of notes,' he said. 'I absorb what I see. I don't remember details. You don't have to copy down like mad if you just get details right.'"

Characteristic of my various chats with Robert Stone, this one contains more than a fair amount of wisdom, insight, and big thoughts—"All the grief of the twentieth century has come from trying to turn life into art." Indeed!

Birnbaum: Your books have been set in New Orleans, Central America, Mexico, Hollywood, the Atlantic Ocean, Jerusalem. Is setting important to your writing?

Stone: Setting is very important. It's the theater where human fate, where human destiny, whatever you want to call it, is acted out. These are all very fateful places.

Birnbaum: Fateful?
Stone: Fate, yes.

Birnbaum: When Lucas [the main character in *Damascus Gate*] is talking to the mother of a drug addict, she says something about sending him to Israel so that he would be less tempted to extreme behavior. Lucas says, "Not tempted to extreme behavior here? Here, in the center of the world where earth touches heaven? Where the destiny of man was written? Where words of fire were made flesh? The prophecy uttered in remote millennia determined the morning? And the place once all we knew of God absconded, promised return, pretended return, promised messengers, whispered messages? Where the invisible wrote fate on stone? Eternally messages, promises. Next year. In the beginning." This suggests an investment in a place somewhat more than I remember about the other places you have written about.
Stone: Jerusalem is the place where earth touches heaven and is the mountain. It is the center of the world. It is more, as I came to realize when I spent more time there. Jerusalem is in a way the place I have been waiting to write about, and that I finally got to. Maybe it's the place I've been looking for.

Birnbaum: Are Israel and Jerusalem equivalents?
Stone: No, no. No.

Birnbaum: Your first acquaintance with Jerusalem was when?
Stone: The mid-eighties.

Birnbaum: And what brought you there?
Stone: I had been doing a travel piece in Egypt, and I had been in Egypt for months. We did a safari—my wife and I—in the Sinai. At that time, after the '75 war, Sinai was being returned bit by bit to Egypt, and we crossed the Egyptian army lines into the Israeli sector. Then we took a bus to Elat. In Elat we took a bus to Jerusalem, so we were arriving in Jerusalem in the morning. It was extraordinary. We had been in the desert for weeks already—and this is the same desert, a continuation of the desert—but we arrived in the

morning with the sun on that rosy-colored stone. As I got to know the city a little and I began to see the people, I said, "These are people I write about." This, in a way, is them being brought to the very place that stands for everything I have been writing about.

Birnbaum: You frame Israel as a mediocre place, and the irony of course is that this nation of seemingly—or not even seemingly—intelligent people—how did they manage to form something that was so mediocre?
Stone: Well, that is almost a cliché. That is a question that is asked so often that it is not original to me. It is the question that everybody asks, that Israelis ask all the time.

Birnbaum: Really? I never had a sense that they were that candid about themselves. The Israelis that I have met and the times I have been in Israel, I rarely found someone who was willing to be critical except about a politician.
Stone: Why do things look the way they look? Why is everything physically to the eye so indifferent? Why is the art so bad? The public art? Why does it all look so second-rate? This is part of the same question. Why is it like the government of some Eastern European country between the two wars?

Birnbaum: You refer to them as mediocre opportunists like the second-rate people in Eastern Europe.
Stone: Yes, well, Netanyahu, make what you will of him, he speaks for himself.

Birnbaum: What about Golda Meir, her concerns that Israelis were becoming like their enemies?
Stone: Well, it's her quote. "If the Arabs make us do this . . ." This is moral kitsch. This is again not original with me; I owe it to an Israeli journalist. I would like to claim it. I have no illusions about my being an outsider in every respect, but it is also a country I know a fair amount about and connect with.

Birnbaum: You're so ready to make the claim that you're an outsider? Israel is a nation of outsiders.
Stone: This is so. Well, maybe I'm anticipating.

Birnbaum: What are you anticipating?
Stone: I'm anticipating trouble.

Birnbaum: From the American Jewish community? Has *Damascus Gate* been published?

Stone: Yes, it is just out. It was just reviewed in the *New Yorker*. Actually, Daphne Merkin gave it an extremely favorable review, for which I am very grateful. I am responsible for my feelings and my attitudes. I know what they are, and I know how I feel about Israel. I know how I feel about the Jewish people. I will be responsible for that, and I don't need anybody to tell me how to feel or to interpret how I feel or to construe how I feel. I know how I feel. And so whatever flak I get, I feel honest about it. I am a friend of Israel. I am not an enemy of Israel. I am certainly not an enemy of the Israeli people or of the Jewish people. I know that perfectly well and so does everyone who knows me.

Birnbaum: I thought that you might have used the quote from the Kabbalah that "to tell the truth without sorrow is the greatest gift" as an epigraph to begin the book.

Stone: There are a great many epigraphs I could have used and didn't. I'm not sure about the one I did use, which is from Melville ["Enigma and evasion grow; / And shall we never find Thee out?"]. But yes, God, there are so many, so many statements in the Kabbalah and Zohar, and so forth. But I resisted, in a way. I thought I wouldn't invoke those words.

Birnbaum: There is a quote by a painter very late in the book, the unnamed painter.

Stone: Gosh, he's unnamed because I can't remember his name.

Birnbaum: "Losing it is as good as having it."

Stone: That absolutely wiped me out. He had a show in the Whitney together with Hopper, and I never forgot that.

Birnbaum: The quote was printed on the wall?

Stone: Yes. I thought that it was extremely wise.

Birnbaum: Tell me why you think it is true.

Stone: That which we have, we invariably somehow lose. And at the same time, it can't be taken away. That is what I take it to mean, and I take it as true.

Birnbaum: Are you satisfied with this book?

Stone: I am satisfied with it. It cost me everything but my sanity and maybe that, too.

Birnbaum: I noticed a page count difference between the advance reader's edition and the final hardcover.

Stone: I went over those proofs and made some changes. I had some mistakes in there. I tried to straighten them out.

Birnbaum: I spoke to you last spring or last summer, and you were still working on *Damascus Gate*. I don't know if you were two minutes away from finishing it or two months away—but maybe it's the same thing; you're not finished.

Stone: I am a lifetime away, it seems.

Birnbaum: What's the process when you finally submit the manuscript? It goes to your editor, an editor, and then it comes back to you . . . ?

Stone: And they say okay, and then it really goes. Then I work on it with Larry Cooper, the copy editor. I don't work much with a regular editor, but Larry is, as Philip Roth once said of him—he would marry him. Larry is the best, the best in the world.

Birnbaum: Is your fiction fact-checked?

Stone: To a degree—they'll say you can't have Passover and Easter the same day that particular year. You do a realistic novel; you can't take absurd liberties. If you're going to do a novel that is not "realistic," that is one thing. But if you're going to do a realistic novel, you have got to make it real. You've got to conform to the rules.

Birnbaum: You've said you feel that there is humor present in your writing. When I read this novel I did find a number of things I thought were funny, including your description of some explosives as a very sophisticated form of pasta. Is there humor here?

Stone: Yes, I think there is humor. What is the difference between the incidental funny things that happen between people and humor?

Birnbaum: In the context of something that is so fraught with the weight of the centuries and the really big questions, and people who are really in trouble, I think that that can overshadow the light things, the funny things.

Stone: I think it does, but there is no life without humor. There was never anywhere, I don't think, that people found themselves without a degree of humor. I think even in the lowest circle of hell.

Birnbaum: "All the grief of the twentieth century has come from trying to turn life into art." Big claim. Big sentence.
Stone: Yes.

Birnbaum: Can you say more?
Stone: Well, I think it is something you have to think about. But the aestheticization of the politics of ordinary life—of being able to wake up every day and be in the play, in a drama, in a political drama—this is what the twentieth century lived for. It is what destroyed civilizations that came before. This is what the communists and the Nazis and the fascists were all offering: be part of this drama, leave your commonplace life behind, and engage in this political drama. And the result was what we've seen.

Birnbaum: The bigger political movements and "isms" of our century were some form of performance art?
Stone: In a way, they descend from people like Wagner—Nietzsche and Wagner. Wagner, I think, was tremendously influential on Marx. Have you ever seen Pierre Chertraus's Marxist ring cycle? You can see how really close Wagner and Marx are. Marx once wrote a long narrative poem that ends with this Götterdämmerung. Walter Benjamin said this about fascism, but it was not only true about fascism. He said fascism is the aestheticization of politics. But it wasn't only fascism; it was all the "isms."

Birnbaum: The music that is mentioned in this book is, of course [from] the anti-Semitic British professor who plays things that are actually banned.
Stone: Orff is banned.

Birnbaum: Strauss is banned?
Stone: Strauss is banned. Not Wagner. But Orff and Strauss.

Birnbaum: How long is the list of banned music?
Stone: I don't know that it extends beyond Orff and Strauss. It is that those two really served the Nazi state. When Zubin Mehta conducted *Tristan and Isolde* at the Israeli symphony, there were demonstrators. But Wagner is not—it isn't played much, but it isn't banned.

Birnbaum: Quite a cast of characters that you put together here. Is anybody here beyond your overreaching sympathy for all human beings in trouble? Is there anyone you really were more fascinated by, more sympathetic to?

Stone: In a way I'd like to think I forgive everybody. I think you can read into the characters for whom I am sympathetic, and a number of people obviously who I am really fond of in this book.

Birnbaum: I couldn't grasp your sense of Zimmer. I am not sure you know he's hardly a . . .
Stone: He's a hard case. He descends in a way—if you remember the character Naftali, he is based on a real guy whom I have known for years. There is a character going to Naftali in *A Flag for Sunrise*. He is sort of like Zimmer.

Birnbaum: Right. Guys just show up. They've got a long, sad story; they have skill and survival.
Stone: And they're mean.

Birnbaum: And they're mean, right. They'll go on surviving. Indestructible. And they are employed by everybody: good guys, bad guys. You also quoted something that was from Cuba—"Have not to die . . ."
Stone: You have not to die, yes.

Birnbaum: The translation was, "You have not to die."
Stone: Yes, that's it . . . the good translation in English is, "What you've got to do is you've gotta not die." When I first handed in the proof, I had, "What you gotta do is you've gotta not kill," which is not the way it goes.

Birnbaum: You have these two half-breed main characters.
Stone: I don't know what you call them, Michelins, mongrels, all this; my family is full of them.

Birnbaum: We're all mongrels. Did you end up in any of the camps in Gaza?
Stone: Oh, yeah.

Birnbaum: Are they grim?
Stone: Yes. They are like Soweto. They are as grim as they could possibly be. They are as grim as anything on earth. 700,000 people—it's truly ghastly.

Birnbaum: Any hope?
Stone: Ever since the beginning they have been trying to make the Egyptians take it. All the Egyptians need is 700,000 more inflamed Islamic extremists, so they are saying, "No thanks." I don't know what will happen

there because they go on having kids. . . . The Israelis kind of played one faction against the other, and they used it for. . . . It was Desolation Row for the Israelis. Dope and guns and so forth. Everything that was conceivably useful, you could always find a guy down in the Gaza Strip who was your guy. It was like the CIA having assets in Mexico or something. And they are terrible, bad guys, but they're my guys and I use them.

Birnbaum: Giving them no shot at a superior moral standing since the Israelis are running people like everyone else is running people. Are you done? You said that you've been wanting to write about Jerusalem for a long time, and now you've done it. Now what?
Stone: Well, you always go on writing about Jerusalem in a certain way. Maybe everything is about Jerusalem. My next book also has a religious dimension, but it is set in Alaska.

Birnbaum: What happens after you've done a book?
Stone: Well, I don't seem to get much rest. I am kind of a workaholic, but I am also a perfectionist. I am also kind of lazy, so . . .

Birnbaum: Good combination.
Stone: In paradise. So I don't know. I don't know where the year went. I was really looking forward to the end of my teaching.

Birnbaum: You're at Yale?
Stone: Yale, yes. I went down to Key West, and it just seemed I started writing other stuff. I started well. So I ended up not having a lot of rest, and I'm obviously facing the road [for a book tour].

Birnbaum: Are you finding it more challenging?
Stone: Yes. I'm sixty. And fifty can feel the same as thirty, but not sixty!

Birnbaum: I'm fifty-one, and I'm not sure I feel thirty.
Stone: Fifty is good. And then you find you're fifty-one and fifty-two, but when you are around fifty you still can feel thirty. Not when you are sixty. That's when you feel like you know you're not thirty anymore. You're really not. So I don't know.

Birnbaum: You have a stature now as a writer—capitalized, italicized, bold-faced—and the *New York Times* calls you to write a little of this, and the book review calls you to write a little of that. And maybe *Harpers* calls. Is this what you want to do? Then the Boston Public Library calls you to come here.

Stone: It's what I thought I wanted. So I guess it must be what I want.

Birnbaum: Is there a way in which you feel like you can slow yourself down or measure yourself?

Stone: I don't know. I may have to try.

Birnbaum: You also strike me as someone who just wants to leave it all out there. You want to use it all up.

Stone: I believe in using it all up. I believe that above all. What are you going to leave behind? Use it up.

Birnbaum: The question is, how do you do that?

Stone: Tough question.

Birnbaum: You don't have a date or a schedule when your Alaska book is going to be done? Two years, three years, five years?

Stone: Oh no, God knows. I hope I live to see it.

Birnbaum: Starting a novel, are there any reference points to the novels you have already written? Does it ever somehow . . . is it there somewhere?

Stone: Oh, yes. I think anybody who reads it is going to see it.

Birnbaum: Do you work at trying to avoid that?

Stone: Yes, I try to make it different. I don't want to be singing the same songs, but a writer has certain concerns. I don't think a writer should have the same characters or anything like that, but a writer will have the same certain concerns, and those concerns will come up.

Birnbaum: Would you call those moral imperatives?

Stone: Yes.

Robert Stone Interview

L. P. Griffith, John Schultze, and Stephanie Anderson / 2006

This interview was edited by L. P. Griffith and conducted by him with John Schultze and Stephanie Anderson on September 29, 2006, as part of the River City Writers Series at the University of Memphis. Printed for the first time by permission.

Schultze: You just finished your memoir *Prime Green: Remembering the Sixties*. In the past you've said you prefer writing fiction to nonfiction because you don't want facts to get in the way of a good story.
Stone: I don't want facts to get in the way of truth, which they have an annoying habit of doing.

Schultze: Were there events in your life that you had trouble making into a good story?
Stone: Yes. In one way for the obvious reason: you can't make a good story out of everything. But there are also things that you don't want to deal with, but it's your job to deal with. And it's a writer's job to say inappropriate things. It's why the dictates of political correctness are so subversive and so dangerous. A writer's function is to force thought and to produce reflection on the part of the reader. You're creating the unexpected, so you use paradox, which is a great instrument of human freedom. Humor and paradox are really important, and I can't really write without them. They take you through the writing process in much the same way that a sense of humor keeps you going through hard times. And you have to be ready to get into trouble if you're trying to stir up a little paradox, a few contradictions.

With some genre writers, even very talented ones, you can see them thinking. For example, the late John D. MacDonald was not a bad writer. His problem was that he didn't seem to know the secrets of the heart. Or if he knew them, he didn't let on. He would always conventionalize his work so that it was acceptable. It is what defined the genre writer of a certain era, in contrast with a writer who was trying to be more serious. The genre writer wouldn't explore the complicated implications of something. In his stories the case got solved and everyone behaved in ways that were acceptable to readers of that period. The serious writer wants to pursue the unacceptable sometimes. He pursues what people are aware of or suspect, but don't speak of or don't want to think of. Yet it is a level that we all share. It is a level that we actually spend a lot of time on and live in.

You also have to give memoir a form. And you remember it in a narrative way. You can't remember things any other way. It's a matter of sensing the story. If it's an anecdote, you have to sense what the anecdote is about. You have to give it meaning because there is no point in writing a bunch of anecdotes that don't add up to anything. Nobody wants to read that. So you try to figure out, "What does this mean?" And what are the aspects about it that are amusing—or potentially amusing—or strange or paradoxical. Because the bottom line is entertainment. It's got to be fun—serious fun—but fun. Readers have got to enjoy it. There is no such thing as a book that is so deep and profound that it doesn't also entertain on some level. That is, if it's going to be worth reading. There is a pleasure principle, and that should always be applied.

Schultze: You kind of touched on aspects of my next question when you said that we remember things in a narrative way. You've said that the main way we know things is through story. I was wondering if you could expand on that epistemological view a little more.

Stone: The basis of story is that life means something. The Bible, for example, presumes that human life has some kind of significance and that what happens to people takes place within some kind of framework. The same thing is true with the literature of the early Greeks. Homeric literature has figures who are exemplars of human behavior, and what they do reflects what the society approves of, what the society disapproves of, and their codes of honor. You take these strange stories in Genesis, for example, and you puzzle over them. What do they mean? Some of them are references to things that have no meaning anymore, or meaning we can no longer penetrate, yet the sense is that they're meaningful. It's human nature to give a meaning to our lives. We want our lives to mean something, but above all, we want our suffering to mean something. Because life is painful, we want that suffering to signify something. And that is, in a way, what literature does.

We, ourselves, are a story. We carry around a sense of ourselves: who our parents were, where our grandparents came from, who they were. All the terms in which we think of ourselves are really a kind of narrative. This happens, and then that happened, and here we are. This sequence is absolutely necessary to comprehension. You can't make any sense out of life without composing it as some sort of story. The whole function of story, whether it is one person saying to another or a grown-up saying to a child or the elder saying to the younger person, "Your situation is what it is and you're having trouble. Well, let me tell you what happened a thousand years ago. Achilles had this problem, and then this happened, and then that happened . . ." Once you hear the narrative, then you can relate to it. You can relate your life and your problems to the problems of Achilles or the migrations of the ancient Hebrews. The whole purpose of story is to provide some meaning for life. You can't comprehend it any other way.

Griffith: You have said that you view the world through a structure of religion, even if it's a world without God, a world you've described as an "empty space from which God has absented himself . . . this enormous mystery before which we are silent and uncomprehending." Can there be great fiction without God or without a struggle to comprehend this mystery?

Stone: I'm not sure I know the answer to that. There certainly can be literature—Conrad's maybe—outside a religious context. And by a religious context I'm not talking about organized religion or a given faith. I don't think faith is what you believe. I don't think faith is saying, "Well there's one God, and there are three persons," and all the rest of the catechism. That's not faith. Faith is an attitude toward things themselves, or the universe that somehow, on some level, there's some kind of meaning.

Just to answer with a story. Proust has a really wonderful section about the death of a critic. The critic is really ill. He reads about a Vermeer show at the museum. He reads this criticism in which there's a patch of yellow that he's never noticed before in *View of Delft*. So he gets out of bed and goes to the museum to look at this painting. He sees it, walks over to the bench, and sits down and dies. Proust goes on to say there was a moment there, but that perhaps all moments are the moments before and moments after. But where is the moment itself, the most elusive thing, the thing that is actually happening? This critic trying to look at the yellow in the painting, what was he after? He was after something much larger than a painting, much larger than an aesthetic, much larger than art itself. He was in pursuit of something of which the traces lie around somehow. In some strange way these traces were put there to make us pursue them, or there's something in our brains that makes us hungry for them. Or maybe they're there for no particular reason at all, but they are there. And we are driven to pursue some kind of resolution to things. Proust doesn't make a statement about this is true or that is true. But that is what I think of when I say my perspective is religious. I think that critic pursuing the yellow in a painting is after something much, much, much greater than what's in the painting. I think art itself, the pursuit of art itself, is or can be the intimation of something enormous, something out there. Or it can *not* be. It can be simply something that was created in the process of evolving man. We don't know. But we know the traces are there, which is what I mean by religious context.

Griffith: You've said that writing cannot be taught, but that principles of rhetoric can. What do you teach your students about rhetoric?
Stone: I think reading is the principal way you learn about writing. You can start in shameless imitation, and then that falls away if you stick with it long enough. One of the things I tell students about, for example, is bathos. The juxtaposition of the absurd and portentousness. The things people will do unconsciously. I also tell them about sound. It is tremendously important in writing. I like to quote what Conrad said, "Fiction must justify itself in every line." Each word has a relationship to the next word. Each sentence has a relationship to the next sentence. It is through these relationships that each line justifies itself. As a writer, you can't put it on automatic. There is no difference in the level of consciousness that you apply to one thing rather than another. You can't drift; you have to be there for every single line.

You also have to be aware of the resonance of words and the associative levels of words. A word has its sound; it has its associations. As the Zen masters say, the mind is a monkey. You're trying to control the consciousness of the reader. You're trying to induce an alternative kind of consciousness. So you do that by exercising as much authority as you can—in a good cause. You're trying to force the reader out of his own awareness and consciousness and replace it with your story. And you can't do that by just reciting the story on the page. You have got to be aware of the music of the words and aware of the levels of association. One word somehow triggers a series of associations in an instant. Words are not neutral; they do not end when you apply them. They continue to resonate. By the time the reader is on the next line, he is still hearing the sound of the line before. It's like pressing the pedal on a piano when you want to keep a note. You keep the sound operative while the reader goes on to the next space. They used to say of Hemingway that he used the white space. I think that it's really important to remember that writing is not a unidimensional process. It is a multidimensional process when it's at its best, and sound amplifies story.

Anderson: You say that you invent a kind of music for each of your characters. Could you explain that process and its significance?

Stone: It's like a leitmotif in music or in an opera whenever a certain character appears. Whenever Siegfried appears in Wagner's *The Ring* you get this passage: [singing, gesticulating] *Ta dumm, da dumm, tada dumm dum, Ta dum* . . . It's an off note there, but it's the music of the character. The prose around the character and the character's dialogue have a certain musical quality that is a leitmotif. In all of opera characters have their own music— a few notes—when they appear on stage. And for Scarpia in *Tosca*, there's always this portentious music around him. That's what I mean.

Anderson: You used to write and perform poetry when you lived in New Orleans, and much of your writing has a lyric quality to it. I was wondering if you listen to music when you write or if lyricism stemmed from your experience as a poet.

Stone: I had this crazed fit once where I threw out all the poetry I had written. Every once in a while, I read poetry and I like poetry and I still write it sometimes. But I always, so to speak, break it down for parts. I write a poem and I come to a situation in prose and I use that image and the sound of that line. In a way, I see myself as being a kind of poet, but I put it in the prose. I don't leave it separate.

Anderson: You've said the only way you can make words evoke "psychological and emotional states effectively is by creating an altered state of consciousness by writing a prose that is close to blank verse." Since a realistic novel can't be composed entirely of poetry, when is it important to put the reader into this altered state? And do you make the decision consciously to become more poetic, or does it happen unconsciously?

Stone: Oh, I think you're going to get in trouble if you make a decision to be more poetic. Dangerous work, that is. No, it has to be there. The situation, what you're describing, has to call forth the poetry.

Griffith: In a *New York Times* article you mention an anecdote about boaters who drowned because they forgot to put down the ladder before jumping into the water. This anecdote seems to be the basis for the short story,

"Under the Pitons." Can you give any advice about how to transform an anecdote into a short story?

Stone: You look for what it means. I don't want to give the story away so I'll talk about it abstractly, but all that particular event means is how lousy life can be. That's all it means. So you look for the extensions of meaning beyond just that. You might ask, "In what ways do these people come together?" You experience this discovery of love by two people. You think about its loss. You think about luck. You think about the vicissitudes of how things can change on a dime. You think about the sea, and how the sea is like everything else, how everything that is true about the ocean is true about life in general. The key is to discover the meaning and the variety of meanings you can find in or impose on something like that. The anecdote, which I guess is true, is a terrible story about a maritime accident. I just tried to impose as much meaning on it as I could. I'm hard-pressed to say exactly how I did that, but I think the answer lies in what I tried to discover in its implications.

Griffith: Was that something you struggled with for a while when you heard that story? Or was it immediately apparent when you heard it?

Stone: I really had to invent around it. The anecdote itself is barbarous. I didn't sit down right away and try to write it. I think one of the things you should do with a story is let it percolate and then one day it comes to you. And then you say, "Oh, I see the way that I can tell it. I see the way I can use this typical story of making a mistake and having to live out the consequences of it, one after another, with everything going wrong because of one mistake." I didn't sit down to write the story right away; it took me quite a while to just think about it.

Anderson: You've compared a good short story to a baseball pitch in its simplicity, complexity, and inevitability. What would you liken a good novel to?

Stone: I think a novel is—musically—more symphonic. It has movements. Sometimes when you're writing a novel you think about plot. It's higher nonsense, this replication of causality, so sometimes plot can seem gimmicky if you don't do it right. A novel has to come together aesthetically, but not in any kind of neat way that misrepresents the way reality happens. But it is important to have what is prefigured to be paid off. So the short answer to your question is, at its best, a novel is symphonic, regardless of the length. A novel can say a lot of things, and if you finish the novel and you feel like you've said them, it's really satisfying.

Schultze: I've got a specific question about *Dog Soldiers*. In it, John Converse muses about the "liberal sensibility" that crumbles in the face of persistence, and in *Bay of Souls* Michael quips that, "The NRA [is] always confusing life and art." Tell us about the role of politics as far as your characters are concerned. Do you find politics a pivotal point in their development? Or do you just need to have politically conscious characters?

Stone: Yes, my characters are politically conscious. They're usually involved in some kind of political situation—as in a way we all are—and they usually have different takes on it. The political situation that I've written about a lot is the impact of America on the world, which is multifarious. Some things are good; some things are not. A country that has an imperial system as we have is in trouble because it's always trying to maintain that imperial system. Some of it is cultural and some of it depends on who's running the country at the time. Some of the impulses are generous, and some of the impulses are breathtakingly cynical and selfish. So my characters have to be aware of this in one way or another. They either have an interest in the political situation, or they're opposed to it, or they're deluded by it, or they have an insight into it. But it's always going on because politics is always going on. We can't escape it. Even if we lie down and pull the covers over our heads and don't read the paper, we're still being acted on by politics. I don't champion any political system—Marxism or the free market or anything of that sort. But I think politics is everywhere.

Griffith: I have difficulty creating characters or drawing upon real people whose background and motivations or conceptions of the world I don't understand or I don't share. So I was wondering how you deal with this problem. Do you grow to understand the character as you write, or do you prefer to remain partly in mystery?

Stone: You have to maintain the mystery of the individual. People are mysteries to each other, and we're mysteries to ourselves. So you can never escape that. But I think it is also a writer's responsibility to imagine his way into just about any quarter of the human experience. I think you have to try to imagine your way into all the characters. And in a way all the characters, finally, are you. At least, they're your voice. It's like ventriloquism. I always think of that line in Dickens's *Our Mutual Friend*, where Betty says of Sloppy, "He do the police in different voices," meaning that he imitates the testimony. He can do the cop answering the judge; he can do the judge. And that's what you're doing as a writer; you're doing the voices. And you really ought to know what the mentality behind the voice is, what the diction is, and how it will sound. Sometimes, it's a character you're utterly out of sympathy with, but you still have to know, in a literal kind of way, where they're coming from. You have to know the mentality, or you have to decide that you know what that mentality is. You have to imagine your way into a character's motivation, and into his language, and kind of into his mind. And in that sense it's ventriloquism. Flaubert said it famously. When they asked, "Where'd you get the idea of Madame Bovary?" he said, "*Madame Bovary c'est moi.*" "It's me. I am Madame Bovary." So, in a way, to a greater or lesser extent, we are all the principle characters in our novels, and to some extent, the minor characters too. Even when these characters are far from the sympathy of the author, they're still the author's voice, in a kind of ventriloquism.

Schultze: Speaking about characters and sympathetic characters, in the end of *Bay of Souls*, Lara tells Michael that he betrayed her. But earlier in the novel, she feels that she betrayed him by bringing him down to St. Trinity under false pretenses. So in that respect, is her final assertion evidence that she did not retrieve her soul as she intended, or is she just a heartless woman who never had a soul in the first place?

Stone: She had a soul. And the way in which she regains it is somewhat mechanical: by engaging in the rites and forcing him to engage in the rites. She gets that soul back, and she purges herself of the spirit, of the sort of demonic figure. And then she becomes an almost metaphysical character herself. For example, she just appears to him on this horse. She's not a heartless woman, but she's obsessive, determined to regain her soul. She lives in a world that in fact is utterly foreign to him. And he's been seized up and thrown in this world and used. He understands what has happened to him, and he's left to try and make a comeback from this. His life has been sort of picked up and turned around and destroyed. No, she had a soul. A dangerous, antic soul.

Anderson: Many of your characters are full of fear and ignorance of other people and the world around them, and they're full of self-delusion. Yet you've said in the past that your overall message is a positive one, not one of despair. So how does that paradox work?

Stone: A lot of people would give me a problem about saying that my message is a positive one. But I would argue that catharsis is positive. The Greek tragedians trying to induce in their audience pity and terror were not simply trying to bring them down and make them feel bad. They were trying to get this process of catharsis. This is how tragedy works. And the fate of a lot of these characters is tragic, but tragedy is, like all stories, a way of looking at our own lives through what happens to characters with whom we can invest some sympathy. I try to elicit sympathy sometimes for people who on the face of it are very unsympathetic. But I want people to see themselves in all kinds of situations. Also, my characters have a way of spotting something out of the corner of their eyes that perhaps is salvific. And that's positive. I think the suspicion of a salvific level of things is positive, and I think catharsis is positive. So that's how I would claim all these awful stories are somehow positive.

Audience: *Dog Soldiers* is one of my most beloved books, and frankly I really like the movie. I think there's a lot to it that perhaps was not apparent upon its initial release. What do you think of the movie, and who would you have liked to have seen, if anyone other than Nick Nolte, play Hicks? For some reason I thought of Roy Scheider.

Stone: That's funny because Roy Scheider was actually considered for that part. He has a kind of—for lack of a better word—a kind of loser's quality that would have been good. But Nick Nolte was really into the book. He read the hell out of it. He's a really good actor, and he's a smart guy. While watching him perform this role it was hard for me not to admire what he was doing. He had just done this television thing, and he'd done *The Deep*. Everybody thought he was just a pretty face. But he really is a smart guy of a lot of complexity with a lot of problems that I can sympathize with, that I can identify with.

There were a lot of good performances in that movie. It has a lot of good things in it, but it doesn't satisfy me because of so many changes in the characters and what happens. But I'm glad you liked it because there was a lot of serious work that the people at what was left of United Artists studios just threw away. One of the breathtaking things about the movie business is not only its fatuousness and cruelty, but the profligate way in which it takes somebody's heartfelt performance and just throws it away. They don't even know what it is. Don't get me started!

Audience: Could you speak a little bit more about character, and how you approach character when you're writing nonfiction versus fiction?

Stone: One process is very close to the other. Fiction and nonfiction are a continuum. There's not a divide between one and the other. You use a lot of selectivity in memoir; you're looking for a significance that connects things.

You're looking for something that signifies about you or somebody else—your relationship. When you create a fictional or nonfictional *character*, you use the same array of characteristics or qualities that you remember in the person. In nonfiction the person might not recognize himself when reading, and he might say, "I'm not like that." But to me, he's like that! It's totally different from his perspective, but to me, it happened that way. I'm not making it up. I'm remembering, but it's still storytelling. That doesn't change. If I write a memoir, I get into a style—I can't shake my style—and that's my voice. As soon as I assume that voice, I'm presenting myself as a character. And that is inescapable.

Audience: How does writing a story or memoir affect you?

Stone: One of the problems with writing is that it's lonely, and you can get into extreme emotional states all by yourself in the middle of the night. You can laugh, you can cry, you can carry on. Suddenly you're really moved by something. I remember one night working on a piece I had already written about eight times over and I finally got it right and I just went to pieces. It was one o'clock in the morning, and I staggered out of the little carrel where I was writing in the college library. I ran right into the security guard. He almost went for his gun because it's the middle of the night, and I looked completely demented. You can get very, very affected. It's one of the reasons writers drink. You gotta shake it; you gotta get out; you gotta get rest. You gotta turn yourself off. You work for a long time, you're in a state, and you want to cool out however you can. This isn't every day, fortunately. But you get very emotional sometimes, and you do it all by yourself.

Audience: If you could put together a Mariners' Writing Society of writers who have an affinity with the sea, and you could get together and talk or sail, who would be in it?

Stone: I can think of some people who would be in it, but I wouldn't want to be caught on a ship with them. It would be a dreadful crew. Nobody would get back alive.

I would include Melville, so let's just talk about him for a minute. *Moby-Dick* is prophecy. Here are these Americans, and they are pursuing this metaphysical whale that also represents an industrial product because whale oil was everything. There were 10,000 people in Nantucket, all of them producing whale oil to oil factory machines, to produce oil for lamps. This was an industrial process. So here is Ahab, this obsessed American over in the Japan Ground, pursuing this creature, trying to subdue it. Trying, in other words, to industrialize it. To Ahab, the whale is everything evil and mindless and uncontrollable and dangerous in the world. The whale is sheer evil because it cannot be subdued. So in *Moby-Dick* there's a constant reversing of roles. The whale is innocent, the whale is good; yet the whale is evil. Ahab is an evil American in pursuit of world domination, yet Ahab is Everyone facing the mindless universe. It's fantastic! It's a breathtaking insight. It's prophecy. Okay, I would include Melville.

Conrad also wrote about the sea beautifully. And Jack London. I think William Golding, the guy who wrote *Lord of the Flies*, wrote a great book about the sea called *Pincher Martin*. Some of the lone sailors wrote very well. It's hard to make a list. They're all different characters, people with whom you wouldn't want to get caught on a ship.

Audience: Ahab's character was formed by this whale, so I'm thinking what Hollywood would make of it in the twenty-first century. Moby Dick's story would be played as a sequel, and it would say, "Ahab—this time it's personal."
Stone: "No more Mr. Nice Guy." It's interesting to go into movies because one thing you can't do in a movie is to have that reversal of roles where you ask, "Is Ahab representative of man's despoiling of the world, or is Ahab you and me?" There's ambiguity. But in a movie you have to cast judgment because you're looking at something photographic. You just can't strike to that level of ambiguity.

Ahab says, "Strike through the mask." In other words, he'll get at what's wrong with the world. Starbuck the mate, who's a Quaker, says, "To be enraged with a dumb thing, Captain Ahab, seems blasphemous." And Ahab says, "Talk not to me of blasphemy, man; I'd strike the sun if it insulted me." This is a strong anti-ecological position! But in a movie you can't have that juxtaposition. Everything about the character—the actor, how he's dressed, how he acts—it compels judgment. Finally there are good guys and bad guys. It's a very exceptional movie that manages to represent a truly ambiguous character. You can have the good/bad gunslinger. You can have the good/bad female, but you can't really do it on a very deep level. You're just compelled to judge good guys and bad guys finally. And that's one of the problems of movies. If it's a good movie, you can go along with it, but there's a certain level that it cannot penetrate to, in my opinion.

Audience: Don't you think it's because the camera is telling the story instead of the language telling the story? Because in Shakespeare you get every kind of character complexity from the language.

Stone: That's a play. That's entirely different. The play is language dependent. It moves on language. It does not require anything else. You can do it on a bare stage. But a movie is photography, finally. One of the very frustrating things for a writer in movies is that the writer is not telling the story. Whoever is controlling the photography—the man with the pictures—is the storyteller. And the pictures, each one of them compels a judgment. You make a judgment every time you see a picture—this is terrible; this is beautiful; the sky is good; the sky is bad. It's just presented to you in that role. So writing a film script is more like writing title cards for a silent movie than it is like writing a play. It's just different.

Audience: That's interesting what you had to say about John D. MacDonald and the secrets of the heart and his inability to put them down on the page. But that could be a definition of all genre fiction in some way. Anytime you write about secrets of the heart you have to slow down the pace of the book, don't you? And that's kind of antithetical to the whole process of reading in genre form.

Stone: It is antithetical. And the secrets of the heart can often be revealed through a reversal, a surprise. The character can suddenly not be the character you thought that character was. And that's not what the readers of John D. MacDonald mysteries want to happen. It does slow it down. It also compels a kind of commitment from the reader that readers of genre fiction—and it may be fairly enough—don't want from what they're reading. My problem with Stephen King, for example, is that I don't think he knows the secrets of the heart. I think his sense of horror is kind of conventional. He's great at scariness, but I don't think he goes very deep. I shouldn't say this because it always sounds like sour grapes . . . he's a *little* better known than I am . . . he sells a *few* more books than I do [laughing]. But I don't think he's a bad writer. He's wonderful at atmospherics. But it's just Halloween scary. I can't say I was a close reader of his book *It*, but I remember he gathers supposed losers, and they're not really losers at all. They were kids who were picked on in high school, and they all become extremely famous and extremely powerful. They oppose this evil clown—I mean, an evil clown, come on! That's a very conventional character. It satisfies expectations in a vulgar way. That's what I have against King, not that sentence for sentence he's such a bad writer.

Audience: You're saying art is about complexity, about dealing with the ambiguities that film doesn't handle as well, especially genre films. Does that mean that those types of movies cease to be art?

Stone: No, I couldn't say that. You don't always have to have ambiguity. Sometimes you go along with a movie, and you know it's a kind of setup. You know it's an ancient drama, a kind of generic story. But if it's atmospheric, if it's good, if it's well-done then you go along with it. There are three basic Western stories a friend of mine was telling me who writes about the West a lot. There's the gunfight at the O.K. Corral, there's the Johnson County War, and there's the Lincoln County War. All Western stories are about or combine those three instances. It really is a genre in that way, and it can be wonderfully done. It can be beautifully executed. There are some great Westerns. *The Searchers* is a great movie, but it does have an ambiguous character, a really troublesome character in Ethan. He is complex. He has some really evil things about him, but he's also heroic. This is not the John Wayne I know. It holds a surprise. So sometimes you can have art and ambiguity in genre films.

Audience: Can you say something about enjoying the writing process versus challenging yourself?

Stone: In a way it's always an act of effrontery to sit down and write something. Before you publish anything you really don't believe anybody's going to read it, except your spouse who either reads it or pretends to read it, and then says, "It's great!" There's a line of Browning that always occurs to me: "That's the wise thrush; he sings each song twice over, / Lest you should think he never could recapture / The first fine careless rapture!" When writing, you get that first fine careless rapture. You don't think anybody else is going to read it; you're just pleasing yourself. But once it gets published you suddenly think, "Oh my god, people are going to write about this. They're going to comment on this. They're going to hurt my feelings." I'm presuming people are going to take the time out of their lives to read what I write. That's a challenge from the get-go. And the satisfaction is in a way overcoming your fears. You finally go down with the hand you're playing, and you hope for the best. All things that are pleasurable are in a way challenging. You have some really bad days, but it feels good to meet and overcome a challenge, to do something good in spite of the difficulties.

Audience: Did you read a lot of Conrad when you wrote *A Flag for Sunrise*, or were you familiar with Conrad?

Stone: I was or I thought I was familiar with Conrad. The relevant book there would be *Nostromo*, set in South America. But no, while I was writing, I wasn't reading a lot of Conrad. I tend to stay away from anyone who is going over the same area that I am writing about because I want to resist influence. But I did know Conrad. He is so eccentric. A guy who started out speaking Polish and then wrote in French and then learned English and wrote in English, so his style is very quirky and eccentric. It's literally inimitable.

Audience: What fiction have you been impressed by in your recent reading?
Stone: In the last ten years I read *All the King's Men*, which for some reason I had not read before, and which I think is just a wonderful, wonderful novel. I really responded to it. Although I'm not a fan of meta-fiction, I think William T. Vollmann's *Europe Central* is an incredible book in its ambition and in what it pulls off. I'm reading *Light in August* again, and I'm really impressed with it. Faulkner's hard to read, and a lot of people have given up on him. Young people don't much read him anymore. It brought back to me a lot of what I had once responded to in Faulkner.

Of the classics that I hadn't read, Turgenev's *Fathers and Sons*, a short novel, is a really wonderful, powerful book. *Billy Budd*—Melville again—is a great novel of the sea. I think Marilynne Robinson's *Housekeeping* is a much neglected by really great novel. Marilynne Robinson is a very eccentric figure, and a very wise person, and really a terrific writer. I wish she had written more. I will think of twenty more books when I walk out the door.

The Total Anti-Totalist

Christopher Bollen / 2013

Originally published in *Interview Magazine*, 2013. Courtesy BMP Media Holdings, LCC.

Not far from seventy-six-year-old novelist Robert Stone's Upper East Side apartment is a model-toy shop. Its shelves are filled with miniature weaponized planes and ships that run the gamut of technological advancement through the United States' various twentieth-century wars. Throughout Stone's long career as a premier voice of American reason and delirium, his novels have brought many of those conflicts home in hallucinogenic, lightning-quick prose, in precise, haunting episodes, and in characters who appear like survivalists extended to the end of their tethers. Whether transporting Vietnam to drug-fueled Southern California in his classic 1974 novel *Dog Soldiers* or taking readers into the dark revolution of a Central American nation tethered on the brink in his 1981 novel *A Flag for Sunrise*, Stone is a writer with a preternatural ability to transform a location into a geopolitical snare trap through which very few pass without a lot of pain or bloodshed. It is in many ways surprising that the writer came of age in the hippie Ken Kesey days of sixties merry enchantment.

Stone's masterpieces are thrilling reads, but they are never easy going. The ground, so intensely described, is always capable of shifting at the reader's feet. Characters are driven by a volatile psychic compression of personal demons, ideological convictions, and social forces beyond their control. He is a complicated literary realist in that what is real is often the least dependable place of all. In this sense, Stone is, perhaps, the most honest living writer America has.

His latest novel, *Death of the Black-Hair Girl*, out this week, might sound like a murder mystery; but, in effect, the title serves to push the plot aside in favor of a deeper focus—not who did it or how, but what remains and what is lost after the body is taken to the morgue. The dead, black-haired girl in question is Maud Stack, an attractive, reckless, overconfident student attending an elite college in an otherwise depressed New England mill town. Maud not only pens an ugly op-ed for the school paper attacking religious anti-abortion activists but also is involved with a married, middle-aged professor, Steven Brookman. Stone turns the college town into an unflinching crucible of class and generational conflict—and all of those twentieth-century systems of ideology spelled out so carefully in his previous books make way for a twenty-first-century penchant for personal irresponsibility and fast forms of love and engagement. By the time the novel fulfills its titular promise, characters swerve between saving what they have and trying to make sense of whatever high obligations keep them from sinking into the quick. Stone's truths are hardly comforting—there is no pull of the thread that releases the knot—but if there is redemption in these pages, it is marked by those outside the wiles of academia willing to look the hard facts in the face.

I visited Stone at his apartment in early November. He was just getting over a cold. We spoke for an hour about his journeyman style of writing, and how the world turns just a bit differently than it did in his early days.

Bollen: I know when you were young, you were a pretty serious smoker.
Stone: I'll tell you a cautionary tale. I quit in the early eighties. I came down with really serious emphysema just a few years ago and quit in the early eighties.

Bollen: How extreme a smoker were you?
Stone: I smoked about three packs a day. So that was a lot.

Bollen: Did you smoke when you wrote? Because when a habit burrows its way into the writing process, it's very hard to weed it out.
Stone: The reason I was able to quit was because of the computer. You couldn't lean a cigarette on a computer, like you could on a typewriter. So it just made it that much more difficult to smoke. So I quit. But this is now thirty years ago that I quit, and it still didn't help me.

Bollen: Maybe the emphysema was due to the chemicals you were breathing during your time in the army?
Stone: I was in Naval Amphibious Force when I was a kid. They put us through all sorts of maneuvers that involved smoke screens. So it is conceivable. I would like to think I got it in a more heroic mode, in the service of the public. But I'm afraid that's not it. I'm afraid it was just smoking, non-stop.

Bollen: Well, if smoking was in the service of your early books, that's still heroic. Or maybe I'm just glamorizing the costs.

Stone: That was an upside. That is glamorizing it, but I'll take it. [laughs]

Bollen: I always think of you as a master of location. Your novels dig into a specific setting and find the conflicting power dynamics and social forces that compose a hostile place. I'm curious why you chose the university for *Death of the Black-Haired Girl*. What intrigued you about the culture of a college town?

Stone: I've been a writer in residence for a lot of places. I've never had tenure anywhere, but I've taught all over—from the University of Hawaii to the Ivy League. I've observed a lot of that dynamic and decided I would employ it. It is a big issue, this abortion topic, which is yet another aspect of town-gown hostilities. And I wanted to bring in the character of Jo, one of my favorite characters who I kind of resuscitated from an earlier book. I wanted to use her and her perspective. I wanted to use the controversy over abortion—that war that was going on. It seemed to characterize the university to me. The university campus isn't my usual stomping ground, but I wanted to discuss it from various perspectives.

Bollen: In a small university town, there is class warfare and generational warfare. There's an industry of privilege erected on top of a dying mill town. And even the motto of your fictional university has to do with eradicating Algonquin Native Americans through the eternal fire of enlightenment. So there's an ethos about taking over the environment, the community.

Stone: It's all gone completely haywire.

Bollen: When I think of your early book *Dog Soldiers*, you describe youths of the time so perfectly. But those youths are countercultural misfits in Southern California during Vietnam. The main character of the new book, Maud Stack, is a different variety of youth. She's confident, educated, self-obsessed, self-righteous. Do you think those two generations of young people are dramatically different, then and now?

Stone: Very different. She's very different than a kid of the sixties or seventies. I've had my eye on kids since I have been teaching and have had several generations of children and grandchildren. I haven't been that removed from them. But the ways in which Maud is different I think were less deliberate than they were just observed. I didn't set out to define differences in these generations. I think they just emerged. She has an arrogance that the kids of the earlier age hadn't developed yet. It's a matter of confidence, arrogance, and certainty. Our generation had that feeling of certainty, but in a way there was something that was skeptical about it. We didn't 100 percent believe what they were saying.

Bollen: Maybe the difference lies in belief systems. There's a line at the end of *Death of the Black-Haired Girl* that I feel is the key to the entire book. It's when Jo Carr, a nun, is talking to Victor Lerner, a psychologist. You write, "Their bond was that they both attempted to subscribe to some of the totalist metaphysical fantasies that had thrived in the previous century." Is the heart of this novel the fact that the "totalist metaphysical fantasies" of the twentieth century have all been destroyed?

Stone: Absolutely. Whether it's Freud, whether it's Marx, whether it's any kind of totalism. I can't remember who it was that coined the word *totalism*. It was one of the great intellectuals of the thirties or forties. What he was talking about was essentially Hegelism—the inner content of history that the totalists believed in. People no longer believe in totalism, which I think is entirely a good thing. They lead to horror shows of all kinds, and they're disappearing, I hope. God knows, they may be replaced by something worse. But I think they are disappearing, and I think that part of this much decried "failing attention span" is responsible for it. Which makes it a good thing.

Bollen: So you're in favor of the short attention span to prevent any cult of ideology?

Stone: In general, I would say, yes.

Bollen: Which is probably why those students who attend Ivy League schools and presumably still have decent attention spans are so often the ones who fall prey to Marxism or left-wing extremism in the name of revolution.

Stone: They're the last to persist in that school of education, within the necessity for history to have an inner core that can be resolved. They're not really buying that, but their professors are. I think most people under a certain age would absolutely deny being a Marxist or a Marxist-Leninist or a post-Marxist or a post-Marxist-Leninist. You have to go somewhere like the *New Left Review* to really even see the jargon anymore.

Bollen: When I started *Death of the Black-Haired Girl*, I thought it might be a murder mystery. But really it's a slide of characters, where the attention turns from the catalysts—Maud and Steven Brookman, the professor she is having an affair with—to the survivors and witnesses, namely Maud's father, Eddie, and Jo Carr. Do you realize when you begin a book which characters are going to overtake the others? Or is it a matter of which ones keep offering you interesting opportunities?

Stone: Maud's father and Jo became tremendously important characters, and I didn't know that was going to happen. I didn't really know that Brookman was going to turn out to be such a self-indulgent asshole as he did, and really undeserving of his wife, who is a bit of a flake herself. But, yes, the key characters are really Eddie Stack and Jo. That developed during the writing. That's often the case with a book of mine, and that was the case here.

Bollen: I think that's why setting seems to be such an essential ingredient to your books. The place does a lot of the telling. Take *A Flag for Sunrise*, about a fictional Central American country on the eve of a revolution that is very similar to Nicaragua. Were you traveling through Central America in the late seventies?

Stone: I went when Somoza was still in charge of Nicaragua. I went to go diving because I used to do a lot of that. I went to the Bay Islands before the cocaine boom, when it was a relatively innocent place. I was really very naïve about Central America, but I traveled there and met various people who explained the situation to me.

Bollen: That was right after you wrote *Dog Soldiers*. Were you consciously on the hunt for a new location to set a book?

Stone: Sort of. And this was certainly a good place for one. I got an offer of a ride from Honduras to Managua when Somoza was still in charge. I rode with the military attaché and his wife and his sister-in-law.

Bollen: A drive like that takes place in *A Flag for Sunrise*.
Stone: Exactly.

Bollen: That must have been an eye-opener. Did you sense the upheaval that was on the way?

Stone: It wasn't happening yet. It was about to happen. People knew it was happening, and you could feel it. You could even hear little bits of it. The first thing that impressed me was that people were very frightened. And when they got scared, I got scared. I could see that really bad things were going to happen, and there's nothing to stimulate a novel like a sense of general fear and paranoia. So that really kicked it off.

Bollen: I could just be speaking from the future here, but what's exciting about a book like *A Flag for Sunrise* coming out in the eighties is that it seems to me that the esteemed American novels of that era are steeped in more internal, national fare—particularly regarding money and wealth and disaffectedness and urban class structures. You were carrying on this idea of the global from the success of *Dog Soldiers* into the eighties with the crisis in Nicaragua. Did you find literature was less accommodating of that kind of larger-perspective book in the eighties?

Stone: I thought it was exciting. I liked doing the locales. I love doing the foreign cities, alien places. That's something I just enjoy. And it was part of a world of struggle when you have the deterioration of Reaganism into Bushism. You could kind of see the blindness, the failure to cope, and that impressed me—even more than the failure to cope at home. If I had been a truly political writer, I would have confined myself to the situation at home. But because I was really into having fun and writing global novels, I took the situation abroad.

Bollen: Did you find that other writers were doing that?

Stone: Other writers, I think, were certainly beginning to do it. Norman Rush was beginning to do it, and then you had British writers who were doing it, like William Boyd. I was aware of their work, but I can't say I was reading it at the time. I always knew I hated Graham Greene, even though I thought he was a really good writer. I really disliked him. My feeling as an American toward Graham Greene was absolutely mutual. [laughs]

Bollen: There's a scene in *Dog Soldiers* in which a character named Gerald wants to try heroin because he's a writer and his ambition is to write about the "drug scene." The main character in the book ends up shooting him up right in the vein as punishment, and Gerald basically collapses and dies because of it. I thought this episode in the book might have been a shot across the bow for you. Like you were warning other writers who were pretending they could write about the dark, drug culture, "Don't pretend you know the inside of the situation like I do."

Stone: It was a gag on me.

Bollen: On you? I thought it was you claiming your territory against literary interlopers.

Stone: Well, that was the kind of message, but it was really a shot across my bow. I was really making fun of myself.

Bollen: It doesn't end well for you, then. You're on the floor of a shack with no pulse.

Stone: When we were working on the movie adaptation, I kept insisting to [director] Karel Reisz that, no, he's not really dead. Reisz said, "You could have fooled me."

Bollen: When you're writing about a place or a group, do you stick to situations you've researched or heard have happened? Or do you give yourself unlimited freedom to tell any kind of story you like?

Stone: I often try to use things that have happened to somebody that I've heard about or things that have actually taken place. I certainly did that in *Damascus Gate*. A lot of what happens in *Damascus Gate* really happened. It really took place. I used a fair amount of history and contemporary information. There's a lot of stuff in *Damascus Gate* that is either historically true or was based on actual plots to blow up the temple.

Bollen: Did you go to Jerusalem for research?

Stone: I hung around with Israeli liberals, Israeli peaceniks, the liberal element of the Israeli left who are activists and who really knew what was going on. I hung out in the café, which is no longer, unfortunately, there, called the Atara in West Jerusalem where everybody would sit all day and talk about the situation. I got a residency in the city of Jerusalem at a really beautiful old Ottoman castle that they made available for a while to writers. But what sent me over there was actually an assignment from *Esquire* to do a piece on the Middle East. Most of the time I was in the Egyptian desert, in Sinai, having a fantastic time.

Bollen: It's so beautiful there. I spent some time in Sinai three years ago. The sunrises are out of this world.

Stone: If you go up the ledge in Sinai, you get this red rock, this sunrise, and you never, ever forget it. It's like you've seen a piece of paradise. So that was a wonderful assignment, and I spent a lot of time in Egypt. I passed very quickly through Jerusalem. The Israelis were just withdrawing from Sinai then. They had taken over all Sinai, not just Gaza. We ended up caught in the riot in the Second Intifada, and we almost got killed. The guides we'd been with, who were Israelis, gave us notes to the Israeli border guards, but it took us forever to get through the Egyptian army lines because, of course, that's the most pompous part of the Egyptian bureaucracy. They finally let us through. And what happens is when you get to the Israeli side, you come through the squalor of the Israeli army camp, and you come to the Israeli border, and this great big beautiful air-conditioned bus comes and picks you up. It's a bit like the border at Tijuana.

Bollen: Who were the writers that were major influences for you early on?
Stone: I was under the influence of the early modern masters—Fitzgerald and Steinbeck and Hemingway, especially, when I was a kid. I reacted against writers like Barth and Hawkes. I did not care for the postmodernist stuff; my allegiance was to realism. I loved Dos Passos when I was younger. When I was at Stanford, there was a great passion for *Revolutionary Road*, which was an old-fashioned realist novel. There was a feeling like, my god, the realist novels are something. What I didn't understand in those days was the difference between realism and what wasn't realism.

Bollen: I'm still often confused by the distinction.
Stone: Utterly confused. But we really were enthusiastic about Yates and *Revolutionary Road*.

Bollen: You found that realism was where you wanted to make your mark?
Stone: Basically, yes. I cast those distinctions aside. I did a lot of work that isn't realist, that can't be called realist . . .

Bollen: Your work is hallucinogenic.
Stone: Exactly. But I felt, to be grounded in realism and to go from there into the hallucinogenic, into what was not realism, was the way to do it.

Bollen: It's interesting to think of Kerouac. Is that realism? Or the polar opposite?
Stone: I don't know. I've never been a Kerouac fan.

Bollen: I know you aren't, although you did surround yourself with some of his associates. He must have been in the air around you at that time, whether you breathed it or not.
Stone: It was a funny situation because I was in the service. My mother,

who was a really strange person, sent me *On the Road*. Not too many people were sent *On the Road* by their mother, but I was. She said, "You have to read this." It was more of her generation in a way, and I liked it because I was a teenager. I was in the Navy, for god's sake. People were yelling at me and oppressing me. I was thinking, what could be more square?

Bollen: Why did you choose to go into the Navy?
Stone: I wanted to go to sea. I was romantic about the sea, and I wanted to see the world. Corny old Navy stuff. I was not successful in school. I was not a good student. I was in Catholic school. I did not get on with the order. I was very unfair to them, I realize now. I look back with regret with the way I mistreated them. I thought they were mistreating me, but I realize now that I was mistreating them. So I dropped out of school and I went into the service. My mother and I, we had zero money. We were living together in this hotel room in the middle of New York, the Chesterfield Hotel on 46th Street. We have this very odd familial relationship. Maybe not odd in any biological way, just odd socially.

Bollen: I just read that the poet Marianne Moore slept with her mother in the same bed until her mother's death when Marianne Moore was nearly fifty.
Stone: It's the innocence of Marianne Moore, and the eccentricity. Well, my mother and I weren't sleeping in the same bed, but we were in the same room.

Bollen: I like that your mother was okay with you dropping out of school and gave you a copy of *On the Road*. Were you a voracious reader when you entered the Navy? You must have shared books on the ship.
Stone: Absolutely. There were always people that you ran into in the service. Especially in the Navy, for some reason, always on Amphibs, those huge ships, you always found people who had read the same books that you did. There was always somebody on the ship who had read *The Great Gatsby* or had read Hemingway. You always found people to hang with.

Bollen: So that was an eduation?
Stone: Yes. They were people whose history was like mine. They had been busted for stealing hubcaps, their father was in prison, and their mother was living alone; something like that. So I actually had a pretty good time in the Navy. I can't say that I had a bad time.

Bollen: What year did you get out?
Stone: '58.

Bollen: Did you come back to New York?
Stone: Yes, I came back to New York and went to NYU. I had a really good freshman English teacher, who suggested the Stegner Fellowship at Stanford in California. I had grown up in New York. I had been a couple of places. I had been to Boston. But California was an utterly different world to me. It was like a garden without a snake. It had snakes, but I didn't know about them at first.

Bollen: You were arriving in California at the right time.
Stone: Oh, I was lucky.

Bollen: Did you get involved in the whole Lawrence Ferlinghetti scene?
Stone: I didn't know Ferlinghetti. Ferlinghetti was a lot older than I was. And Kerouac was older; this was a somewhat older generation. [Ken] Kesey was my age. Neal Cassady was a little older, but Neal Cassady was hanging with Kesey. Neal Cassady was looking for the latest scene. I got out there in '62. We were beginning to take acid. It was like the first acid generation.

Bollen: Did you seek this out, or was it around you at Stanford?
Stone: It was around. I just fell in with certain people who said, "You gotta try this stuff, peyote," and I had never done it. I thought, well, sure. [laughs] Woo! God. What a day that was.

Bollen: Do you think that those hallucinogenic experiences informed your writing? For example, the scene at the end of *Dog Soldiers* is filled with ecstasy and agony and mind-warps.
Stone: Yes.

Bollen: In college, I used to think you could split the population of the world into two categories—people who had tried LSD and those who hadn't. Because once you try it, you realize that the entire world is basically chemicals in your brain—religious chemicals. Well, that was a while ago. It's been years since I've done LSD.
Stone: Me too. But, yes. You would say if somebody were coming to a party, "Are they cool?" You were mainly talking about dope, just about smoking dope. But you had to know. Are they cool, or are they going to be shocked

out of their senses that people are doing drugs at this party? But that was the division among the literary or humanist students at Stanford. Are they cool or are they not?

Bollen: You were part of that world, but you have a rare career in that you moved beyond it. A lot of those writers fell victims to their own excesses, or kept repeating themselves. You managed to move outside of it—beyond the prankster van. How?
Stone: I really, really wanted to write. I loved language. I loved literature. I loved reading. I never read a foreign language, I'm afraid, but I loved Flaubert. I loved the nineteenth-century classics. I love Thomas Hardy. I wanted to be a goof on the bus, but I wanted to write more.

Bollen: Did you use a typewriter or did you write in longhand for your first book?
Stone: I was a radioman when I first went into the Navy, so I learned to type by taking Morse code. So I was using the typewriter from day one. My handwriting wasn't any good anyway.

Bollen: Morse code is a strange system that I don't think anyone in my generation understands. It's extinct. It's something you learn and read about constantly, but I don't have the slightest idea what three dots and a dash means.
Stone: It's funny, every once in a while I swear I'm hearing it and I think it must be a hallucination.

Bollen: Maud Stack is a character without any sort of nostalgia—as is her roommate, an actress. I feel for a long time young people have had a nostalgia about the sixties and seventies, but maybe that's gone from the young now.
Stone: It's gone. Those hopes, I think, . . . they're gone. Every once in a while, you get some kid who thinks Occupy Wall Street is going to bring it back. It's not going to happen.

Bollen: You don't think so?
Stone: I really don't, just because the degree to which it's occupied with totalism. Some people see the hope to restore Marxism and Occupy Wall Street, anti-capitalism. What can you do about capitalism? Capitalism is with us. If we don't have debt, we don't have the business society that we have, which is hateful. But life is shit. What're you going to do?

Bollen: It's like Nicaragua. If you go there today, it's extremely poor, and yet the government is trying to promote American tourism to its beaches. It seems like history went the long way to arrive at a rather sad place. Maybe American capitalism was always going to happen. I don't know.

Stone: They don't know either. But it is the only country in the world where you get to swim in a lake with sharks.

Bollen: I swam in that lake! Do you still travel?

Stone: Well, I can't travel as much. I really have bad emphysema, I'm afraid. It keeps me from getting around. You know, I can do things. I'm reduced to situations where I take cruises because I don't have to walk very far and I like being at sea.

Bollen: Your 1992 novel *Outerbridge Reach* is about sailing, being at sea. How did you learn the sailing lingo? Was that from your time in the Navy? You have a great ear for authentic dialogue.

Stone: I had a couple of advisors. One was the guy who designed a boat in the World Cup competition and who keeps a boat at Darien, a real, kind of independent Canadian. I'm a pretty quick study, and I do sail a little. Maybe I could get across Long Island Sound as a lone sailor. I'm afraid the scope of the earth is beyond me. I might make it to Port Jefferson. That would be an accomplishment. I'm not an accomplished sailor. I did pick up the lingo, and I did work at it. My other advisor was Peter Davis, the documentary filmmaker. So from my two experts, my documentary filmmaker and my lone sailor, I had advice that I cultivated.

Bollen: Do you always seek out advisors for subjects? Or do you ever fact-check your books? *Damascus Gate* possessed a lot of detail to double check.

Stone: I live in dread, because I don't fact-check. I went to dinner at the consulate. There's nothing like going to dinner at the consulate. It's just great. You hear everything. Everybody talks. And going to dinner at the consulate, I once saw the two consulates in Jerusalem—one on the east side, one on the west side—just talking to the reporters, and the people who were there are mostly the press, so you pick up enormous amounts of scuttlebutt. And hanging out at the Atara Café and being introduced to people—the Israelis are very voluble. They like to talk and the Arabs, too. So you learn a lot.

Bollen: But what's interesting about *Damascus Gate*—and most all of the novels—is that you're picking hot zones that people have very strong opinions about. Do you ever get a reaction on it? Or are you trying to be fair in all the writing?

Stone: I try very hard to be fair, and I look for ironies. In a way, I live on ironies as a novelist. One critic from the *Times* picked up on a moment in the book where I say, "People look at Gaza and they say, 'This is the equivalent of Auschwitz. This is the payoff for Auschwitz.'" How wrong is that, to say what happens in Gaza could ever be the equivalent or the payoff from what happened in Auschwitz? So what do I get in the *Times*? "Stone says that what happens in Gaza is the payoff for what happened in Auschwitz." I'm not going to sit down and knock myself out writing a letter saying, "Hey man, read the thing straight."

Bollen: It's always bad when the writer responds to the critic. It never ends well.

Stone: I've got some pretty mean reviews in my time. Some are really, really mean reviews. I don't let them hurt me anymore. Some people just don't like what I do. I have to face that fact. They just don't like it. [laughs] What are you going to do?

Bollen: Maybe that attitude is why you've managed such a long career. You aren't writing for the critic. Maybe you'd have stuck to writing about Southern California druggies if you listened to the advisors of the day.

Stone: Right, and I think that helped me. Maybe it also helped that I'm not a very famous writer.

Bollen: Come on, yes you are.

Stone: Well, I have felt that I'm not risking my life and fortune, and "Oh my god, this is going to be it." I think I long ago reached the point where I'm going to do it, and I'm going to do the best I can. I'm going to try and enjoy doing it. If I'm not enjoying doing it . . .

Bollen: After your first novel *A Hall of Mirrors* came out in 1967, how did you get to Vietnam to start the groundwork for *Dog Soldiers*?

Stone: I was young enough and I went to England. For some crazy reason I went to Europe, and I was batting around Europe. I shouldn't have done that. That was not a good career move. I was doing more hanging out, more goofing, I don't know what I was trying to escape after the first book came out. Then I had to do yet more goofing around. But then I knew I had to go to Vietnam.

Bollen: And you were in Vietnam as a reporter?

Stone: Yes, for an English magazine called *Ink*. That was the only way I could get there. And I wanted to. That was deliberate, premeditated—"I gotta go. I gotta see this."

Bollen: I'm still trying to get a copy of *Who Will Stop the Rain?*, the film based on *Dog Soldiers*. And *A Hall of Mirrors* was made into a film too, wasn't it?

Stone: Yes, and that was one of the most horrible movies you can conceive. Conceive the most horrible movie you can and you've more or less got it.

Bollen: Why is it so bad?

Stone: I could say that all the reasons that it was bad have to do with other people, and all the reasons it's good have to do with me. The director was Stuart Rosenberg. I always felt bad about [Paul] Newman because Newman was a friend of mine and really was a good guy. I miss him a lot. It was a bad movie, and he was in it. I felt partly the fault was mine. But the writer is of absolutely no consequence around a movie. They changed my script at whim, ad hock, ad lib. It was awful. It was a terrible experience, and I was also very young. This was another part of my bad-good fortune. The movies were changing. It was Charlie Manson time. The movies were changing. They were using bad language. The crews were shocked. The makeup girls, the grips, were shocked at the language we used. They were shocked at the presence of hippie-dip characters like me wandering around the set with their friends. My secretary would be shocked by people calling me up at the studio and saying, "Could you connect me with Mr. Stone's office?" And she goes, "Just a moment, please." [laughs] My friends thought it was such a riot that they could call up a Hollywood studio and ask for me. It was really ridiculous, but it was the changing of the movies. The movies at that time—this is the late sixtiess, beginning of the seventies—they were clueless. They had no idea what their audience wanted to see. They had no idea. They were trying anything. They thought there was this hippie stuff, so they would try to do that by dressing extras in weird clothes. Oh, it was absolutely pathetic.

Bollen: Did it get bad reviews?

Stone: [laughs] Pauline Kael probably wrote the most eloquent bad review she ever wrote about any movie over that movie. Oh god. It was awful. That was the first one.

Bollen: Finally, you use Catholicism repeatedly as a subject in your books. You were raised a Catholic, and so was I. I've personally noticed that a lot of Catholics who fall away from the church when they're younger return to it later in life. Do you find that you've changed on the subject of religion over your life?

Stone: Yes, very much. I think that the element of whatever you want to call faith doesn't really attach to doctrine or dogma or spiritual entities like Father, Son, and Holy Ghost. I think there's a necessity for some attachment to the spiritual world and, in a way, people really have to have it. They come back to it through whatever liturgical or non-liturgical means that they require. I think people are drawn back to it, and I think it's understandable. It's not at all regrettable or regressive. I think it's the way it is.

Bollen: At the end of *Death of the Black-Haired Girl* there's this very sad scene in which Eddie Stack tries to bury his daughter's ashes in the same crypt as his wife, but the Catholic Church won't allow it because of her stance on abortion. Did you see that as the cruelty of the Church, its inability to offer consolation or its narrow understanding of its service to the community?

Stone: It's a problem with the Church. That just came from my general disgust for the mediocrity of the Church, to which I once committed my spiritual life, and its intense mediocrity and utter failure. That's where that came from.

Index

www.ingramcontent.com/pod-product-compliance
Lightning Source LLC
Chambersburg PA
CBHW020654030726
47498CB00002B/505